"Warm, witty, wise, and winsome; theologically rigorous, rhetorically convincing, and pastorally helpful, this book is not to be missed. Taking the reader through the narrative of the exodus, Carmen Joy Imes shows us that it is our story, not an arcane, ancient document as dry as last year's bird nest. The genre of Law speaks today. You will see the name Carmen Joy Imes regularly in the future as she continues to bless the church with accessible and edifying scholarship."

Jeffrey D. Arthurs, Haddon Robinson Professor of Preaching and Communication at Gordon-Conwell Theological Seminary and author of *Preaching as Reminding*

"Rarely do we encounter scholars who are able to distill the essence of complex notions and recast them in forms that are both accessible and compelling for lay readers. Carmen Imes's skills in this regard are extraordinary. In the academy, people who have read her published technical monograph on bearing God's name have been quick to celebrate the stellar quality of her work. In this volume Carmen introduces lay readers and serious students of Scripture to her major findings through writing in engaging and persuasive prose—with plenty of ideas for application. For readers who long to recover the life-giving message of grace in the Torah, this book will be a great place to start."

Daniel I. Block, Gunther H. Knoedler Professor Emeritus of Old Testament, Wheaton College

"If you are ready to be transformed by a book, read this one! Like Lucy and Edmund in C. S. Lewis's *The Voyage of the Dawn Treader,* Carmen Imes plunges her reader deep into the world of the Old Testament (and the New). The journey will reshape what you know about God's name, Israel's law, and our identity as Christians who bear God's name."

Beth Stovell, associate professor of Old Testament at Ambrose University and national catalyst for theological and spiritual formation, Vineyard Canada

"Professor Imes refuses to divide the Bible into a simplistic dichotomy of rigid law and abounding grace. Her goal is to highlight continuity between Sinai and Calvary; between lawgiver Moses and grace-dispenser Jesus. . . . Imes skillfully highlights the teachings of Sinai law throughout the New Testament. Yes, grace and mercy win out, but within a proper understanding of the foundation which was laid by Yahweh in the first covenants. My favorite emphasis of Imes's writings centers on her exposition of 'chosen people.' Yes, Israel, but now all tribes, all races, all linguistic flavors can be included in the massive throng of the new chosen people who will one day gather at the Throne of God and sing in glorious unison, 'Hallelujah, for our God almighty reigns!' Well done, Professor Imes."

Phil Parshall, former president of International Christian Fellowship, active missionary among Muslim people for forty-three years

"Carmen Joy Imes's *Bearing God's Name* is a marvel. Imagine a scholar who writes for the church, a member of the academy who cares deeply for the parish. However you phrase it, Imes has done it—given the gift of both accessibility and accuracy to the church. I learned much in this text and look forward to returning to it again and again. I suspect your experience will be the same."

Talbot Davis, pastor of Good Shepherd UMC in Charlotte, North Carolina, and author of *Simplify the Message: Multiply the Impact*

"Get ready to receive an abundance of insight from the story of Israel's exodus and dedication to their divine calling. Carmen Imes brings this ancient story to life in a sharp and approachable read that will help you understand the divine calling in your life."

Jonathan Collins, cofounder of The Bible Project, author of *Why Emotions Matter*

FOREWORD BY **CHRISTOPHER J. H. WRIGHT**

BEARING GOD'S NAME

WHY SINAI STILL MATTERS

CARMEN JOY IMES

IVP
Academic

An imprint of InterVarsity Press
Downers Grove, Illinois

InterVarsity Press
P.O. Box 1400, Downers Grove, IL 60515-1426
ivpress.com
email@ivpress.com

InterVarsity Press® is the book-publishing division of InterVarsity Christian Fellowship/USA®, a movement of students and faculty active on campus at hundreds of universities, colleges, and schools of nursing in the United States of America, and a member movement of the International Fellowship of Evangelical Students. For information about local and regional activities, visit intervarsity.org.

All Scripture quotations, unless otherwise indicated, are taken from The Holy Bible, New International Version®, NIV®. Copyright © 1973, 1978, 1984, 2011 by Biblica, Inc.™ Used by permission of Zondervan. All rights reserved worldwide. www.zondervan.com. The "NIV" and "New International Version" are trademarks registered in the United States Patent and Trademark Office by Biblica, Inc.™

While any stories in this book are true, some names and identifying information may have been changed to protect the privacy of individuals.

"Prayer to Any God" translation copyright Benjamin R. Foster, Before the Muses, CDL Press. Used courtesy of Benjamin R. Foster.

Cover design and image composite: David Fassett
Interior design: Jeanna Wiggins
Cover images: abstract watercolor: © Pobytov / DigitalVision Vectors / Getty Images
poster paper background: © spxChrome / iStock _Getty Images
sand: © svedoliver / iStock / Getty Images Plus
cracked wall: © man_kukuku / iStock / Getty Images Plus
grunge white paper: © duncan1980 / iStock / Getty Images

ISBN 978-0-8308-5269-7 (print)
ISBN 978-0-8308-4836-2 (digital)

Printed in the United States of America ♾

InterVarsity Press is committed to ecological stewardship and to the conservation of natural resources in all our operations. This book was printed using sustainably sourced paper.

Library of Congress Cataloging-in-Publication Data
A catalog record for this book is available from the Library of Congress.

P	25	24	23	22	21	20	19	18	17	16	15	14	13	12	11	10	9	8	7	6	5	4	3	2
Y	37	36	35	34	33	32	31	30	29	28	27	26	25	24	23	22	21	20						

For my parents,

Dan and Verna Camfferman,

and for Danny,

my partner for life,

and for our children,

Eliana, Emma, and Easton,

who have known for a long time

what it means to bear God's name.

CONTENTS

FOREWORD

Christopher J. H. Wright

"And you call yourself a Christian!" That was about the worst thing we feared hearing as young Christians in my Northern Ireland childhood. If you were caught cheating on a test, or saying a bad word in your anger, or getting into a fight on the playground, or telling a dirty joke, or just showing off in front of the girls . . . whatever it was, the most stinging rebuke from other kids (or worst of all from a teacher) would be, "And you call yourself a Christian!" From another kid, that would mean, "See! You're no better than the rest of us. Holier-than-thou. Hypocrite!" From a teacher it was more sobering: "That's not the sort of behavior we expect from you of all people, Christopher." Either way it was a pretty excruciating humiliation. There you were with your little Christian lapel badge for the Scripture Union or whatever, advertising that you were a Christian. But you'd let the team down again, let Jesus down again.

In our late teenage years the terminology changed a bit, but the inference was the same. There were many things that a "real Christian" simply didn't do, places you didn't go, music you shouldn't listen to, clothes you shouldn't wear, and so on, because if anybody saw or heard you, it would spoil your testimony. How could you bear witness to being a follower of Jesus, if you were just as "worldly" as all the other young folks?

Now of course I recognize that an unwholesome dose of legalism lurked in that kind of Christian culture, and sadly there were those who so reacted against it that they rejected the very faith it was trying to protect. But there was a genuine biblical truth underneath those assumptions and restrictions, namely this: how those who claim to be the people of God *behave* is an essential and inseparable component in the credibility (or otherwise) of what they say they *believe* about the God whose name they bear. If you *call yourself* a Christian, you'd better behave like one (or at least bear some resemblance to how people think Christians should behave). "Let every one that *nameth the name of Christ* depart from iniquity" (2 Timothy 2:19 KJV, emphasis mine), was a memory verse impressed on us and rightly so.

Learning the Ten Commandments by heart, word-perfect from the KJV, was also part of my upbringing. So we chorused, "Thou shalt not take the name of the LORD thy God in vain; for the LORD will not hold him guiltless that taketh his name in vain." And of course, we knew what taking God's name in vain meant. It was using the name of God, or Jesus, or Christ as a swear word or in any kind of exclamation. So we just didn't! And we tutted and frowned very disapprovingly at anybody who did.

Well, again, I don't regret or reject those childhood admonitions to watch our language. But having now read this book by Carmen Joy Imes, I do wonder what difference it would have made if those renowned KJV translators had been more literal and rendered the verb in its natural meaning: "You shall not *bear* the name of the LORD thy God in vain." It might, of course, have simply increased the agony of those "And you call yourself a Christian" moments. But if Imes is right, it would have been much closer to the strong ethical thrust of the commandment than merely verbal abuse or misuse of God's name (not that that is a trivial matter by any means).

And I have to say that I am convinced that Carmen Imes is right. Her case in this book (and argued in great exegetical detail in her published dissertation, *Bearing YHWH's Name at Sinai: A Reexamination of the Name Command of the Decalogue*), is that "bearing the name of Yahweh" is comparable in meaning to the High Priest bearing the names of the tribes of Israel on his breastplate and bearing the name of Yahweh on his forehead. He represents—in both directions—those whose name he bears. Similarly, those who bore the name of Yahweh, like those who bear the name of Christ, represented that name before the watching world. Israel was called to live in the midst of the nations as the people who bore the name of Yahweh and made Yahweh "visible" in the world by walking in his ways and reflecting his character. To bear the name of the Lord was not merely an inestimable privilege and blessing but a challenging ethical and missional responsibility. This makes eminent sense to me. And its New Testament parallels are obvious.

A little more of my own story may explain why I resonate so enthusiastically with the message of this book. My parents were missionaries in Brazil before I was born, so I grew up with a houseful of missionary artifacts and a headful of missionary stories. ("And you a missionary's son!" was an even more stinging rebuke for the mildest bad behavior, since it felt like bringing disgrace on my own father, let alone the Lord Jesus.)

I studied theology in Cambridge University. But in my undergraduate years there seemed no connection between theology and my missionary interests. I then went on to do doctoral research in the field of Old Testament ethics. That was a rich field of exploration in which I became ever more convinced that much of the weakness of the modern church is owing to its neglect of the profound ethical message and principles that God has woven so pervasively into the life and scriptures of Israel—and that filter through into so much of the ethical teaching of Jesus and the apostles in the New Testament. But again, this did not particularly connect with mission in my thinking.

Then I went to teach the Old Testament in India for five years in the 1980s. I remember vividly the moment I encountered the remarkable divine soliloquy that is Genesis 18:18-19.

Abraham will surely become a great and powerful nation, and all
nations on earth will be blessed through him. For I have chosen
him, *so that* he will direct his children and his household after
him to keep the way of the LORD by doing what is right and just,
so that the LORD will bring about for Abraham what he has
promised him. (emphasis mine)

There, in the three clauses of that single sentence of verse 19, with
its two explicit indications of purpose ("so that"), we have God's *election* ("I have chosen him"), and God's *mission* (the fulfilment of God's
promise to Abraham that all nations on earth will be blessed through
him), and right in the middle connecting both of those, we have God's
ethical demand (that Abraham's community should walk in the way
of the Lord—not of Sodom and Gomorrah—by doing righteousness
and justice).

That verse united in my mind (and heart) the two great loves of my
life in my biblical thinking and teaching: mission and ethics. They
became like two sides of the same coin. God's mission for Israel was
simply that they should *live* as the people of Yahweh in the midst of the
nations, bearing his name in their worship, prayer, and daily lives. And
for that purpose, they must *walk* in the way of the Lord. And that was
why God had chosen them in the first place, in Abraham, so that through
them he could ultimately bring redemptive blessing to all nations. This
single verse breathed missional election and missional ethics—and I
was doing missional hermeneutics, though none of those terms seem
to have been invented back then.

And that is what Carmen Joy Imes is doing in this book (though
fortunately she does not use that kind of language!). She is helping us
to relish once again the wondrous depths of truth and challenge that
are there *for us Christians* in that great epic narrative of Old Testament
Israel—whether those stories are familiar to us already or not. She not
only shows what a horrendous and misleading fallacy it is when church
leaders either ignore the Old Testament, or even worse, assure us that

we can easily do without it and still be good Christians. The very idea would have appalled Jesus, Paul, Peter, James, and John.

Carmen also indirectly exposes the folly of some of the dichotomies that still plague the Christian West, particularly in the evangelical community—dichotomies I strive to overcome in speaking and writing. There is for example that tediously long-lived debate about whether "real mission" is primarily a matter of the evangelistically proclaimed word or also includes social, economic, and cultural engagement in works of compassion, justice, creation care, and so on. Why push asunder what God has joined together? For bearing the name of the Lord (in proclamation) will surely be "in vain" if it does not proceed from those who bear the name of the Lord also in lives and works that demonstrate his character. And then one hears of Christian pastors who never preach from the Old Testament or about any moral issues or even the ethical demands of Jesus and the apostles, for fear of undermining "the gospel" of justification by grace and faith alone. What do they think Paul means by "the obedience of faith" or "obeying the gospel" or being saved as "God's handiwork, created in Christ Jesus to do good works, which God prepared in advance for us to do" (Ephesians 2:10), or "so that those who have trusted in God may be careful to devote themselves to doing what is good" (Titus 3:8)? The dichotomizing of so-called gospel and ethics is damagingly unbiblical and might be said to constitute in itself a form of bearing the name of the Lord in vain.

So you call yourself a Christian? I trust that reading this book will give you a deeper and more biblical understanding of what it ought to mean to bear that name, and not to bear it in vain.

INTRODUCTION

AN INVITATION

In the opening to *The Voyage of the Dawn Treader*, C. S. Lewis crafts an arresting scene: Edmund and Lucy Pevensie are upstairs in their cousin Eustace's home, lamenting that they are stuck with him for their summer holidays rather than somewhere far more interesting, such as Narnia. Their grief is sharpened by a painting on the wall—a ship at sea that seems remarkably like a Narnian vessel. Eustace overhears the siblings talking and begins to mock them for their childish imagination. He thinks the painting is downright rotten.

As they stare at it, the children fall silent. Something peculiar happens. They can almost see the undulating waves, almost feel the wind blowing, almost hear the sound of the ship slicing through the waters, and almost smell the air of the sea. Suddenly, they are splashed with sea spray and water pours through the frame into the bedroom. In a matter of moments, there is no bedroom at all, and the children are gasping for air in a tumultuous Narnian sea.

Perhaps without meaning to, Lewis demonstrates the nature of Scripture. At first glance, the Bible is only a book, telling us of lands and peoples long ago and far away. But like the Narnian painting, as we look more closely, it comes to life and sweeps us into its story.

You're holding in your hands a book about Sinai, the mountain where the ancient Israelites met their God, Yahweh. It revisits their story as they trudge through the wilderness from a grueling past to a promising future. Chances are slim that you've ever been to Sinai in person, and slimmer that you are there as you read this. The people in this story lived over 3,000 years ago, spoke a different language, and lived by a radically different rhythm, with different values, customs, and concerns. However, these differences cannot erase the fundamental connection between their ancient story and your own. My prayer is that as you read you will experience what the Pevensie children experienced on that hot summer day in England—that you'll be drawn into the biblical story and find that it is very much alive and that you're a part of it—that it's *your* story.

A WORD TO THE SKEPTIC

You may already be skeptical about the value of time travel to Sinai. You may be reading this book only because someone shoved it in your hand and said, "You need to read this." If so, I understand your hesitation.

The Old Testament has been given a bad rap for lots of reasons. Too violent. Too confusing. Too remote. Too legalistic. Too outdated. Oh, there are a few inspiring stories tucked in between the head-scratchers. These we like to pull out and hold up to the light briefly before high-tailing it back to the New Testament. But the rest? We might not be willing to say it out loud, but large portions of the Old Testament are not just boring, they're downright embarrassing. It would be easier to defend our faith if most of the Old Testament would just disappear.

An example of this ambivalence comes from Atlanta megachurch pastor Andy Stanley. He enjoys wide popularity, and for good reason. He has a special gift for communicating spiritual truths in a way that attracts the unchurched. He gets people in the door, and he holds their attention. He recognizes that the Old Testament is a significant barrier for many who might otherwise want to follow Jesus. His solution to this problem is to set it aside. The word he used was "unhitch." In a sermon on Acts 15, Stanley said, "[Early] church leaders unhitched the church from the worldview, value systems, and regulations of the Jewish Scriptures . . . and my friends, we must as well." He claimed, "The Old Testament was not the go-to source regarding any behavior for the church." In the same sermon he went so far as to say, "When you read the Old Testament, when you read the old covenant, when you read the story of Israel . . . you don't see much [grace]."[1]

> The book of Exodus overflows with grace.

But as I read it, the book of Exodus overflows with grace. It turns out that Stanley realizes this too. In an interview with Dr. Michael Brown a few months after Stanley's controversial sermon, he explained that what he wants his listeners to "unhitch" from is not the Old Testament *properly understood*, but the Old Testament as people have come to imagine it.[2] In other words, he'd like people to leave aside the Old Testament *temporarily*, just long enough to be captivated by the resurrected Lord. Once they've encountered Jesus, they'll rediscover the value of the Scriptures Jesus loved.

With this book, I'm taking a different approach. I believe that we need the Old Testament as Christians, not later, but *now*. Rather than unhitching, I want to make the case that we should re-hitch to Israel's Scriptures so that we can truly understand who Jesus is and what he came to do. Without some guidance, we might easily conclude that the Old Testament is a terrible burden to pull and wish to walk away from it. We need an experienced guide who can help us see the enduring value of the Old Testament for the life of faith. I've had many such guides who have helped bring the Old Testament to life, and this book is my means of passing along to you their most important insights along with my own. I hope it will change your mind about the relevance of the Old Testament for Christians.

We especially need help with Old Testament law. Most of us do not perk up when we hear the word "law." Boring, irrelevant, primitive, harsh, patriarchal, ethnocentric, cruel—all these charges are leveled against it. Laws are dry and tedious, and they take away freedoms we'd rather have. Laws keep us from parking in the most convenient places and require us to take off our shoes at airport security checkpoints. Laws cramp our style—*do not climb this or sit here or talk loud there. Silence your cell phone and no flash photography and don't chew gum and don't bring in outside food or drink and keep your hands and arms inside the car.*

This is why Moses' response to the law catches us off guard. Here he is, with tens of thousands of former slaves, exhausted after trekking through the wilderness with everything they own. They've been hungry, thirsty, and attacked along the way. They set up camp at the base of Mount Sinai, where the Lord first spoke to Moses in the flaming bush and promised to deliver his people from Egypt. Moses climbs up the mountain to talk with God again, now that he's carried out God's instructions to lead the people out of Egypt. The people have arrived. And God gives them *rules*?

I would expect Moses to push back a bit. *Um . . . Lord? Isn't this the part where you bless us? Or at least give us a break? These folks have had a long journey and, frankly, a hard life. What they need is a rest. Couldn't you cut them some slack? Do you really think it's fair to saddle them with a bunch of rules when they've only just tasted freedom? Couldn't this wait until later?*

But the way Moses sees it, other nations will actually be *jealous* of the law Israel gets at Sinai:

> See, I have taught you decrees and laws as the Lord my God commanded me, so that you may follow them in the land you are entering to take possession of it. Observe them carefully, for *this will show your wisdom and understanding to the nations*, who will hear about all these decrees and say, "Surely this great nation is a wise and understanding people." *What other nation is so great as to have their gods near them the way the Lord our God is near us whenever we pray to him?* And what other nation is so great as to have such righteous decrees and laws as this body of laws I am setting before you today? (Deuteronomy 4:5-8, emphasis added)

Wisdom? Jealous? If Moses' words strike us as odd, then we need to take a second look at Sinai because we have failed to catch what's actually happening there. That's where we'll begin in Part One. First, we'll ask, "What's the big deal about Sinai? Why should we care what happens there?" These questions are answered by the narrative frame within which the Sinai experience is set: the wilderness stories leading up to it mirror those that follow Sinai. This literary context makes Sinai the high point of the Torah (the first five books of the Bible, also called the Pentateuch) and the event that sets the agenda for everything that follows.

Once the frame is in place, in the rest of Part One we'll study the "painting" itself. The Sinai narratives span fifty-seven chapters from Exodus 19 to Numbers 10. Much happens here, and it's crucial for the formation of Israel's identity and vocation. Israel cannot be God's people without Sinai. (Neither can we, but that's getting ahead of ourselves.) Most people have a general familiarity with the most famous declaration that takes place there: the Ten Commandments. Nevertheless, misunderstandings abound about their purpose and meaning. We'll tackle some of these misunderstandings along the way, zeroing in on a single command that has been largely misinterpreted—the command not to "take the name of the LORD thy God in vain" (Exodus 20:7 KJV). Then we'll look at the other laws that lay out God's covenantal expectations, including instructions for building the tent in which he is to dwell.

That brings us to Part Two. We'll look at the story after Sinai—how Israel largely fails at living as the people of God, how the prophets hold out hope for future covenant renewal, how Jesus adopts the vocation of the people of God as bearers of Yahweh's name, and how the story opens up to include those of us who are non-Jews, enabling us to become who we were meant to be. Rather than abandoning the Old Testament, the New Testament church turns to it again and again as their primary source for ethical reflection. They see themselves in continuity with the Old Testament people of God, carrying forward their mission to represent God to the nations. Their story becomes ours when we join the family of faith.

WHO IS "THE LORD"?

We'll want to get one thing straight at the outset so there's no misunderstanding. "God" (*elohim* in Hebrew) and "Lord" (*adonai* in Hebrew) are not names. *Elohim* is a category of beings who inhabit the spiritual realm; angels are *elohim* and so are the gods of other nations. *Adonai* is a title that means "master," whether human or divine. Both words can describe Israel's deity. However, the God of Israel also revealed his name, inviting the Israelites to address him personally as "Yahweh."

Scholars today aren't precisely sure how to pronounce God's name because in Hebrew we're given just four consonants, YHWH. Later in history Jews adopted the practice of replacing the divine name YHWH with other words out of reverence. When reading the biblical text, they might refer to YHWH as "Adonai," which means "Lord," or "Ha-Shem," which means "the Name." In order to remind people not to say God's name, Jewish scribes attached the vowels of "Adonai" to the consonants of YHWH, resulting in a nonsense word, YaHoWaH, that was meant to remind people to say *Adonai*. Later still, Christian scholars trying to read ancient Hebrew sounded out this nonsense word, coming up with "Jehovah." Our English Bible translations follow Jewish tradition of avoiding pronunciation of the name by representing the Hebrew YHWH with LORD in all capital letters.

Whenever you see LORD throughout this book (or in your Bibles!), remember that you're looking at God's personal name, Yahweh.

DIGGING DEEPER

If you're relatively new to the Bible or if you're rusty on the overall storyline, it would be a good idea to pause your reading and check out the appendix. There I've provided links for videos from The Bible Project that will help orient you to the message of Scripture. The first two video links will be especially helpful before you dive into the next chapter. If you are already quite familiar with the Bible, then I'd recommend the third video for you. All three will help you get the big picture in mind before we dive into the particulars. If you can read QR codes with your smartphone or tablet, these will take you straight to the videos. Alternatively, you can type in the url or google the title of the video, joining the hundreds of thousands of people who have seen the Bible come to life with the help of The Bible Project. You'll find other codes that correlate with each chapter in the book in the appendix. The videos nicely complement each chapter of the book, but should not be considered an endorsement from The Bible Project.

PART 1

BECOMING THE PEOPLE WHO BEAR GOD'S NAME

1

LEAVING EGYPT

Deliverance as Grace

CONTEXT IS EVERYTHING

The first and most commonly made mistake with the Old Testament law is to ignore where it appears. Many Christians assume that in the Old Testament era the Israelites had to *earn* salvation by following the Sinai law, while Jesus did away with that notion, making salvation available for free. This is a terribly unfortunate caricature of the Old Testament, but it is easily resolved by taking a closer look at the story. Israel arrives at Sinai in chapter 19 of Exodus. That's where Yahweh will give them the law. However, God's elaborate deliverance of the Israelites from Egypt takes place in chapters 3–14. If the law were a prerequisite for salvation, then we would expect to see Moses in Egypt making a public service announcement: *Hey, everyone—Good news! Yahweh plans to set you free from slavery to Pharaoh. There's just one catch. You're gonna have to agree to live by this set of rules. If you just sign on the dotted line saying that you agree to these conditions, Yahweh will spring into action. Who's in?*

Of course, this is not what happens. Instead, God appears to Moses in the wilderness, reveals his personal name, Yahweh, and gives Moses this message for those living under oppression in Egypt:

of your fathers—the God of Abraham, Isaac
ed to me and said: I have watched over you
t has been done to you in Egypt. And I have
_____ ω υιιιg you up out of your misery in Egypt into the
land of the Canaanites, Hittites, Amorites, Perizzites, Hivites and
Jebusites—a land flowing with milk and honey. (Exodus 3:16-17)

Yahweh delivers them "with an outstretched arm and with mighty
acts of judgment" (Exodus 6:6) without first checking their homes for
idols or performing an audit of their morality. His deliverance has to
do with his character and his promise to their ancestor, Abraham, rather
than with their righteousness. True, God had given instructions to
Abraham and his sons, which they were to obey, but he had not given
them any permanent code of conduct.

God made a covenant with Abraham back in Genesis. He promised
as many descendants as the stars in the sky (Genesis 15:5), along with
a vast tract of land that would become theirs (Genesis 15:18-21). He also
had spoken of Israel's future enslavement in Egypt:

> Know for certain that for four hundred years your descendants
> will be strangers in a country not their own and that they will be
> enslaved and mistreated there. But I will punish the nation they
> serve as slaves, and afterward they will come out with great pos-
> sessions. (Genesis 15:13-14)

Now they've done their time. Yahweh is ready to put his plan in
motion. Abraham's descendants have become a great multitude
(see Exodus 1:7), and they're about to be rescued. The only requirement is for each family to eat a lamb together and spread its blood
on their door frame as a sign for God to protect them from the
destroying angel.[1]

Whatever Sinai represents, it cannot be a prerequisite for salvation.
Israel has already been delivered when they arrive. In order to understand what the law at Sinai is for, we'll need to take seriously where and
when it is given and how it is framed. And timing is everything.

PASSOVER

We know this event as the "Passover," but the English word "Passover" is not a great translation of the Hebrew *pasakh* in Exodus 12:13. It gives the unfortunate impression that Yahweh is "passing over" them and his attention is elsewhere. While the word *can* mean pass over, in this context the meaning "protect" makes more sense. Yahweh protects, or covers, the Hebrew households from the destroying angel who has been commissioned to carry out God's judgment.[2] Yahweh's gracious protection of his people shows faithfulness to his promise to save them. Exodus 12:23, 27 and Isaiah 31:5 are other examples where *pasakh* means "cover" or "protect" rather than "pass over."[3]

FRAMING SINAI: THE WILDERNESS JOURNEYS

You've likely seen Leonardo da Vinci's painting titled "The Last Supper."

Figure 1.1. da Vinci's *The Last Supper*

In it, Jesus sits at the center of a long table with six of his disciples on either side, grouped in clusters of three. The twelve are not insignificant, but Jesus matters more. He is the center of focus. All the perspective lines point toward his face, which is framed by the window behind him. That window is flanked by windows and four columns on either side of the room, drawing the viewer's eye to the center. This framing technique is not only effective in visual art. It also works in stories.

Each culture has its own set of expectations for how stories ought to be told. In the Western tradition, the climax belongs at the end. Other cultures arrange their stories differently, some with the climax right in the center. This technique is sometimes called a "ring structure," "mirror imaging," or "chiasm," and it was commonly used in ancient writing. I like to think of it as a literary sandwich. While the climax of a chiasm is not always found in the middle, the turning point of the narrative often is.[4]

The flood narrative in Genesis 6–9 is an example of mirror imaging on a smaller scale. The way the story is told mirrors the actual event; the symmetrical ebb and flow of the story matches the rise and fall of the water. The structural center of the chiasm, or literary sandwich, is also the theological turning point: "God remembered Noah" (Genesis 8:1).[5]

A closer look at the wilderness stories immediately before and after Israel's camp at Sinai reveals a surprise: they deliberately mirror each other, creating a narrative frame that draws our focus to Sinai in the center (see Figure 1.2). If we were tempted to think of the Sinai instructions as a boring appendix to the story of deliverance from Egypt, this framing technique wakes us from our delusion. We'd miss it if we only read parts and pieces of the Torah. But when we read large chunks of text in one sitting, we can begin to see what's there. As a result, the Sinai

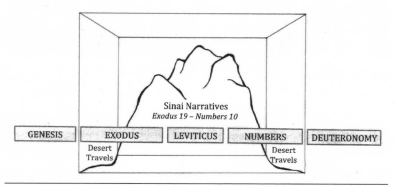

Figure 1.2. The framing of the Sinai narratives

narratives take their place as the crown jewel—the center of focus—of the Torah. Let me show you what I mean.

Numbers 33 lays out the full itinerary of Israel's hike from Egypt to Canaan. There are forty-two camping spots on that itinerary. But if you carefully read the narratives that actually describe those travels before and after Sinai (Exodus 12–18 and Numbers 11–32) you'll discover that only six campsites are mentioned on either side, each introduced by the same Hebrew phrase: "and they set out."[6] This is not to suggest that one account is more reliable than the other. The itinerary and the narrative serve different purposes. If you made a scrapbook of your summer road trip, you might include a page with your full itinerary. But you might not have taken great pictures at every stop along the way. Some places were more significant than others, so they'll get more attention on the pages of your scrapbook. So, too, with Israel. The narrator has selected six representative campsites before Sinai and six after, putting Sinai right in the middle, like Jesus in da Vinci's "The Last Supper." With Sinai deliberately in the center, our eyes are drawn to it. But this is only the beginning of the literary symmetry.

The itineraries mention "desert" seven times before Sinai and seven times afterward. On the way to Sinai we read about God's provision of manna and quail (Exodus 16), as well as two requests for water satisfied by a gushing rock (Exodus 17:1-7). After Sinai? The same pattern: one story about manna and quail (Numbers 11) and two requests for water satisfied by a gushing rock (Numbers 20:1-16). We're told that God provided manna daily in the wilderness as they traveled from Egypt to Canaan (Exodus 16:35) and obviously the people would have needed regular access to water, but the narrator's selective telling contributes to the literary framing effect that points to Sinai.

But there's more. God's angelic messenger protects the Hebrews from a foreign king once before Sinai and once afterward (Exodus 14:19-20; Numbers 22:21-35). Before Sinai, Israel fights the Amalekites (Exodus 17:8-16). After Sinai? Again, Israel fights the Amalekites (Numbers 14:39-45). Before and after Sinai, Moses meets with a Midianite family member and receives guidance (Exodus 18; Numbers 10:29-32). Before and after Sinai, Moses is weighed down with leadership responsibilities (Exodus 18:17-18; Numbers 11:10-15) and begins delegating those responsibilities to others (Exodus 18:24-26; Numbers 11:16-17). This example involves a deliberate quotation. In Numbers 11, Moses explicitly reuses Jethro's language from Exodus 18. Speaking of Moses' leadership responsibility, Jethro had said, "For this thing is too heavy for you. You are unable to do it alone" (Exodus 18:18, author's translation). Moses takes up these words after Sinai, saying "I myself am unable alone to carry this whole people for it is too heavy for me" (Numbers 11:14, author's translation).

What's more, the Israelites' response to the report of the scouts in Numbers 14 mirrors the response to Pharaoh's army before they crossed the sea (Exodus 14:10-12)—they lament ever having left Egypt. With such a close match between stories that took place before and after Sinai, you might begin to wonder if anything has changed during Israel's year at the mountain. Indeed, it has.

MIDDLE OF NOWHERE: A PLACE OF BECOMING

In spite of the similarities before and after Sinai, a great transformation has taken place. The Hebrews fled Egypt as a mixed multitude, refugees and former slaves seeking a better life. They leave Sinai as a well-organized army, registered and marching tribe by tribe. But change wasn't easy. Big questions plagued the first part of their journey. Are we safe? Where are we going? What's on the menu? Who's in charge? What sort of god is Yahweh? And what does Yahweh expect of us?

We can relate. It's like being lost on a hike. You know where you want to end up, but you can't figure out how to get there because you don't know which direction you're facing. Or maybe you've felt lost in life, stuck in between where you've been and where you're going. You know what you're cut out to do, but you can't get the traction you need to get there. There's a word to describe this state: *liminality*. It's from the Latin word *limen*, which means "threshold."[7] Imagine yourself standing in the doorway, neither in nor out of a room. That's liminal space. An airport, for example, is a liminal space. Nobody lives there. We're all passing through on our way to somewhere else.

The first people to start talking about liminality were anthropologists. They used it to describe a stage in rituals that change someone's status or identity. Sociologically speaking, a liminal place is a transitional space where a person lacks social status and is reduced to dependence on others. Every human ritual the world over includes an element of liminality, from coming-of-age rituals to funerals. Liminality has since been applied more broadly to psychology, politics, popular culture, and religion. In a moment, we'll explore Israel's experience of liminality. But first, I want us to think about the ways *we* experience liminality, because all of us do! For example, a wedding ceremony sets the bride and groom apart and lingers in liminal space. During the ceremony the couple is neither married nor unmarried. They wear new, symbolic clothes and explore other symbols of their new life together (rings, candles, vows, kiss). The congregation witnesses their change of status as the minister pronounces them "husband and wife" and welcomes them to rejoin the community with a new identity.

When a woman becomes pregnant, she enters liminality. She is officially on the threshold of motherhood, and yet she has not yet experienced most of its aspects—nighttime feedings, diapering, discipline, pushing a stroller, singing the ABCs. Liminality is usually temporary, but it can be prolonged. My first pregnancy ended in miscarriage. Part of my grief was because I found myself in the strange position of having been pregnant, but lacking a child to hold. Mother's Day that year was especially awkward and painful. Was I a mother? Or wasn't I? I didn't really belong in either category.

Few people actually enjoy liminality. We have an inborn desire to seek order and belonging and predictability. Just a few months after that awkward Mother's Day I became pregnant again and happily left that liminal state behind. My grief largely dissolved when the ambiguity of my status was resolved. Others are not so fortunate. Immigrants or refugees sometimes spend long stretches of time in a liminal state—lacking papers to legally work or even stay in their host country, always feeling like an outsider, and never knowing if they should put down roots or start packing.

College intentionally creates liminality. Students leave home and enter an entirely new environment with a new set of expectations and roles. With the help of faculty and staff, they scrutinize themselves in order to reshape their identity and discover their vocation. But they are not welcome to stay. Just when they feel like they know the ropes, they are thrust into the "real world" to begin the process all over again as full-fledged adults. Graduation is a ritual designed to mark that transition between academia and the outside world. To some extent, it redefines students by qualifying them for new roles in society. Crossing the stage, they cross the threshold to a new season of life.

For Israel, the wilderness journey from Egypt to Canaan is liminal space. Far more than just a place to pass *through*, it is the workshop of Israel's *becoming*. The wilderness is the temporary destination that makes them who they are. Liminal places always do this. They change us.

The Israelites have been liberated from slavery in Egypt, but they have not yet arrived at their final destination. Everything they know about who they are, how to survive, and what is expected of them is stripped away on that fateful night when they make their escape, leaving them vulnerable and uncertain. They don't know how to live under these new arrangements. But God is not in a hurry to lead them out of liminal space and into the land he promised to give them. They're not ready yet. Into this vacuum, Yahweh speaks. He answers the basic questions of human existence in surprising new ways, offering himself as the solution to their needs for leadership, guidance, protection, and provision, and revealing his name as the key to their identity and vocation as his people. Yahweh invites them to begin walking in a new direction by trusting him. Sinai is part of their liminal experience. In the wilderness of Sinai they are free from the mind-numbing distractions of Egypt and Canaan. In their isolation,

> God is not in a hurry to lead them out of liminal space and into the land he promised to give them. They're not ready yet.

they can hear the voice of God. Having lost their old identity, they are ready to become what they are meant to be.

ARE WE SAFE? FINDING SECURITY

We may be long centuries removed from Israel's wilderness wanderings, but we share many of the same basic human instincts. Like the Israelites, we want to know if we can close our eyes at night and fall asleep in safety. Uncertainty breeds anxiety.

As I read the wilderness narratives with students, the question I'm asked more than any other is this: "How can the Israelites so quickly forget God's power to deliver them?" The people who've seen ten dramatic plagues on Egypt, whose own households were spared devastation, whose neighbors have willingly given them silver and gold and clothes for their journey, who've heard Pharaoh's command to "Get out!"—these are the same people who quickly change their tune as Pharaoh chases them in hot pursuit. The Hebrews are terrified. They cry out:

> Was it because there were no graves in Egypt that you brought us
> to the desert to die? What have you done to us by bringing us out
> of Egypt? Didn't we say to you in Egypt, 'Leave us alone; let us
> serve the Egyptians?' It would have been better for us to serve the
> Egyptians than to die in the desert! (Exodus 14:11-12)

If this response surprises us, it's because we underestimate the disorienting effect of liminal spaces and because we overestimate our own stability. Perhaps a thought experiment would help. Imagine you are a college student. One day your professor ends class with a special announcement: "Attention Students! I have fantastic news. A generous donor has arranged to cover the rest of your tuition payments this year as well as all the school loans you have accumulated so far."

Incredulity melts into celebration as you all realize she is dead serious. The classroom erupts with cheers of joy and (for some) tears of relief. When the commotion dies down, your professor gives some instructions. "All who would like to take advantage of the donor's offer need to gather up their belongings and follow me." Of course, you pack your bag and follow. How could you pass up the opportunity? But you're not sure where she's taking you. The class files out into the hallway, down a back staircase, and down the sidewalk behind the cafeteria to the parking lot.

"Wait here," she says. "I'll be back."

She disappears into the administration building and she's gone . . . for a long time. For the first few minutes everyone is jovial and curious, wondering where she's gone and how long the wait will be. But as the minutes stretch on and the sun gets higher, your stomach reminds you that it's lunchtime. The longer you wait, the more you begin to wonder if this is some sort of practical joke. You crane your neck to see if there's a video camera set up somewhere, capturing your gullibility on film.

What if this happened to you? How long would you wait in the parking lot for your professor to reappear? How quickly would you begin to doubt the sincerity of her announcement? A wonderful promise becomes much harder to believe when we are tired and hungry, or when we can't imagine how things will play out. Abraham Maslow claimed as much in his 1943 essay, which popularized a hierarchy of needs.[8] He posited that certain needs are fundamental, such as physiological needs (food, water, air, sleep) and the need for safety. Without these in place, people are less motivated to focus on higher-level needs, such as love, esteem, and self-actualization. Some criticize Maslow's hierarchy as reflecting an individualist, rather than collective, society, making it potentially less pertinent for understanding Israel's wilderness wanderings. We could also disagree with Maslow's humanist perspective. He insists on the essential goodness of any human desire, failing to recognize how our inclination toward those desires may be corrupted by sin. Contrary to Maslow's assumption, we do not become who we are meant to be by seeking to fulfill every felt need. Still, his overall idea is helpful—without fulfillment of basic needs such as food, water, and a safe place to live, people will very quickly lose interest in promises relating to higher-order thinking about values or beliefs or opportunities. Remember when Moses delivered God's great promise of deliverance to the

Hebrews in Egypt? "Moses reported this to the Israelites, but they did not listen to him because of their discouragement and harsh labor" (Exodus 6:9). The promise was glorious, but they weren't buying it.

Hunger, thirst, and fear are powerful masters. (These days, so is the lack of internet access.) Yahweh knows this. Remarkably, he does not chide the Israelites when they complain or panic as they travel toward Sinai. He simply provides for their needs. He utilizes this trek to demonstrate to them his trustworthiness. Here are a few examples of Yahweh's care from these chapters:

> When Pharaoh let the people go, God did not lead them on the road through the Philistine country, though that was shorter. For God said, "If they face war, they might change their minds and return to Egypt." So God led the people around by the desert road toward the Red Sea. (Exodus 13:17-18)

Yahweh first ensures Israel's safety.

> By day the LORD went ahead of them in a pillar of cloud to guide them on their way and by night in a pillar of fire to give them light, so that they could travel by day or night. (Exodus 13:21)

In the hot and dusty desert, traveling in the cool hours of night may be preferable. God provides unmistakable guidance day and night. He has thought of everything.

> [God said to Moses,] "Raise your staff and stretch out your hand over the sea to divide the water so that the Israelites can go through the sea on dry ground. I will harden the hearts of the Egyptians so that they will go in after them. And I will gain glory through Pharaoh and all his army, through his chariots and his horsemen. The Egyptians will know that I am the LORD when I gain glory through Pharaoh, his chariots and his horsemen." Then the angel of God, who had been traveling in front of Israel's army, withdrew and went behind them. The pillar of cloud also moved from in front and stood behind them, coming between the armies of Egypt

and Israel. Throughout the night the cloud brought darkness to the one side and light to the other side; so neither went near the other all night long. (Exodus 14:16-20)

Two things are worth noting: First, God provides the Israelites a way of escape. He does not choose the easiest route, but rather the one that will demonstrate his power and bring him the most glory. Second, God provides safety all night long, even lighting their camp to dispel the fear of attack in the darkness.

> Trust is not automatic, and God does not expect it to be. He patiently works on Israel's behalf until they can see that he is worthy of their confidence.

Trust is not automatic, and God does not expect it to be. He patiently works on Israel's behalf until they can see that he is worthy of their confidence. God's guidance and protection of the Israelites cultivate their trust in him and in Moses (see Exodus 14:31). The wilderness is his classroom. He has work to do in the Israelites that can only be done in a state of dislocation, in liminal space.

WHAT'S ON THE MENU? LEARNING TO TRUST

The Israelites haven't traveled far—three days, in fact—when they become desperate for water (Exodus 15:22). I think Maslow would agree that it doesn't matter how dramatic last week's breakthrough when your throat is parched today. And so they begin to grumble against Moses. The right response would have been to pray and ask God for help. This is what Moses does, and God provides. The incident is even more striking when read against the plague narratives. In Egypt, the outcome of the first plague, when the Nile turns to blood, is "water they cannot drink" (Exodus 7:24)—a judgment against Egypt. When the Hebrews arrive at Marah, they find "water they cannot drink," but Yahweh shows Moses how to transform it from bitter to sweet (Exodus 15:23-25)—a blessing for his people.[9]

Six weeks later, they run out of food. Despondency sets in. "If only we had died by the LORD's hand in Egypt! There we sat around pots of meat and ate all the food we wanted, but you have brought us out into this desert to starve this entire assembly to death" (Exodus 16:3). Again, God's response is full of mercy. He announces his plan to provide bread from heaven. In Egypt, God had "rained hail" (Exodus 9:18, 23), but here he "rains bread" (Exodus 16:4). In Egypt, locusts "came up" and "covered" the ground, devouring all the produce (Exodus 10:14-15), but now God provides meat for the people to eat in the form of quail that "comes up" and "covers" the ground (Exodus 16:13).[10]

The bread God provides is not just any bread, however. It doubles as a "test to see whether they will follow his instructions" (Exodus 16:4). Rather than filling their pantries to bank against future famine (this is a road trip, after all!), God invites them into an exercise of daily trust. Each morning, he provides a day's worth of food, as much as each one needs. In this way, they learn how to depend on him daily. Those who disregard his instructions find maggots the next morning in the extra food they've collected.

On the sixth day of every week, God provides twice as much. In this way, Israel also learns the rhythm of Sabbath observance—six days of work, one day of rest, repeat. Like a parent with a toddler, patiently teaching obedience and reward, Yahweh trains an entire nation. His provision of food demonstrates his glory and cultivates habits of obedience and trust for forty years straight! Their need in the wilderness supplies the opportunity for a greater display of Yahweh's character. God has things to teach that can only be learned in a state of dislocation. On the way to Sinai, the Hebrews find out what sort of God he is and how to live in dependence on him.

God taught me a similar lesson in the first few months of marriage. Never having lived on my own off campus, I was nervous about money. I was still getting the hang of grocery shopping, paying rent, and living by a budget. One day, I went shopping for food to make a spaghetti dinner. I remember standing by the rack of French bread in the bakery department. Garlic bread sounded tasty, but a whole loaf for one meal? Was that wise? It seems strange now that I wrestled so hard over this one 99-cent item. In the end, I left the store without bread, feeling poor. Not long after I arrived home, I heard a knock on our back door. Our next-door neighbor stood there with a loaf of French bread. "I bought too much bread. Can you use this?" Never before or since has someone brought me French bread. On that day, God sent me a message loud and clear: "I am your provider. I've got this." That bread was more than manna for my stomach. It was manna for my soul. Like Israel, I was learning to trust God to provide.

WHO'S IN CHARGE? APPOINTING LEADERS

Another question that rises to the surface in liminal places is "Who's in *charge*?" Anyone who has tried to do a group project for school can relate. Nothing gets done until somebody takes the lead. A similar leadership vacuum results whenever an elementary school teacher is absent and requires a substitute. The children face a measure of uncertainty about how the day will go. What is this substitute like? What will be expected of me? Will he be a harsh taskmaster or will he be funny and kind? Inevitably, a student or two steps into the vacuum and asserts their own authority, attempting to control the substitute.

Ultimately Yahweh calls the shots. It is he who appointed Moses to a leadership role. He inevitably bears the brunt of Israel's complaints. But he recognizes that their protest is actually resentment against God himself, merely deflected toward him (Exodus 16:8). Still, it's not easy being the target of their grumbling. Moses reaches a breaking point at Rephidim, where the Israelites complain again about thirst: "What am I to do with these people? They are almost ready to stone me!" (Exodus 17:4). On this occasion, God answers the people's prayer directly through the hand of Moses, telling him to strike the rock at Horeb. Water flows in the sight of the elders. The same staff used to strike the Nile, making Egypt's water unfit to drink, now supplies liquid grace for the Israelites.[11]

Up next is the battle against the Amalekites, for which Moses and Joshua both receive credit. Joshua fights the battle on the ground, but he only prevails as long as Moses' hands are raised on the mountain (Exodus 17). Both of these incidents publicly underscore Moses' God-given authority to lead.

Moses consistently shoulders the burden of responsibility for the people, bringing their requests to Yahweh and announcing his response. When his father-in-law, Jethro, stops by for a visit, he is alarmed that Moses serves as judge for the people from morning until night (Exodus 18). They come to him whenever they want to know God's will. Jethro advises Moses to delegate the bulk of these responsibilities to trained officials, reserving his energy for the most difficult cases.

With divine approval for Moses' leadership and a structural hierarchy in place, the people's basic question "Who's in charge?" is answered. Moses' authority is vindicated by God and supported by a network of leaders serving under him. The resulting clarity provides security for the people, helping them as they learn to trust God and his appointed leaders. It's a lesson they'll revisit later, when jealousy sets in.

But now, we arrive at Sinai.

DIGGING DEEPER

Resources with an asterisk (*) are accessible to a broad audience. Resources without an asterisk are written for scholars.

*Peter Enns. *Exodus*. NIVAC. Grand Rapids: Zondervan, 2000.

*Terence E. Fretheim. *Exodus*. Interpretation. Louisville: Westminster John Knox, 2010.

*Jeff Manion. *The Land Between: Finding God in Difficult Transitions*. Grand Rapids: Zondervan, 2010.

Mark S. Smith. *The Pilgrimage Pattern in Exodus*. JSOTSup 239. Sheffield: Sheffield Academic, 1997.

Related video from The Bible Project: "Torah: Exodus 1–18."

2

SURPRISED AT SINAI

Law as Gift

DIVINE APPOINTMENT

After three months of walking through the wilderness and following the cloud, the Israelites arrive at Sinai, sweaty, dirty, and tired (Exodus 19:1). I wonder if the people had any idea what was in store for them. Had Moses told them about the bush-in-flames? Had he told them about the audacious promise God had made to him on those slopes?

Let's recap the story. Moses was a Hebrew, but he had grown up in the royal palace in Egypt, thanks to a fortunate series of events in which the household that was trying to kill Hebrew babies rescued him instead. However, when Moses was grown, he had an altercation with an Egyptian who was mistreating a Hebrew. Moses killed the man, hid him in the sand, and immediately became "Pharaoh's Most Wanted." He fled for his life, crossed the Sinai Peninsula, joined a Midianite family, and became a shepherd. He stayed away from Egypt for forty long years.

One day, while Moses was herding sheep in an area known as Horeb, God showed up as fiery flames from within a bush that did not burn up. Moses was surprised, intrigued. He approached the bush, and Yahweh called Moses by name. Not only did God know his name, but he knew the names of his father, grandfather, and great-grandfather. (Talk about a long-time family friend!) To announce that he's the God of Abraham, Isaac, and Jacob instantly brings to mind the promises God made to Abraham and reaffirmed to his descendants—promises that had not yet come true. The Hebrews were not out-of-sight, out-of-mind in Egypt. God was still at work bringing his promises of land, descendants, and blessing to fruition. It was time to announce his plan of deliverance.

This divine appointment had two sides to it. Not only did God show up to meet Moses. He also asked Moses to step up and take responsibility. Moses was God's designated special agent for this rescue operation. But Moses was not buying it. "Who am I that I should go to Pharaoh and bring the Israelites out of Egypt?" (Exodus 3:11). After forty years as a fugitive, he thought God was making a mistake. Yahweh's response sidestepped the question. "I will be with you," he said, teaching him an important lesson. It doesn't matter who Moses is. It matters only that God is with him. At that moment, in that sacred encounter, God gives the awestruck shepherd a promise: "This will be the sign to you that it is I who have sent you: When you have brought the people out of Egypt, you will worship God on this mountain" (Exodus 3:12).

And that's not all. At the burning bush, God also revealed his personal name to Moses. This is a big deal. Most gods were known by a pseudonym that kept others at

> It doesn't matter who Moses is. It matters only that God is with him.

arm's length. Knowing the proper divine name offered access to power. For example, in an ancient Egyptian myth called "The Legend of Isis and Re," one god is trying to get control of another, but he can't get the upper hand without knowing the other's real name.[1] But Yahweh, rather than hiding his name and maintaining a measure of distance, invites Moses into his counsel. He and the Hebrews are welcome to address Yahweh directly. They're on a first-name basis.

Before he leaves Sinai to return to Egypt Moses unveils his fears in God's presence: *What if they ask me questions? What if they don't believe me? I'm horrible with words. I'd really rather you send somebody else*

(Exodus 3:13; 4:1, 10, 13). But God has a further surprise in store for him. He works through Moses' staff to validate Moses' leadership, giving a dramatic demonstration of his power. And Yahweh had already designated Aaron as Moses' assistant: "He is already on his way to meet you" (Exodus 4:14)—a divine appointment if ever there was one. God had already started answering Moses' prayer before the words formed on his lips. Aaron was on his way.

Moses must have treasured this encounter during the difficult months ahead—leaving his wife's family, returning to Egypt, trying to rally the Hebrew slaves, and confronting Pharaoh. All the while did he keep thinking about that mountain and Yahweh's promise to bring them all to Sinai?

> At Sinai, everything changes. At Sinai, the Hebrews discover who they are and, more importantly, *whose* they are.

And the people—did they know this is where they were headed? Do they realize they'll camp here almost a full year? I suspect that the Hebrews have Canaan on their minds and hope to get there as soon as possible. If so, they are in for a big surprise. On this divine road trip, the detours are essential. The people are not yet ready for Canaan.

WORSHIP IN THE WILDERNESS

Worship was not only the stated reason for their desire to leave Egypt but was the sign that God had kept his word. Moses didn't ask Pharaoh to let them go forever. He simply asked for a few days to hold a worship celebration to Yahweh (Exodus 5:1). This request was no farce. Though God had promised to completely deliver the Hebrews from slavery and bring them into a new land, Moses' scaled-back request to Pharaoh reveals the stinginess of Israel's Egyptian master. It is not just that he overworks and oppresses the people, depriving them of freedom. He also deprives Yahweh, their God, of worship. Pharaoh's response is a direct challenge to Yahweh. And God's reply is decisive: Yahweh is worthy of worship, and he will tolerate no rivals.

At Sinai, everything changes. At Sinai, the Hebrews discover who they are and, more importantly, *whose* they are. The agenda for this stop is *worship*. For most of us, the word "worship" is synonymous with singing on Sunday morning. However, in the Old Testament era, worship meant presenting God with animal sacrifices as a demonstration of repentance and gratitude for his provision. This is what the Hebrews intended to do in the wilderness—animal sacrifice. Away from forced labor, they would be able to devote themselves fully to a celebration of God's forgiveness.

So Yahweh brings his people out to worship him. He has kept his word. They've been set free! And now they've come to do what they intended, to make things right with God and give him the honor he deserves. It's a divine appointment. And in the process of learning how to honor God, they discover their own vocation. It's not what they expect.

PROFILE UPDATE

Words are powerful.

Whether you like where you are in life or not, there's a very good chance that you can think back and remember a time when someone said something about you that stuck. "You're really good at that." Or, on the other hand, "Don't quit your day job." I remember a particularly dark time in my doctoral studies. Severe interpersonal challenges sapped me of my strength. Just when I was ready to limp across the finish line, my advisors lovingly pulled me aside and told me that I had quite a bit more work to do. I was crushed.

It was during those difficult days that a senior faculty member met me for lunch. She told me, "Carmen, I have every confidence that you will graduate. You will find a great job and you will thrive." Those words meant the world to me. I clung to them for the next eighteen months as I labored to finish my research and writing. And she was right. I did finish, and I did find a job, and I am thriving. But if she had said, "Carmen, jobs are very scarce. You should think about heading in a new direction," I might have walked away. Words are powerful.

God's first message at Sinai lays the groundwork for all the rest of his instructions. These words set a new trajectory for the nation of Israel. If we miss it, we'll likely mischaracterize everything else. Moses heads up the mountain to meet with Yahweh. God gets right to the point:

> This is what you are to say to the descendants of Jacob and what you are to tell the people of Israel: 'You yourselves have seen what I did to Egypt, and how I carried you on eagles' wings and brought you to myself. Now if you obey me fully and keep my covenant, then out of all nations you will be my treasured possession. Although the whole earth is mine, you will be for me a kingdom of priests and a holy nation.' These are the words you are to speak to the Israelites. (Exodus 19:3-6)

Grace in Exodus? Absolutely. When Yahweh responded to the cries of the Israelites in Egypt, he didn't blame them for their predicament. He didn't tell them they were naive or spineless or gullible. He said they were a treasure set apart for a special purpose. We miss the grace because we too often see the Ten Commandments without the glorious context of deliverance. We miss the grace because we read the judgment stories in isolation, without the long litany of second chances. When we read the laws on their own, without the deliverance, we come out with a skewed picture of the Old Testament God. Israel didn't see Yahweh like that. Exodus 19:3-6 is a prime example of grace. In this single passage, four major grace notes are sounded:

1. Yahweh's decisive military victory over Israel's oppressor: "You yourselves have seen what I did to Egypt." God triumphed over Egypt to set his people free.

2. Yahweh's loving care for Israel in the wilderness: "I carried you on eagle's wings and brought you to myself." He carried them, keeping them safe.

3. Yahweh's invitation to covenant faithfulness: "If you obey me fully and keep my covenant." God is no harsh taskmaster. He drew

Israel to himself, offering the Israelites his commitment to bless them.

4. Yahweh's selection of Israel as his ambassador, set apart from other nations for special service: "Out of all nations you will be my treasured possession."

To fully grasp the significance of Israel's new status, I need to teach you my favorite Hebrew word: *segullah* (pronounced SEH-gull-ah). In the NIV, it's appropriately translated as "treasured possession," but it helps if we understand the wider use of this word. *Segullah* appears eight times in the Old Testament. Twice it refers to the king's personal treasury (1 Chronicles 29:3; Ecclesiastes 2:8). The other six occurrences are figurative, referring to Israel as Yahweh's "treasured possession" (Exodus 19:5; Deuteronomy 7:6; 14:2; 26:18; Psalm 135:4; Malachi 3:17). Equating people with a savings account seems odd. In what sense can a group of people be considered a treasure?

The Bible is not alone in using this term to refer to people. The related ancient languages of Ugaritic and Akkadian both employ an equivalent word to refer to someone who enjoys a special status in relation to the king, a covenant partner who is especially treasured and entrusted with greater responsibility.[2] Just as a person carefully puts away his or her earnings for a special purpose and then treasures what they have patiently saved, so Yahweh is said to have selected and saved Israel from among all the nations to be his treasured people. From slaves to treasure. In the Aramaic translations of the Old Testament, the *segullah* is described as "beloved."[3]

The immediate context in Exodus 19:5-6 describes what role Yahweh's *segullah* is expected to play in relation to the rest of the world as a result of their treasured status. They are to be a "kingdom of priests," serving as his ambassadors to the nations, and a "holy nation," set apart for God's purposes. In my all-time favorite book, *The Mission of God*, Christopher J. H. Wright emphasizes that Israel was chosen in order to bless the nations. He says, "They have a role that matches their status. The *status* is to be a special treasured possession. The *role* is to be a priestly and holy community in the midst of the nations."[4]

This is a high calling indeed. And it's not forced on them. Many have the impression that Yahweh's law is heavy-handed, but note the people's reaction to this new arrangement: "So Moses went back and summoned the elders of the people and set before them all the words the Lord had commanded him to speak. The people all responded together, 'We will do everything the Lord has said'" (Exodus 19:7-8). They sign on willingly.

Then, lest the leadership lessons of the previous three months be forgotten, Yahweh arranges a public demonstration of Moses' authority: "The Lord said to Moses, 'I am going to come to you in a dense cloud, so that the people will hear me speaking with you and will always put their trust in you'" (Exodus 19:9). In preparation for this dramatic display, the people wash their clothes and abstain from sexual relations. This is their means of consecration, or being set apart to witness the glory of God. However, only Moses and Aaron are allowed to approach God by climbing the mountain. Thunder and lightning, thick clouds, smoke, and an earthquake are the signs of Yahweh's awesome presence. In the midst of this awe-inspiring scene, Yahweh speaks directly to Moses, who mediates his messages to the people. This should put to rest any lingering questions about who is in charge.

Moses delivers another message, preparing the community to hear directly from Yahweh (Exodus 19:20-25).

And then God speaks again, this time directly to the people. He gives them . . . rules.

SOMETHING TO CELEBRATE

Now we've come to the part that most of us would like to skip over. Dare I say it? The law. After Exodus 19, a single exciting chapter with lightning, thunder, glory, and verses inspiring enough to paint on the wall, we enter the weeds—twenty chapters of detailed instructions about what's allowed and what's not, how to build a tabernacle, and how to dress the high priest. A few stories interrupt this sober litany, for instance, the golden calf, but these are chapters that most of us would be quite content to skip.

However, as I've already noted, Moses' attitude toward these lists of instructions is strikingly positive. For him, law is a gift to be received gladly. And Moses is not alone in this sentiment. In fact, the longest chapter in the whole Bible, Psalm 119, is an extended celebration of the law as a *gift*. Check out this unbridled enthusiasm (emphasis added):

- *Joyful* are those who observe his rules and seek him with all their heart (v. 2 NLT).
- I have *rejoiced* in your laws as much as in riches (v. 14 NLT).
- I will walk in *freedom*, for I have devoted myself to your commandments (v. 45 NLT).
- How I *delight* in your commands! How I *love* them! (v. 47 NLT).
- Your laws are my *treasure*; they are my heart's *delight* (v. 111 NLT).
- As pressure and stress bear down on me, I find *joy* in your commands (v. 143 NLT).

Psalm 119 is an acrostic poem. Each stanza is connected to a letter of the Hebrew alphabet, and every verse of each stanza begins with the same letter. Somebody spent a lot of time crafting this poetic celebration of the law. The poet held it in high esteem. He thought it was the best thing since manna.

But why? Why would the people of Israel consider these rules a treasure? What's the big deal? To understand their enthusiasm, we need to walk a mile in their sandals. The Israelites lived in a time when people were desperate to know what the gods were saying. Since the gods didn't normally *speak* audibly as you and I do, priests were trained to read the signs they left in the natural world. Sometimes they manufactured situations in which the gods could reveal things to them, such as the elaborate rituals in which they dropped oil or flour into water and interpreted the results. They sacrificed animals and studied their livers or intestines (yes, their bloody guts) for clues about what the gods were thinking or what they would do next. They watched for strange births or newborn animals with defects. They studied the stars. They contacted the dead, doing whatever it took to forecast the future or discern the will of the gods. An answer was not guaranteed. Sometimes they simply could not figure out what the gods wanted. Check out this excerpt of an ancient prayer written in Akkadian, the language of ancient Assyria and Babylon. Dating roughly to the same time as the Exodus, the "Prayer to Any God" is characteristic of the literature of this period, which depicts humans as unable to comprehend the ways of the gods.[5]

May (my) lord's *angry heart* be reconciled,

May the *god I do not know* be reconciled,

May the *goddess I do not know* be reconciled,

May the god, *whoever he is*, be reconciled,

May the goddess, *whoever she is*, be reconciled. . . .

O (my) lord, many are my wrongs, great are my sins,

O my god, many are my wrongs, great my sins,

O my goddess, many are my wrongs, great my sins,

O god, *whoever you are*, many are my wrongs, great my sins,

O goddess, *whoever you are*, many are my wrongs, great my sins!

I do not know what wrong I have done,

I do not know what sin I have committed,

I do not know what abomination I have perpetrated,

I do not know what taboo I have violated![6]

The prayer is soaked in anguish. The one praying is not at all certain to whom he is even praying—"whoever you are"—or how he has angered the gods—"I do not know what wrong I have done." His prayer is a scramble to cover all his possible bases. He was desperate to know the deity and to please him or her.

Not so with Israel. God took the initiative. He chose them, rescued them, established them as his people, and then told them exactly what he expected. God *spoke*. No more guesswork. No wondering what would make him happy or angry. He made it all clear up front. How freeing! Why did people breathe a sigh of relief over twenty long and boring chapters of laws at Sinai? This is why.

I am *not* saying that salvation comes through obedience to the law, or that the gospel depends on our effort. Remember—the Israelites had already been rescued from Egypt when they were given the law. God did not say to them, "Do all these things and I will save you from slavery." He saved them first, and then gave them the gift that goes with salvation, instructions on how to live as free men and women. Moses and the psalmist both realized that they were better off for it. They realized that true freedom requires clearly communicated boundaries. They recognized the grace of God's law. It was a gift!

Imagine that your community is planning to build a new playground with easy public access, right beside a busy intersection. Wouldn't it be odd if someone argued that children would have more fun on this playground if there weren't any fences to cramp their style? No, putting a fence between the cars-in-motion and kids-in-motion just makes sense. It ensures that children can play freely without fear of harm. It provides parents with a respite from watching their every move. A good playground includes physical boundaries. These ensure that everyone can have fun and fewer children end up in the emergency room. The fence is a gift! A playground with no fences isn't really freedom; it's an accident waiting to happen.

Israel's laws are the fences within which life can flourish. They make possible a distinctive way of life so that other nations

> Israel's laws are the fences within which life can flourish.

can see what Yahweh is like and what he expects. The law was never the means by which Israel earned God's favor. The Israelites were saved the same way we are—by grace through faith. But their obedience expressed their covenant commitment, or allegiance, to Yahweh. And it kept them in a position to experience the benefits of the covenant relationship.

The covenant promised wonderful blessings for the Israelites—a fruitful land, many descendants, and the opportunity to represent Yahweh to the nations and be a conduit of his blessings. None of those privileges could be realized if they were worshiping other gods or acting treacherously toward their neighbors. For their society to point others to Yahweh's character, they would need to reflect that character in all their relationships. If they allowed greed or lust or idolatry a foothold in their community, Yahweh would need to discipline them, calling them to repentance. Rebellion on their part would activate the other side of the covenant—the stern warning expressed in curses (see Deuteronomy 28). The invitation to covenant with Yahweh was itself a gift, not something they earned by good behavior, but it was not a blank check to fill out how they pleased.

The Old Testament laws related to virtually every facet of Israel's life—business, agriculture, cooking, diet, dress, worship, governance, relationships, health, even the yearly calendar—because being God's covenant people meant being transformed in all these areas. The law envisions a different kind of life, characterized by self-discipline and self-giving love. Imagine a community where every member actively worked to love and protect their neighbor!

Keep this in mind as we enter the maze of instructions at Sinai. This law is a *gift*. It's *good* news. Yahweh *speaks*. And he sets up boundaries so that his people can experience the joy of living in freedom.

LAYING DOWN THE LAW? HOW LAW FUNCTIONS IN ANCIENT ISRAEL

When my son completed fifth grade at Prairie Christian Academy, the school held their annual awards assembly. The occasion was more significant than the usual advancement ceremony because his teacher, Mr. Andries, was retiring after thirty-eight years of teaching. Mr. A. addressed the class, casting a vision for the lifelong project of following Jesus. He inspired them to keep growing and to remain faithful. But Mr. A.'s last words to them were startlingly mundane: "Don't forget . . . ," he paused, allowing the students to chime in and finish his sentence, "to make your bed." It was obvious that this had been his daily mantra.

Mr. Andries had a reason for his advice. He recognized the power of ordinary faithfulness and daily responsibility. Inch by inch, over time it adds up because we become the kind of people who have the discipline and organization to bring lasting change. Picky as some of them seem, the Old Testament laws have the same effect as Mr. A.'s admonishment. After the first inspiring speech at Sinai, where Yahweh calls the Israelites his "treasured possession," the list of rules must have felt rather anticlimactic. At least it does to modern readers. But is it really?

Before we read these laws, let's be sure we know what we're talking about. The English word "law" is both too narrow and too misleading to accurately translate the Hebrew word *torah*. It is better translated as "instruction." Torah encompasses a wider scope of material than just laws. And "law" is not the best word to describe what the Torah contains. Here's why:

In modern Western society, "law" refers to a statute codified by the legislature that indicates either required or prohibited behavior, containing specific penalties that are enforceable by the executive branch of government. Often, their precise details are specified at length. "Buckle up—It's the Law" means that not only is it a good idea to wear a seatbelt in a moving vehicle, it is also unlawful not to do so, leading to a prescribed fine or even the loss of driving privileges. In the state of Oregon, the seatbelt law is statute 811.210, punishable as a Class D traffic violation. On its own, this single statute contains enough small print to fill an entire page. Another section lists eleven exceptions to the rule.

Ancient "law" didn't function in the same way.

Scholars studying ancient cultures are beginning to recognize that ancient laws were often hypothetical, rather than legislative.[7] Lists of any kind were the primary means of demonstrating wisdom. You may have heard of Hammurabi (or Hammurapi, as his name is sometimes spelled). He ruled Babylon in the eighteenth century BCE and is best known for his law code consisting of 282 laws. Copies of Hammurabi's code continued to be produced for centuries, indicating that a ruler such as Hammurabi was held up as the paragon of wisdom in governance. His law code was not legislatively binding, and therefore not cited in court, but rather a collection of wise deliberations on civil society, meant to be studied by judges to inspire reflection on justice. A judge or elder may have found a particular stipulation useful, but they were not bound to apply it across the board.

Could it be that the laws at Sinai fit this ancient category of "law as wisdom"? I think so. Significantly, in spite of the huge number of laws (613 to be exact), we rarely read about their enforcement in ancient Israel.[8] In Old Testament times, the instructions at Sinai would have been understood as the paragon of wisdom—a portrait of a covenant-keeping Israelite. These instructions issued an invitation to a life worth living. Yes, he calls for their commitment, but not without his own. Yahweh's instructions are embedded in a loving relationship.

My husband, Danny, and I require our children to do chores around the house. They clean their rooms, help with dinner, and complete their homework before play time. It would be odd for us to begin giving orders to other kids in the neighborhood. "Hey, Colton! Come take the trash out." Or, "Theron, pull up these dandelions before you play basketball." They would look at us perplexed. We lack the authority to give them chores. We also lack the relationship. At home, our relationship with our children is defined by a lot more than chores. We also eat together, play games together, go on walks, and have late-night conversations. There are hugs and tears and birthday parties and vacations. Chores are only one aspect of being a family.

I wonder if sometimes we read the Old Testament law as though God is that parent giving orders to other neighborhood kids. He's overstepping his bounds or being too demanding or negative. His instructions aren't random, though, and they don't overreach. They are the "house rules" for Yahweh's family. They ensure peace between family members. They are not the main thing, but rather the backdrop for the main thing, the loving relationship. We don't have families so that we can do chores and have rules. We do chores and have house rules to facilitate life in a family.

God's instructions at Sinai are set in a context of redemptive relationship involving mutual commitment. When we fail to realize this, it's no wonder we get bent out of shape.

DIGGING DEEPER

Daniel I. Block. *How I Love Your Torah, O LORD!: Studies in the Book of Deuteronomy.* Eugene, OR: Cascade, 2011. Chapter 1.

*Roy Gane, *Old Testament Law for Christians: Original Context and Enduring Application.* Grand Rapids: Baker, 2017.

Michael LeFebvre. *Collections, Codes, and Torah: The Re-characterization of Israel's Written Law.* LHBOTS 451. New York: T&T Clark, 2006.

Austin Surls. *Making Sense of the Divine Name in Exodus: From Etymology to Literary Onomastics.* Winona Lake, IN: Eisenbrauns, 2017.

John Walton. *Ancient Near Eastern Thought and the Old Testament: Introducing the Conceptual World of the Hebrew Bible.* 2nd ed. Grand Rapids: Baker, 2006. Chapter 13 on Law and Wisdom.

*Christopher J. H. Wright. *The Mission of God: Unlocking the Bible's Grand Narrative.* Downers Grove, IL: IVP Academic, 2006.

Related videos from The Bible Project: "Reading Biblical Law," "Shema: YHWH," "Sacrifice and Atonement," and "Torah: Exodus 19–40."

3

MAJOR DEAL

Covenant as Vocation

WRITTEN IN STONE: WHY TWO TABLETS?

With Yahweh's dramatic appearance and gracious invitation as a prelude, God issues instructions to the people appointed as his representatives (20:1-17). He later calls these instructions the "Ten Words" (Exodus 34:27-28). They are the official terms of the covenant Yahweh is making with Israel (see Exodus 31:18). Unlike all the other commands given at Sinai, God speaks them directly in the hearing of all the people.

DECALOGUE

Although it's standard to call them the "Ten Commandments" in English, the Bible never does. They are always the "Ten Words." This is where the term "Decalogue" comes from—it's made up of the Greek words *deka* (ten) and *logos* (word). "Word" in Hebrew (*dabar*) has a wider range of meaning than "word" in English. It can refer more generally to a "matter" or "thing" as well as a word. As we will discover, the Ten Words contain more than ten commands.

Later, he inscribes them on two stone tablets. Why two? One of the biggest misconceptions about the Ten Commandments is that they did not all fit on one tablet. The vast majority of artistic representations of Moses and the two tablets presume that he's holding "Volume 1" and "Volume 2." However, we know from the biblical text that the commands were written on both sides of each tablet: "And Moses turned and he went down from the mountain, and the two tablets of the covenant document [*eduth*] were in his hand, tablets inscribed on both sides, inscribed on front and back" (Exodus 32:15, author's translation).

The Hebrew word *eduth*, sometimes translated "testimony," is a plural technical term for treaty documents. As with *segullah* above, *eduth* is a word found in related languages, such as Akkadian, to refer to treaty documents.[1]

Given the brevity of the Ten Words in Hebrew, just 171 words total, they easily could have fit on two sides of a single stone tablet, even if that tablet was not much larger than Moses' hand. (This paragraph and the next total 200 words.) So why produce two tablets? For the answer we must turn to other ancient Near Eastern treaty documents. What we find is that it was standard practice to make duplicate copies of a treaty document, etched in stone. One copy belonged to each party, who would put it on display in their respective temple.[2] This way, each of their gods could see the terms of the treaty and watch to ensure that both parties remained faithful. Here's a Hittite example from a treaty between Suppiluliuma of Hatti and Shattiwaza of Mitanni (try saying those names five times fast!). In each king's respective territory, the tablet is deposited in the temple so that the gods can oversee the agreement:

A duplicate of this tablet has been deposited before the sun-goddess of Arinna, because the sun-goddess of Arinna regulates kingship and queenship. In Mitanni land [a duplicate] has been deposited before Teshub, the lord of the [sanctuary] of Kahat. At regular [intervals] shall they read it in the presence of the king of the Mitanni land and in the presence of the sons of the Hurri country.[3]

In the case of Israel's covenant, only one deity can ensure the covenant faithfulness of both parties: Yahweh. For that reason, both copies of the treaty will be placed in the most holy place of the Israelite tabernacle, under God's watchful eye. The duplicate tablets indicate that both parties—Yahweh and Israel—are bound by the covenant between them.

Another myth about the Ten Commandments is that they divide neatly into two groups of laws—one pertaining to God and another pertaining to people. This unfortunate, deeply entrenched misunderstanding goes back many centuries. To cite just one example, the Heidelberg Catechism states:

Q. How are these commandments divided?

A. Into two tables. The first has four commandments, teaching us how we ought to live in relation to God. The second has six commandments, teaching us what we owe our neighbor.[4]

The artificial division between commands demonstrates an inadequate view of how covenants work. In the covenant community, every part of life is an expression of worship and loyalty to the God who has committed himself to these people. How they treat others reveals their heart toward God. Consider this example: after David sins by lusting after his neighbor's wife, committing adultery with her, and then murdering her husband (breaking three of the Ten Commandments), he responds to the prophet Nathan's confrontation by saying, "I have sinned against the LORD" (2 Samuel 12:13). Later he prays to Yahweh, "Against you, you only, have I sinned and done what is evil in your sight" (Psalm 51:4). For David, the so-called interpersonal commands have everything to do with God.

> In the covenant community, every part of life is an expression of worship and loyalty to the God who has committed himself to these people. How they treat others reveals their heart toward God.

Conversely, if just one Israelite rebels against Yahweh, it puts the entire community at risk of God's judgment. An obvious example is

Achan, who kept some of the plunder of Jericho in spite of God's clear instruction not to do so, making Israel vulnerable to defeat at the battle against Ai (Joshua 7). All ten of these commandments reflect a proper disposition toward God, and all ten affect the entire covenant community. By keeping them, the Israelites not only honor God but also ensure that the community of faith can flourish.

I'll never forget a sermon I heard as a child shortly following the Jim Bakker scandal. The television personality and founder of PTL was caught embezzling funds, lying to donors, and allegedly raping a woman. Our pastor did not go into detail, but lamented that "Christians have become the butt of every joke." He was right. One pastor's fall into sin reflected poorly on evangelicalism as a whole, confirming what many suspected: Christianity is full of hypocrites, and preachers can't be trusted. It happened again in 2006 with Ted Haggard, then president of the National Association of Evangelicals, when he was caught in a sex-and-drug scandal involving a male escort.

Like it or not, that's what happens when one member of a company, a sports team, a club, or a faith community behaves badly. It reflects on the entire group and what they represent. There is no such thing as private sin. What we do matters. Not just to us, but to everyone on our team.

With Israel, the problem is even more serious than guilt-by-association. Because the whole nation collectively entered into the covenant with Yahweh, one person's unfaithfulness put everyone else at risk of punishment by defiling the land (see Leviticus 18:28). It was all-for-one and one-for-all.

People often assume that because the Ten Commandments were written in stone, they apply to everyone throughout history, unlike the myriad specific laws in the Torah, which were intended for ancient Israel. But based on what we know of treaties from that time, it should be clear that this line of thinking is out of touch with ancient culture. The Ten Commandments are prefaced with a clear statement of their specific audience: "I am the Lord your God, who brought you out of Egypt, out of the land of slavery" (Exodus 20:2). The commands contain language very specific to that ancient culture ("Do not covet your neighbor's ox"). They are never communicated to other nations. When the Old Testament prophets pronounce judgment on neighboring peoples (e.g., Amos 1–2), they are not measured against the Ten Commandments. Instead, they are measured against a standard of basic human decency. Are they arrogant jerks? Have they taken advantage of other nations' misfortune or been unduly violent? These standards do not clearly arise from the Ten Commandments.

No, the commands in this ancient context are for the Israelites alone.[5] The torah was a gift to Israel, the people of Yahweh. They signed on to it. But what exactly have they agreed to do?

THE GIFT OF LAW: A MANDATE TO FREEDOM

The Ten Commandments are among the most famous passages of the Bible. Even those not raised in the synagogue or church often have a vague idea of what they are—God's divine decree about what people are *not* supposed to do. The unfortunate thing about this is that the commands are usually divorced from their context. If taken alone, people focus on the "Thou shalt nots," and they miss the dramatic story of God's deliverance that sets the stage.

Context is everything. I grew up with the most frugal grandparents on the planet, I thought. We were not allowed to turn on lights until the eye strain became unbearable. We could not waste paper, or water, or any bites of food. Leftovers were always saved for the next meal. Laundry was hung outside to dry. Old clothing was mended first before becoming quilts or perhaps rags. Old carpet became walkways between rows of beans and carrots in the garden. Zip-lock bags were washed for reuse. Scraps of wood were burned in the wood stove, upon which the tea kettle whistled and the pot of porridge cooked. All this frugality made much more sense to me when, as an adult, I visited "the old country" with my Dutch grandma, whom we called "Oma." The Netherlands is a land reclaimed from the sea, where wind is harnessed to pump water, grind grain, press oil, and produce electricity. During

World War II, when Oma was a young woman responsible for her motherless siblings, food was so scarce that they ate tulip bulbs. Walking in her wooden shoes for two weeks helped me to understand why she valued frugality so highly. In context, it made more sense to me.

To understand the Ten Commandments, we must read them in context. We've already considered the larger context, noting that they don't receive the law until *after* their deliverance from Egypt. Now we'll consider the immediate context. The first statement is not "Thou shalt not," but rather "I am"—"I am the LORD your God, who brought you out of Egypt, out of the land of slavery" (Exodus 20:2). *Remember me? I'm the one who rescued your people after 400 years of oppression.* This declaration sets the agenda for everything that follows. If we post these commands in public but leave off verse 2, we could easily give the impression that these commands are a burden or form of bondage for those unlucky Israelites. But no, these commands are given to them by a God who rescued them from slavery, a God who has entered into a committed relationship with them, a God who reveals his personal name. Whatever follows must be a dimension of the freedom made possible by these ten boundaries, within which their lives can flourish. The God who saved them is giving them a gift!

COUNTING TO TEN: THE FIRST COMMAND

Counting the Ten Commandments is surprisingly tricky.[6] We know there are ten because Exodus 34:28 and Deuteronomy 4:13 both say so. Special notations in the Hebrew text preserve two possible ways of counting them. The history of interpretation has introduced still others. Differences revolve around how to handle the first five and the last two verses. Jewish interpreters often consider the preamble (Exodus 20:2) as the first "Word." (Since the Bible never refers to these as "Ten Commandments," but rather "Ten Words," it's plausible to have a "word" that is not actually a command.)

Among Christians, there are two main approaches: the Reformed and the Catholic/Lutheran. The Reformed take "no other gods" and "no idols" are the first two commands, whereas Catholics and Lutherans take these together as the first command. They still end up with ten commands because the last command, "Do not covet," is split in two (note that "do not covet" appears twice).

The way we count the commands makes a difference in our interpretation of them. Consider the traditional Reformed view:

> Preamble: I am Yahweh your God (verse 2)
> Command #1:   You must have no other gods (verse 3)
> Command #2:   You must not make an image (verses 4-6)

The Reformed branch of the church, which counts the command against "images" as its own command, concludes that no images of any deity can ever be made, including Yahweh. The walls of a Reformed church typically contain no pictures of God, Bible characters, or saints.

When I was newly married, I remember a phone conversation with Oma. I mentioned that I was hunting for a nativity scene that we could put out during the Christmas season. I was frustrated because all the options I found were light skinned, blond haired, and blue eyed. She was frustrated for another reason.

"Well," she chided on the other end of the line, "You should skip it altogether. We are not to make any graven images."

I was startled. A nativity scene a graven image? With her Dutch Reformed upbringing, any pictures or other representations of God were off-limits, even if they were not an object of worship, and even, apparently, if they were of Jesus. I argued that because Jesus was God-become-human, an artistic depiction of Jesus did not violate this command. Still, Oma wouldn't budge.

The Catholic church counts the commands differently:

> Preamble: I am Yahweh your God (verse 2)
> Command #1:   { You must have no other gods and
>   You must not make an image (verses 3-6)

Because the Catholic tradition counts "no other gods" and "no images" as a single command, they read the command against images as a command against images *of other gods*. As a result, they permit lavish artistic representations of the one true God and great men and women of faith. Show me the inside of your sanctuary, and I'll tell you how your church counts the commands.

My solution to counting the commands is a combination of all three approaches described above. While most interpreters split Exodus 20:2-6 into two or three separate parts, I count these verses as a single command.

Command #1: {
I am Yahweh your God, so
You must have no other gods and
You must not make an image (verses 2-6)

I take the preamble (Exodus 20:2) as part of the first command, providing a rationale for limiting worship to Yahweh: I am the God who set you free, therefore you should worship me alone. Likewise, "no image" belongs together with "no other gods." I see two reasons for this—one historical and one grammatical. The historical reason is that worship and images went hand in hand in the ancient world. It would be impossible to properly worship a deity without an image of that deity, just as it would be nonsensical to possess an image that you did not worship. The point of images is worship. The means of worship are images.

The grammatical reason to read these commands together is found in verse 5: "You shall not bow down to *them* or worship *them*." The recipients of worship are *plural*, but "image" in the previous line is singular. This prohibition must be continuing the thought of the preceding sentence, a prohibition of other gods (plural). A chiasm (or literary "sandwich" pattern) in Exodus 20:2-6 (or Deuteronomy 5:6-10) reinforces my claim that they should be read together.[7]

> The point of images is worship. The means of worship are images.

A I am Yahweh your God (verse 2)
  B You must have no other gods (verse 3)—*plural*
    C You must not make an image (verse 4)—*singular*
  B' You must not bow down to them or worship them
     (verse 5a)—*plural*
A' I, Yahweh your God (verse 5b)

The prohibition of images underscores the seriousness of the command to worship only Yahweh. The commands make no effort to convince the Israelites that Yahweh *is* the only God. Instead, they call Israel to *worship* only Yahweh. In a sea of options, Yahweh is the only legitimate deity deserving of worship. Rather than *mono*theism (the *existence* of one God), the Ten Commandments teach *heno*theism (the *worship* of one God). This is not to say that there *are* other gods, but the Israelites and their neighbors regularly assumed that they existed by seeking divine favor in pagan shrines. The uniqueness of Yahweh is that he calls for exclusive worship.

So that's the first command: Worship no one but Yahweh. The second command is vitally important for us to understand. There may be a whole lot more at stake with the command not to "take the name of the LORD your God in vain" than you've been told.

INVISIBLE TATTOO: THE SECOND COMMAND

I grew up thinking that "taking the Lord's name in vain" was using "Jesus" or "God" as a swear word. At our house, even "gosh" or "holy cow" cost me a fat twenty-five cents. Both were too irreverent. "Cows aren't holy!" my dad would say. And he was right, of course. Substitute swear words thinly veil the real thing, and they exhibit the same toxic attitude. After Danny and I got married, I picked up on his habit of saying, "Oh, Lolly!" Here was a winner! It had no resemblance to any of God's names and had the advantage of sounding quite cheerful. It functioned as the equivalent of "Silly me!" That word worked well until we joined a new Sunday school class at church and met a new friend named . . . you guessed it . . . Lolly. Now we thought we were taking *her* name in vain and had to come up with an alternative.

Clearly, it's not advisable to use God's name as a swear word—dishonoring God in any way is a serious matter, indeed. But after further study, I'm now convinced that most of us have misunderstood the command concerning God's name, what I call the Name Command. To explain what it really means, we'll have to go back to the Hebrew and attempt a new translation:

> You must not *bear* (or *carry*) the name of Yahweh, your God, in vain, for Yahweh will not hold guiltless one who *bears* (or *carries*) his name in vain. (Exodus 20:7, author's translation)

Most translators have decided that this makes little sense. After all, names aren't lifted or carried, they're spoken. These interpreters conclude that something must be "assumed" in this statement—something that would have been obvious to the Israelites but is not so obvious to us. And most conclude that the missing something has to do with *speaking* God's name, so that the command is prohibiting the spoken use of God's name in some situation.

Some suggest that we should assume the name is being lifted "on the lips" (i.e., spoken), others suppose that a *hand* is being lifted to the name (i.e., raising the right hand to swear an oath). They often point to other passages inside and outside of the Bible to make their case for one reading or the other. The problem is that virtually all of these interpreters overlook the closest and most relevant passage of all, one that illuminates this command without adding anything.

The passage is Exodus 28. Buried in the instructions for building a tabernacle (more on that later) is the plan for what the high priest will wear. As the authorized officiant of the holy place, the high priest cannot dress however he wants. Unlike pastors in evangelical churches today who may wear either a suit and tie or jeans and sandals while preaching, the high priest has a specific costume to wear (more on that later, too). His most striking item of clothing is his elaborate apron, woven with gold threads and set with twelve precious stones, each engraved like a seal with the name of one of the twelve tribes. And Moses is told that the high priest is to "*bear* (or *carry*) the names of the sons of Israel" as he moves in and out of the tabernacle (Exodus 28:29). Moses' brother Aaron, who becomes Israel's first high priest, literally "carries" these tribal names whenever he's on duty.

Aaron also wears a name on his forehead—the name "Yahweh." Tied to his turban is a gold medallion engraved with the words "Holy, belonging to Yahweh." It's just two words in Hebrew: *qodesh layahweh*. The "L" in front of the name Yahweh is the customary way of indicating ownership. If you want to make sure everyone knows that this is your book, you could write your name inside the front cover with an "L" in front

SEALS IN THE ANCIENT NEAR EAST

In the ancient Near East, a common way of declaring ownership of something or of affirming its authenticity was to seal it with a signet ring. Clay tablets often bore the stamp seal of those authorizing their contents or agreeing to its stipulations. Jars of wine or olive oil were sealed shut by means of a blob of clay bearing the authorized seal of a producer, confirming the quality of the product. Seals have even been found bearing the name of a deity. These would have been used in the temple precincts to conduct official business on behalf of the temple.

Some seals were purely pictorial, but others, especially in Israel, were engraved with words. The vast majority of Israelite seals with writing used the letter "L" (called *lamed* in Hebrew) plus a personal name to indicate the owner of the seal. In this context, the "L" is a preposition that means "belonging to." The gemstones worn by the high priest are "each engraved like a seal" (Exodus 28:21), and the medallion on his forehead contains the language we would expect to see on a seal: "holy, belonging to Yahweh" (Exodus 28:36, author's translation). These imply that he is the authorized representative of the tribes to Yahweh as well as the authorized representative of Yahweh to the tribes.

of it, and that would be the normal Hebrew way to say it's yours. With *layahweh* on his forehead, it's clear that the high priest is set apart for service to Yahweh. He belongs exclusively to Yahweh. He serves no other.

So what does this have to do with the Name Command? We've already noted that most interpreters assume it makes no sense for Israel to be *carrying* the name of Yahweh, so they look for other possibilities. But right here in close proximity to the Name Command is the high priest, set apart to belong to Yahweh, *carrying* the names of the twelve tribes. The key to understanding the Name Command is right here!

The twelve gemstones indicate that the high priest represents the entire nation before Yahweh. The medallion on his forehead indicates that he is Yahweh's authorized representative to the nation. Now think back to the dramatic declaration of Exodus 19, when Israel first arrived at Mount Sinai. There God bestowed titles on his people like *treasured possession, kingdom of priests, holy nation.* As his treasured possession, Israel's vocation—the thing they were born to do—is to represent their God to the rest of humanity. They function in priestly ways, mediating between Yahweh and everyone else. They are set apart for his service.

We can see how this connects to the high priest. He is a visual model of the vocation of the entire nation. Just as the high priest represents Yahweh to them, so they represent Yahweh to the nations. By looking at Aaron, every Israelite is reminded of their calling as a nation. Just as he is set apart for service ("holy"), so are they ("a holy nation"). At Sinai, Yahweh claims this nation as his very own and releases them to live out their calling. That calling is to *bear Yahweh's name* among the nations, that is, to represent him well.

At Sinai, he warns the people not to bear his name in vain. Keeping this command, then, involves much more than not saying "Oh, Yahweh!" when someone cuts in front of you on the freeway, or a disgruntled "Jesus Christ!" when your team misses a touchdown pass. Keeping the command not to bear Yahweh's name in vain changes *everything* about how we live.

If that's so, how does the Name Command fit in with the rest of the Ten Commandments? Compared to the rest of the commands, doesn't this one seem a bit too broad to belong on God's Top Ten?

FORMULA FOR SUCCESS: THE FIRST TWO COMMANDS

One of the key differences between the Ten Commandments and all the other instructions that Yahweh gives at Sinai is the mode of delivery. Moses is the mediator for all the other commands; God speaks to Moses on the mountain, and Moses delivers the message to the people. Not so with the Ten Commandments. When we carefully trace Moses' movement up and down Mount Sinai, he has just descended the mountain to warn the people one more time not to climb up when God begins speaking. That puts him with the people, who hear the Ten Words directly from God.

If I'm right about how to count the commands and what the first two are saying, then we begin with the two weightiest commands—the ones that set the stage for all the others. Stated positively, they say:

1. *Worship only Yahweh.*

2. *Represent him well.*

Together they echo Yahweh's declaration to the descendants of Jacob in Egypt repeated so often through the Old Testament, especially by the prophets: "I will take you as my own people, and I will be your God" (Exodus 6:7). Jeremiah and Ezekiel repeat this formulaic statement so frequently that it becomes shorthand for covenant renewal: *I am yours; you are mine.*[8] Unlike the gods of other nations, Yahweh could not be represented by a carved image (20:4); instead he was to be represented by the people to whom he had revealed his name (20:7). Since he had claimed them as his own, their words and actions were to reflect his lordship. The first two commands and the covenant formula they express indicate how Israel should fulfill its vocation obligations successfully. They were to worship him exclusively in order to demonstrate his greatness. If they worshiped other gods, his glory would be diminished. They were to be all in, all his.

These two commands bring the covenant relationship into alignment. Yahweh is the only God worthy of worship. Israel must see itself as belonging to him, representing him to the world. To bear his name in vain would be to enter into this covenant relationship with him but to live no differently than the surrounding pagans. Israel's fate in the succeeding narratives always comes down to breaking these two commands, either failing to worship Yahweh alone or failing to represent him well.

The rest of the Ten Commandments flow from the covenant formula established by these first two commands, fleshing out what covenant faithfulness looks like in every conceivable area of life: work, family, conflict, marriage, property, and reputation. Daniel Block calls the Ten Commandments a "bill of rights."[9] However, unlike the Bill of Rights in the US Constitution, Block points out that these ten do not focus on a person's *own* rights but the rights of one's *neighbor*. The job of every Israelite is to protect other people's freedoms. And it's done by keeping the Ten Words. Let's dive into a discussion of the remaining eight.

> The job of every Israelite is to protect other people's freedoms.

BILL OF (OTHER PEOPLE'S) RIGHTS

With the first two commands in place, the covenantal "formula for success," we can explore the other eight commands.

3. Remember the Sabbath Day. The Sabbath command is the one Christians are most likely to think is no longer relevant. But why wouldn't we want it? The Sabbath command protects the entire household's right to rest, ensuring a rhythm of sustainable living. No one (including animals!) in this new society is to slave away 24/7. Slavery is a thing of the past. Each Sabbath is an expression of trust in Yahweh's provision, put into practice first in the wilderness with the collection of manna six days a week. It's not just the master of the house who gets a day of rest, while everyone else waits on him. Rather, the entire household is free to participate in this rhythm of grace.

Sabbath requires advance planning. Meals prepared ahead, house in order, chores done, homework complete. Sabbath is not simply ceasing from labor, but actually enjoying its results from the other six days. In Exodus 20, God's creative work is the model for Israel's Sabbath. Like a king who rests on his throne after enemies have been defeated and the realm is at peace, so Yahweh rests after he brings order to the universe. It's not that he's tired and needs a nap. Rather, he can sit back and enjoy the fruit of his success.

4. *Honor your father and your mother.* We tend to think of this command as the one for children, but nothing signals a change of audience. Adults must honor their parents too. This is especially critical in a culture with multigenerational households, such as ancient Israel. A friend of mine is engaged in a daily adventure following this command. He and his wife and their four children live in a modest house with both of their mothers and one of their grandmothers. Though having four mothers from three generations in one household is a challenge, to say the least, this family is convinced that they must find ways to honor each one.[10]

Protecting parents' honor ensures that the Sinai covenant will be passed from generation to generation. The New Testament calls this "the first commandment with a promise" (Ephesians 6:2): "so that you may live long in the land the LORD your God is giving you" (Exodus 20:12). But what does this mean? That individuals will live to a ripe old age? Not necessarily. We can all think of godly, parent-honoring people who have died young. No, this command doesn't promise old age. It promises that an entire nation will continue to enjoy living in the land as long as the covenant is kept. Discarding their parents' faith would have disastrous consequences, making the people vulnerable to exile and perhaps death.

The remaining commands all contribute to a community characterized by mutual trust. If every individual covenant member ensures the protection of his neighbor's life, spouse, property, and reputation, then everyone will have space to live and flourish.

5. You must not murder. This command protects the neighbor's right to life and to a fair trial in the case of a dispute. Individual Israelites may not take matters into their own hands, disregarding those with God-given authority to settle disagreements. Tempers do not guard justice. Revenge has no place in the covenant community.

6. You must not commit adultery. Each neighbor has a right to a marriage free from competition. For the covenant community to flourish, relationships between neighbors (and spouses!) must be built on mutual trust. Every man's job is to protect his neighbor's marriage and his neighbor's wife, rather than preying on her.

Sexual intimacy is reserved for marriage because marriage is a reflection of the covenant with Yahweh. In both, two enter into an exclusive commitment: "I am yours; you are mine." For marriage to work as God designed, both parties must give themselves wholly to each other and to no one else.

7. You must not steal. Every Israelite has a right to personal property, free from the greed of the neighbor. As with marriage, the protection of a neighbor's property is everyone's business. "Neighborhood watch" is a very old idea, and it's biblical. By taking what's yours, I demonstrate a lack of gratitude and a lack of trust in God to provide for my needs.

8. You must not give false testimony. In an age without DNA testing, fingerprinting, video surveillance, and lie detector tests, a person's word held a great deal of weight. It was crucial to the maintenance of a just society that no one wrongly implicate a fellow Israelite. Each person's reputation depended on truth. Slander would eat away at the community like acid. Even with all of our technological advances, false accusation still deals a harsh blow, sometimes with devastating consequences. Your word against my word—who is right?

9-10. You must not covet your neighbor's house, and you must not covet your neighbor's wife or any other household member. The Ten Commandments close with two surprising commands that are totally unenforceable. How can anyone prove that someone craved their neighbor's house or wife when lust is a heart condition? The internal nature of these commands hints at the function of the entire law. This is not legislation in a modern sense, but character formation. These instructions paint an ideal picture of a covenant-keeping Israelite, including both outward behavior and inward motivation.

A friend in college posted these words on her dorm-room wall: "Happy is the woman who wants what she has." It's true. Contentment does not lie in gaining more, but in cultivating gratitude for what we already have. Another friend posed the question, "What if we awoke tomorrow with only what we thanked God for today?" To crave what we lack makes us bitter and sullen. It builds a wall between us and the God who has given us so much.

And that's it. Those are God's Top Ten. The stipulations of the covenant—the source or seed of all the rest of his instructions at Sinai.

These first words the Israelites hear directly from Yahweh make quite an impression on them. To put it lightly, they are intimidated. "When the people saw the thunder and lightning and heard the trumpet and saw the mountain in smoke, they trembled with fear" (Exodus 20:18). Given the drama of Yahweh's appearance, the people are glad to have Moses as a mediator. They insist, "Speak to us yourself and we will listen. But do not have God speak to us or we will die" (Exodus 20:19).

Moses reassures them in an odd way. First he says, "Do not be afraid" (Exodus 20:20). But he follows this immediately by letting them know that their fear is part of God's goal: "God has come to test you, so that the fear of God will be with you to keep you from sinning" (Exodus 20:20). So which is right? To fear or not to fear?

In his commentary on Exodus, Peter Enns paraphrases it this way: "Do not be afraid. God is giving you a taste of himself so that this memory will stick with you to keep you from sinning."[11] In other words, you can trust the God who has thundered on the mountain. He is not out to get you. Yes, he's calling you to a high standard of behavior. He expects a lot of you. But he wants you to succeed at covenant faithfulness. He's *for* you. That's why he's letting you see how awesome he is.

If anything, we learn in Exodus 20 that the law is not an end in itself. It is Israel's means of knowing Yahweh, and of living out their vocation in the world. When Moses climbs back up the mountain, God gives him a much longer list of instructions. We quickly discover that the Ten Commandments are not the final word.

DIGGING DEEPER

Daniel I. Block. *How I Love Your Torah, O LORD!: Studies in the Book of Deuteronomy.* Eugene, OR: Cascade, 2011. Chapters 2 and 3.

Daniel I. Block. *The Gospel According to Moses: Theological and Ethical Reflections on the Book of Deuteronomy.* Eugene, OR: Cascade, 2012. Chapters 4, 5, and 8.

Carmen Joy Imes. *Bearing YHWH's Name at Sinai: A Reexamination of the Name Command of the Decalogue.* BBRSup 19. University Park, PA: Eisenbrauns, 2018.

Michael Harrison Kibbe. *Godly Fear or Ungodly Failure?: Hebrews 12 and the Sinai Theophanies.* ZNTW 216. Berlin: de Gruyter, 2016.

*Jan Milič Lochman. *Signposts to Freedom: The Ten Commandments and Christian Ethics.* Translated by David Lewis. Eugene, OR: Wipf & Stock, 2006.

*Sandra L. Richter. *The Epic of Eden: A Christian Entry into the Old Testament.* Downers Grove, IL: IVP Academic, 2008.

Related video from The Bible Project: "Law."

4

NOW WHAT?

Appointed for Service

FROM NOW ON: THE NEED FOR ONGOING GUIDANCE

So much has already happened—the rescue from slavery in Egypt, care for Israel in the wilderness, Yahweh's self-revelation at Sinai, and his invitation for Israel to be his treasured possession, representing him among the nations. In chapter three, we explored the Ten Commandments, discovering that they are central to the covenant relationship between Yahweh and those who bear his name. But what about all the other laws that follow? And how does the tabernacle fit into this picture?

On their own, the Ten Commandments are incomplete. Many areas of life remain untouched. A long list of other instructions from God at Sinai stretches from Exodus 20:22 to Exodus 23:19. Scholars often refer to these three chapters as the "Covenant Code" or "Book of the Covenant." The instructions flesh out what covenant faithfulness looks like in a host of areas: proper worship, fair employment practices, reasonable penalties in case of injury, penalties for theft or loss of someone's property, responsibility toward the community's most vulnerable members, proper conduct in a lawsuit, celebration of holy festivals.

But what's most striking to me about these chapters is what comes next. Lest the Israelites assume they've heard everything they need to know, Yahweh promises to continue to guide them as they leave the mountain:

> See, I am sending an angel ahead of you to guard you along the way and to bring you to the place I have prepared. Pay attention to him and listen to what he says. Do not rebel against him; he will not forgive your rebellion, since my Name is in him. (Exodus 23:20-21)

The angel who functions as Yahweh's authorized deputy, bearing Yahweh's name, meets important needs in four areas (Exodus 23:20-23): (1) protection on their journey; (2) direction to the promised land; (3) ongoing instruction; and (4) leadership in battle. We're told very little about the angel after this passage, so it's impossible to know exactly how this worked in practice, but the point is clear: The law is not the be all and end all for Israel. It does not replace ongoing guidance. They are not "set" now that they know what God expects. Real life is messy. They will continue to have questions, and Yahweh anticipates their need for his direction.

We're offered a few glimpses of what this might have looked like in the months that followed. Leviticus 24:10-23 recounts

> The law is not the be all and end all for Israel.

a fight between two men in which one cursed Yahweh. This should have carried an obvious penalty, but the elders were not sure what to do because the man was only half Israelite. They needed clarification. Do the laws at Sinai apply to non-Israelites or half-Israelites? We're told, "They put him in custody until the will of the LORD should be made clear to them" (Leviticus 24:12). Moses inquired of Yahweh and received clear instructions they could apply to any future case involving a non-Israelite as part of the covenant community: "You are to have the same law for the foreigner and the native-born" (Leviticus 24:22). That settled it.

I remember my first real job in high school. I worked at a Christian bookstore, initially in the office filing invoices, then on the floor ringing up sales. As you'd expect, I first went through orientation. Martin, the store manager, gave me a tour of the store, introducing me to each of the employees, and showing me how product was organized. I learned how to keep track of my hours, where to turn in my timecard, what my responsibilities entailed, and how the computers worked. But that orientation was not the last I saw of Martin. Each day when I reported to work, my first task was to find him. Martin had a clipboard with a legal pad and a pen on a string. He called it his "To Tell" list. On the left-hand side of the page was a list of things he needed "to tell" every employee. Across the top were our names, each of us with our own column. The result was a grid. I would arrive, find Martin, and ask him what he had "to tell" me. He would check his chart to see what he told me last and pick up from there, checking off each item under my name as he did so. "The new shipment of Mother's Day gifts arrived from Thomas Nelson. They're on display to the left of the front door." *Check.* "Inventory is next Thursday evening from seven to ten. Can you be here?" *Check.* "If anyone asks about the new Gaither Vocal Band album, it's on backorder." *Check.* And so it would go. Martin was a great boss. Part of his success, I think, is that he made sure we all had access to the information we needed to succeed. He was available for the duration of the job. When he was away, he appointed someone else to stand in as manager and tell us what we needed to know.

Of course, God is much more than a boss to Israel. The relationship is more intimate, more permanent, and more significant than any working relationship. However, if we stick with the illustration, Sinai was Israel's orientation. They learned about their God, their identity, and their role. Yahweh's expectations were outlined in detail. But, like a job orientation, the law was not enough on its own. Sinai was just the beginning of a long-term working relationship that promised far more than a static list of instructions, as valuable as those were. As Israel faced future challenges, they would need further instruction. And as Israel's context changed, sometimes God's instructions changed, too.[1]

Their relationship with Yahweh was just beginning. The next step, now that they knew his expectations, was to make it official.

SEALING THE DEAL: THE COVENANT RATIFIED

The Sinai instructions sketch the boundaries of the covenant Yahweh initiated with Israel. Technically speaking, this is not a new covenant. Yahweh had sealed the deal with Abram in Genesis 15, promising a vast tract of land for his descendants. Now Yahweh was taking action to fulfill that commitment, outlining the particular stipulations that flesh out what it means to "walk before me faithfully and be blameless" (Genesis 17:1). People often assume that this is a different covenant, but Yahweh directly indicates his purpose in rescuing Israel. He's fulfilling the oath he swore to Abraham and repeated to Isaac and Jacob. No new promise is made here. We simply have a new generation that needs to be aware of the declaration God made and what's entailed if they want to benefit from it. Before Israel's arrival at Sinai, Abram's descendants had only been sojourners, living among other peoples in Canaan and Egypt. As God calls his people out of Egypt, he remembers his covenant again, "I will bring you to the land I swore with uplifted hand to give to Abraham, to Isaac, and to Jacob. I will give it to you as a possession. I am the LORD" (Exodus 6:8).

The book of Deuteronomy sets the Sinai instructions in the context of a sermon, Moses' last words before they enter the land God promised them. While Deuteronomy is not itself a treaty document, it bears some similarity with other ancient Near Eastern treaties. Like Hittite treaties, Deuteronomy's recital of the covenant includes a title (1:1-5); a historical prologue (1:6–4:49); a list of stipulations (chapters 5–26); instructions for depositing the document in the temple (31:9-13); description of the ceremony (chapter 27); a list of witnesses (31:26); and blessings and curses (chapter 28).[2] In spite of these similarities, a few differences between Israel's covenant and ancient Near Eastern treaties stand out. International treaties typically regulate behavior between nations. A greater king (called the suzerain) would make a treaty with a lesser king (called the vassal). In a suzerain-vassal treaty, the suzerain called all the shots, usually in exchange for his military protection of the vassal. *Do not make alliances with other nations. Do not attack our allies.*

Do not fail to send your required tribute. For the Israelites, a different dynamic is in play.

In this case, instead of a "greater king," the suzerain is a deity. God is the great king. His treaty partner is a nation with no king. In effect, each individual Israelite functions as a covenant partner.[3] Therefore, the obligations of the treaty, or covenant, pertain to interpersonal, rather than international, relations. *Do not murder* because your neighbor is also my vassal, whom I have pledged to protect. *Do not worship other gods* because that would constitute disloyalty to the suzerain, the equivalent of making alliances with another nation. *Do not bear his name in vain* because you have been appointed as Yahweh's vassal, charged to represent him among the nations. *Do not steal* because Yahweh is committed to protecting your neighbor from marauders. Stealing puts you at odds with him.

The Israelite covenant has an interpersonal, rather than international, focus because each household has been drawn into relationship with

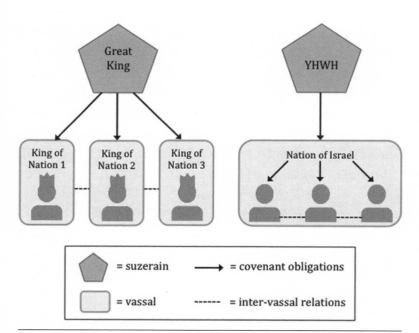

Figure 4.1. Comparison of ancient Near Eastern suzerain-vassal treaty and Yahweh's covenant with Israel

Yahweh and enjoys his protection. Figure 4.1 attempts to illustrate these differences.

Israel's response to the Ten Commandments and the Book of the Covenant is unanimous. "When Moses went and told the people all the LORD's words and laws, they responded with one voice, 'Everything the LORD has said we will do'" (Exodus 24:3). Accordingly, Moses takes steps to ratify the covenant (24:4):

- He writes down Yahweh's instructions as a witness to future generations.
- He builds an altar for animal sacrifice to underscore the seriousness of the agreement.
- He sets up twelve pillars, representing the twelve tribes as party to the covenant.

The entire rite of passage is loaded with significance. A burnt offering cleanses the community of sin. A fellowship offering restores communication with Yahweh. Half of the blood from those offerings is splashed on the altar. Moses then reads the Book of the Covenant to the people. Again, they respond, "We will do everything the LORD has said; we will obey" (Exodus 24:7). Moses sprinkles them with the rest of the blood. We are likely to be more grossed out by this picture than impressed. We can easily get caught up in how foreign this seems and lose sight of the symbolic significance of this action. Blood is an important symbol of life and of purity. The blood spiritually cleanses the people, sealing the covenant, and publicly signifying their position as covenant members. It may also remind them of the blood of the Passover lamb painted over their doorposts in Egypt to invoke God's protection, as the roasted meat would remind them of their last meal in a foreign land.[4]

If we have in mind a typical ancient Near Eastern treaty, the sprinkling of blood on the entire population should strike us as very profound. Treaties

> The blood spiritually cleanses the people, sealing the covenant, and publicly signifying their position as covenant members.

made between kingdoms would have had scarcely anything to do with the general population and would have little effect on them, other than a tax hike so that tribute could be paid. But *every* Israelite is a covenant member. Everyone is responsible to ensure the covenant is kept. And therefore everyone is sprinkled with blood.

In fact, blood is not normally sprinkled on people as part of the sacrificial system. The exception is the ordination of the priests, who have blood splattered on them during the ceremony (Leviticus 8:30). Thus, the sprinkled blood at this ratification ceremony reinforces Israel's priestly vocation. The Israelites constitute an entire kingdom made up of priests, a nation set apart, Yahweh's *segullah*.

That this covenant is ratified outside the land is also significant because all twelve tribes start on a level playing field. No tribe gets to serve as host to this important moment.[5]

After the ratification, Moses brings the elders partway up the mountain to eat a covenant meal in Yahweh's presence. Moses ascends the rest of the way himself to receive the two stone tablets and the tabernacle instructions, delegating authority to Aaron and Hur in his absence. If Yahweh is to be their God, preparations must be made that will facilitate his dwelling among them. But it doesn't take long for Israel to fail at keeping their end of the bargain. By the time Moses returns, the community is courting chaos.

SHATTERED: THE COVENANT BROKEN

While Moses is gone, the Israelites get restless. As hours stretch into days and days stretch into weeks with no sign of Moses' return from the mountain, people become uneasy. He has disappeared up the mountain, and his god is therefore inaccessible. A leadership vacuum yawns. Israel's lessons in the wilderness are recent, but fading. They want something tangible to rely on. They want a god they can see and a leader present to assist them. No matter that they had agreed not to make images of any god; they pitch their idea to Aaron: "Come, make us gods who will go before us" (Exodus 32:1).

It's hard to imagine how Aaron can justify his compliance with the people's request. Of all people, he should know better. Moses, when he later arrives on the scene, wonders the same thing: "What did these people do to you, that you led them into such great sin?" (Exodus 32:21). Perhaps in his mind, he is not making an image of another god, but an image of Yahweh's mode of transportation. In surrounding cultures, some worshiped a deity in the form of a calf or bull and others imagined their deity riding a bull. Maybe Aaron is trying to strike a delicate compromise between the commands of Yahweh and the demands of the people. However, I have already suggested that worshiping other gods or making an image are both violations of the same command. Either way, Aaron is out of bounds. After shaping the calf from gold the people supplied, Aaron says nothing. His silence is the occasion for the people's announcement: "These are your gods, Israel, who brought you up out of Egypt" (Exodus 32:4). Aaron's immediate response is to build an altar and announce a festival to Yahweh. Is this his attempt at damage control, a sleight of hand to turn them back to proper worship?

In any case, it doesn't work. The people present offerings on the altar, but also "indulge in revelry" (Exodus 32:6), an indication that the festival turned into a wild party.[6] Yahweh is not fooled by their show of piety. His statement to Moses, who is still on the mountain, is almost comical: "Go down, because *your* people, whom *you* brought up out of Egypt, have become corrupt" (Exodus 32:7). Can you detect the disassociation? Now they are *Moses'* people. Whatever Aaron's intentions, Yahweh interprets the golden calf in no uncertain terms as an idol to which the people bowed down. He calls them "stiff-necked," or intractably stubborn, and announces his plan to destroy them and make Moses into a great nation. God is ready to start from scratch.

Moses turns down this once-in-all-of-history opportunity. Instead, he turns things right around, saying, "Why should your anger burn against *your* people, whom *you* brought out of Egypt with great power and a mighty hand?" (Exodus 32:11). He clings to what is true: these are Yahweh's people, and therefore Yahweh's reputation is on the line. He addresses God as naturally as if he is in a conversation with a colleague: "Why should the Egyptians say, 'It was with evil intent that he brought them out, to kill them in the mountains and to wipe them off the face of the earth'?" (Exodus 32:12). Moses can just imagine the headlines back in Egypt: "Escaped Slaves Slaughtered by Yahweh!" The implications of this news would be far worse than the frustration of Israel's momentary rebellion. The nations would get the wrong impression about what sort of God Yahweh really is. After all, Yahweh swore by himself to Abraham, Isaac, and Jacob that he would make Israel into a great nation and give them land. Although he is right to be angry, to destroy them now would be a negation of his own character, a breaking of his word. For Moses, no personal glory could possibly outweigh these disastrous results.

Moses' attitude bears further consideration. What would motivate any of us to turn down an opportunity to be a star and at the same time get revenge on all those who've made life difficult? Anything at all? For Moses, the dishonor to God himself that would result from God's proposed actions overrides everything else. Maybe this is why Moses is called "more humble than anyone else on the face of the earth" (Numbers 12:3). At Sinai, he refuses to put himself ahead of God's reputation.

The greatest mystery of this story is that Yahweh repents (Exodus 32:14). In response to Moses' plea, God decides not to wipe out his people. This raises so many questions for me. *Is Moses' prayer effective mainly because he calls on God to act in accordance with his own character? If so, why does God need a reminder to act consistently with his own self? What would have happened if Moses hadn't prayed?* We're simply not told.

The story becomes even more complex when Moses gets down the mountain and sees their rebellion with his own eyes. The text tells us "his anger burned and he threw the tablets out of his hands, breaking them to pieces" (Exodus 32:19). His anger burned? This is exactly what Yahweh had said of himself on the mountain: "Leave me alone *so that my anger may burn* against them" (Exodus 32:10). One wonders if Moses was able to be calm and reasonable on the mountain because he hadn't yet seen what God could see. Now he sees and lets it fly. He smashes the covenant tablets, demonstrating vividly that the covenant itself had already been broken.

Moses' shattering of the tablets certainly would have seized their attention. Aaron's response is a classic picture of human nature at work: "You know how they are." He quotes their request exactly, but paraphrases his own response, deemphasizing his role in their rebellion: "They gave me the gold, and I threw it into the fire, and out came this calf!" (Exodus 32:24). The narrator has already told us how invested Aaron was in the project: Aaron "took what they handed him and made it into an idol cast in the shape of a calf, fashioning it with a tool" (Exodus 32:4). Aaron is the artisan, a fact he conveniently leaves out of his report.

The story ends with the valiant actions of the Levites to bring an end to the orgy and with Moses' earnest plea for God's mercy. Not only is he willing to give up being the head of a new nation; he is willing to forfeit his own record in the book of life to spare the obstinate nation (Exodus 32:32). How inspiring! But Moses is not alone in his mercy toward the Israelites. Yahweh already has a rescue plan in place. Their rebellion was no surprise to him.

BLUEPRINTS OF MERCY: PLANS
FOR THE TABERNACLE

What's most remarkable to me about the golden calf incident is what immediately precedes it. The seven chapters we skipped over contain detailed plans for the construction of a tabernacle—a special tent that simultaneously enables the presence of Yahweh to dwell among the Israelites while providing relief from the devastating effects of their own rebellion. The Israelites had agreed to the terms of the covenant, but God's first order of business was articulating to Moses the means by which they could be forgiven for breaking that covenant. Wow. That's grace.

My husband and I celebrated our twentieth anniversary in the Colombia River Gorge. The Colombia forms a boundary between Oregon and Washington and is home to some of the most breathtaking views on the continent. We revisited our favorite honeymoon spot, Bridal Veil Lodge, a short walk from Bridal Veil Falls, one of many stunning waterfalls along the Gorge. Each morning we would step out our door, cross the scenic highway on foot, and wind our way through the trees to the overlook. From that vantage point we could see the Colombia River, the busy interstate that traces the river's southern banks, and the tree-laden mountains to the north on the Washington side. We were a good one hundred feet above the freeway, which lay at the bottom of steep cliffs. Wise park rangers installed a strong fence along the edges of the overlook. Rather from preventing our enjoyment of the view, these fences made it possible for us to soak it all in without fear of falling. We could safely get right up to the edge.

The tabernacle was like this. The hot spot of Yahweh's presence was hidden in the innermost chamber of the tabernacle, guarded by the outer tent, which only the priests could enter. The entrance to the holy place was further protected by an outer boundary of curtains with an entrance near the altar. No toddler could accidentally wander into sacred space and tip over the menorah with its seven burning lamps. No sin-stained Israelite would suffer a violent death by getting too close to God's holy presence. The outer boundary of the tabernacle kept them from danger while enabling them to live in close proximity.

The layout of the tabernacle allows them to gaze at Yahweh's glory from a safe distance and have the assurance of his attentive presence without constant fear of ritual violation. Just like the law, the tabernacle offers grace by putting up protective fences.

YAHWEH'S DANGEROUS PRESENCE

It seems contradictory to say that Yahweh is both good and dangerous. Yet both are facets of his character. Because he is loving, he cannot tolerate wickedness. He is a God "who does not leave the guilty unpunished" (Exodus 34:7). When we approach God humbly, repentant for our sin, he is gracious to forgive us. But if we enter his presence unaware of our sin or in a state of rebellion, his holiness demands purification.

We might think of it like the sun, which provides light and warmth for the earth. But if we got too close to the sun, we would be burned.[7] What makes Yahweh's presence dangerous is his purity—in the face of our impurity. The Israelites need a barrier between them and God because their moral and ritual impurity makes them unfit to be near God.

"Ritual purity" is a foreign concept to us today, so it requires some explanation. Leviticus outlines two major categories of impurity for the Israelites—ritual and moral. Leviticus 18–20 instructs the Israelites in the area of *moral* purity. This category is not as difficult for us to understand because it connects with our sense of right and wrong, even if a few of the commands given may still seem arbitrary. God cannot tolerate immoral behavior. When he moves into the neighborhood, the Israelites need to live rightly. Laws for *ritual* purity are outlined in Leviticus 11–15. It was not considered sinful to be ritually unclean, but ritual purity was a requirement for participation in temple activities (that is, rituals). Ritual impurity was caused by substances associated with death, such as dead bodies, reproductive body fluids (menstrual blood, afterbirth, semen), mold, mildew, and skin disease, as well as by eating unclean foods outside the prescribed diet.[8] Impurity was temporary. A person simply had to wait a set period of time, bathe, and offer a sacrifice to be clean again.

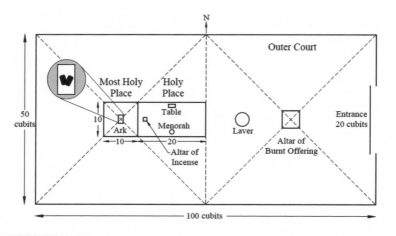

Figure 4.2. Diagram of the Tabernacle

The outer boundary, made of white linen, ensures the sanctity of the courtyard. Only those bringing sacrifices or offerings enter. The priests are prevented from accidental contact with dead bodies or mildew or anything else ritually unclean. The tent itself is more elaborate, made of brightly colored fabrics, signaling the elevated importance of its contents. The tent houses and protects the symbolic implements that enable a sensory worship experience—lampstand for sight, incense for smell, sacred bread for taste. When the high priest enters, the bells on his garments jingle and blood is sprinkled for consecration, involving the senses of sound and touch. Behind the most elaborate curtain, woven with designs of cherubim and held in place by gold-plated wood posts, is the inner sanctuary, entered only once a year by the high priest. Inside is the ark of the covenant, an ornate wooden box, plated with gold, that contains the stone tablets of the covenant and various mementos of God's provision in the wilderness.

With that, the tabernacle plans are complete—a gracious provision for the maintenance of Yahweh's covenant with Israel. But just when we think we've made it through the most boring passage in the entire Bible, the seven chapters of building instructions before the golden calf incident, in Exodus 35–39 they are repeated again almost verbatim! This fact alone has ensured that most of us will skip reading the second half of Exodus altogether. Why say everything twice? In fact, there's an important reason: to underscore the seriousness with which Moses treated God's instructions.

The tabernacle is no free-for-all, choose-your-own-adventure means of creative self-expression. Every aspect of the project is thoughtfully scripted in advance. Each furnishing holds theological significance. Even the color scheme is intentional (more on that later). God invites us to exercise creativity in many areas, but when it comes to his dwelling place, he's the designer-in-chief. Moses' job is simply to communicate the vision and ensure that it is carried out. This he does with scrupulousness, as these chapters demonstrate.

In an age that prizes self-expression, we may have difficulty appreciating this attention to detailed obedience. A rough modern-day equivalent might be building codes. My husband worked as an architectural draftsman before we became missionaries overseas. He remembers the tedious work of trying to follow building code—the right number of parking spaces, each the right width, the right number of spots designated for handicap access, proper sidewalk width and curb height, handrails, and stair tread. This all seemed like a bother until we moved to Manila, capital of the Philippines. Living in a city of eighteen million people with little-to-no building code was hazardous! Walking somewhere was "at your own risk." Gaping holes in the sidewalk—if there *was* a sidewalk—were left unfilled. Step heights were uneven and inconsistent. Stairs often had no railing at all. Many businesses had no parking and no handicap accessibility.

One aspect of our service in Manila was to help a local outreach team with a kindergarten program in an impoverished neighborhood. One summer, the director of the kindergarten had travel plans and asked if I could help oversee construction workers who were replacing the floor of the second story in the concrete building. I knew absolutely nothing about building safety. I was merely to show up every few days and pretend to scrutinize their work. That experience gave me a new appreciation for the value of building inspectors who know what they're doing.

Israel's tabernacle instructions are not a building code with the primary purpose of physical safety, though there are physical repercussions if proper protocol is not followed. Instead, they ensure the spiritual health and safety of a people among whom the most powerful being in the universe has chosen to dwell. These instructions are God's measured and patient way of bringing order to chaos and making it possible for his presence to dwell among them.

DRESSED FOR SUCCESS: AARON AND THE PRIESTS

Another way God brings order to chaos is by designating priests to work within the sacred space of the tabernacle. Aaron does not volunteer for his job as high priest. Neither do his sons. Yahweh chooses them by name. They come empty-handed. They bear no special qualifications. They do not even put on their own uniforms. They become caretakers of the presence of God, responsible for the maintenance of the tabernacle and experts in the procedures that ensure forgiveness for sin. But first they have to be dressed.

The ordination ceremony during which they become authorized to enter the tabernacle and perform sacrifices is commanded in Exodus 29 and carried out in Leviticus 8–9. It may seem like an odd ceremony to us, but it contains all the elements of a bona fide ritual: separation, liminality, and reintegration.[9] A ritual, by definition, changes someone's status in a community and gives them a new identity. For that to work, the person in question must be set apart from everyone else and taken to a neutral zone, a liminal space where the ritual may be performed. Afterward, the person can rejoin the community with the new status. This is precisely what occurs in the priestly ordination ceremony. Aaron and his sons are separated from the people by bringing them to the "entrance to the tent of meeting"—literally a "liminal" space (remember, *limen* is the Latin word for *doorway*). There, Moses publicly washes and dresses them in their carefully crafted uniforms. Aaron's sons wear white linen underwear, caps, and tunics tied with a multi-colored sash.

Aaron himself wears the most elaborate of garments (see Figure 4.3). Over his white tunic (1) and multicolored sash (2) he has a blue robe (3), the hemline of which is decorated with alternating bells and tiny pomegranates made of bright thread. Over that he wears a multicolored apron threaded with gold (4). On his shoulder straps are two gemstones, each listing six of the twelve tribes (5). An attached chest panel is studded with twelve more gemstones (6), each one engraved with the name of one tribe. These gemstones daily remind Yahweh of his covenant commitment to the twelve tribes of Israel, and they ensure that each of the twelve has a place in his ministry. None can be marginalized or forgotten. They all belong. They are all Yahweh's treasured possession. On his head, Aaron wears a turban (7) with a gold medallion tied with blue cords (8). The medallion reads "Holy, Belonging to Yahweh," just two words in Hebrew, *qodesh layahweh.*

These clothes make him what he is—a representative of every Israelite before Yahweh and a representative of Yahweh before the people. Aaron becomes part of the tabernacle, capable of carrying out effective rituals on Israel's behalf. He traverses the space between the outer courtyard and the inner sanctuary, mediating between worlds. In fact, his clothes are an "inside-out tabernacle":[10] his most elaborate garments, woven with purple, blue, red, and gold thread corresponding to the materials of the innermost sanctuary, are his outermost layer. Underneath this, he wears the plain white linen of the outer curtains of the courtyard.[11]

The high priest enters the center of God's presence, the holy of holies, only one day a year, the Day of Atonement. When he goes in, we might expect him to bear the names of the Israelite tribes, but he does not. Rather, Aaron is instructed to wear only his plain linen tunic and turban, perhaps

Figure 4.3. High priestly garments

to symbolize his mediatory role between two worlds. On the Day of Atonement, he comes into Yahweh's presence without pretense, wearing common clothes appropriate for the outer courtyard. Perhaps his simple clothes remind him that he doesn't really belong in the most holy place.

OPEN FOR BUSINESS: THE SACRIFICIAL SYSTEM

Leviticus 1–7 may read like the priests' employee handbook, but these chapters are actually everybody's business. I'll never forget listening to these chapters on audio with my son Easton when he was only seven. Nobody had warned him that Leviticus is boring. Much the opposite: we had watched The Bible Project Read Scripture video on Leviticus and the theme video on Atonement, so he was pumped and ready. As the narrator spoke, Easton was totally mesmerized. I could see the little wheels turning in his head as he tried to follow the logic of this ancient procedural text: *intentional sin, unintentional sin, goat without defect, pair of birds, grain offering.* Once, he asked me to stop the audio, puzzled: "Mom, I thought if they were too poor to bring birds, they could bring a grain offering. But it didn't say that this time." Easton's absorption in these chapters was a demonstration to me of how ancient Israelites would have heard them—with great interest. This was a matter of both national security and personal well-being.

> The sacrificial instructions are laced with grace. Yahweh provides clear steps for restoration of a broken relationship and forgiveness of sin.

The sacrificial instructions are laced with grace. Yahweh provides clear steps for restoration of a broken relationship and forgiveness of sin. The repeated refrain of these chapters is the jubilant proclamation, "and they shall be forgiven."

The priest's training must have been somewhat like the training for a bank teller today. Rather than creativity, the job requires strict conformity to protocol. Money must be carefully accounted for using uniform methods. A teller cannot give money away when she's in a generous mood, nor refuse service to customers if she's feeling cranky.

She cannot come up with her own system for tracking funds. The slightest deviation from bank rules will get her fired.

The elevated status of Aaron and his sons does not allow them to do whatever they want. Like bank tellers, the Israelite priests dare not diverge from their training even a smidgen. There is no room for creativity in their work. They are guardians of procedure and caretakers of protocol. To illustrate just how seriously they were to take their job description, Leviticus 9 offers a sobering account of their first day on the job. After preparing the necessary sacrifices to cleanse the community, "the glory of the LORD appeared to all the people. Fire came out from the presence of the LORD and consumed the burnt offering and the fat portions on the altar" (Leviticus 9:23-24). God's fire was proof that he accepted their offering. By consuming the sacrificial animal, the fire symbolically consumed their sin.

The very next story in Leviticus 10 shows what happens when the priests take their own initiative in worship. Apparently, Aaron's sons, Nadab and Abihu, have a creative itch, so they put unauthorized fire and incense in their censers and offer it before Yahweh. It's not the time or the place or the method God commanded. He is not impressed. He strikes them dead: "So fire came out from the presence of the LORD and consumed them, and they died before the LORD" (Leviticus 10:2). The same fire that consumed sin in the form of an offering in chapter nine, now consumes sinners who have the audacity to think they know a better way to worship Yahweh than what he commanded. Innovation is welcome in other areas of Israel's communal life, but Yahweh cannot tolerate it in the tabernacle—the stakes are much too high. The purity of the entire community is on the line, and therefore their ability to live peaceably with a holy God in their midst.

Perhaps this bothers you. If so, consider occupations in our world today that require strict adherence to policy, such as tax preparation or pharmaceuticals or nursing or aviation. Deviance from policy could be fraudulent or downright dangerous.

Just ask Nadab and Abihu.

DIGGING DEEPER

Michael J. Chan and Brent A. Strawn, eds. *What Kind of God?: Collected Essays of Terence E. Fretheim*. Siphrut 14. Winona Lake, IN: Eisenbrauns, 2015. Part 2.

*Peter Enns. *Exodus.* NIVAC. Grand Rapids: Zondervan, 2000.

*Terence E. Fretheim. *Exodus.* Interpretation. Louisville: Westminster John Knox, 2010.

Carmen Joy Imes. *Bearing YHWH's Name at Sinai: A Reexamination of the Name Command of the Decalogue.* BBRSup 19. University Park, PA: Eisenbrauns, 2018.

Related videos from The Bible Project: "Covenants," "Exodus, part 1," "Exodus, part 2," "Holiness," and "Torah: Leviticus."

5

READY TO ROLL

Prepared for the Promised Land

GOD WITH US

The Israelites had camped at Sinai for some time. It was a season filled with surprises. They discovered who they were—a federation of twelve tribes appointed as Yahweh's unique representatives. They also discovered what Yahweh expected of them in this role: a way of life that protected the rights of each neighbor and worshiped Yahweh exclusively. They learned how to deal with their moral failures as well as how to maintain ritual purity so they could enter God's presence. These lessons were crucial in their formation as God's people. However, Moses had another surprise at Sinai, something infinitely more important this. He met Yahweh face to face.

A. W. Tozer once wrote, "What comes into our minds when we think about God is the most important thing about us."[1] A study of cross-cultural Christian workers by Duncan P. Westwood demonstrates a strong correlation between the picture one holds of God and one's resilience in the face of difficulty.[2]

What picture comes to your mind when you think about God? Westwood developed an exercise in which participants drew images of God in four window panes, depicting how their picture of God had developed over major life stages. His research indicates that the three healthy signs of a God image are:

1. The presence of intimacy

2. Movement or growth through the various stages of life

3. A capacity to embrace the mystery and expansiveness of God[3]

If our picture of God includes these things, we're far less likely to struggle with anxiety and depression and we'll be more resilient in the face of difficulty. Life presents us with a wide range of experiences. If we see God as distant and full of wrath, we will imagine he is against us, which will make us susceptible to a crippling sense of failure or a drivenness to earn his favor. If we see God as exclusively compassionate, we may struggle with him if we experience injustice. How could a compassionate God allow this? Or how could he let the perpetrators of oppression go free? If we instead conceive of God more holistically, we'll be able to release our grip on understanding his ways, and we will be able to trust him to ultimately bring justice. This hope makes us resilient.

How has Sinai changed the Hebrews' picture of God? Their picture began taking shape in Egypt. Each of the plagues demonstrated to Egypt and Israel alike who Yahweh was—a deity more powerful than the gods of Egypt, who holds people accountable for mistreating fellow human beings. Already in Egypt, God's justice and mercy are demonstrated side-by-side.

At Sinai, they encounter Yahweh's glory in an awe-inspiring storm. Moses hears from God on the mountain and then regularly in a tent outside camp. But something is still missing. Moses fervently expresses his desire to know Yahweh more fully: "Teach me your ways so I may know you and continue to find favor with you" (Exodus 33:13). When God promises to go with them as they leave Sinai, Moses insists, "If your Presence does not go with us, do not send us up from here! How will anyone know that you are pleased with me and with your people unless you go with us? What else will distinguish me and your people from all the other people on the face of the earth?" (Exodus 33:15-16). For Moses, Yahweh's personal presence with them was non-negotiable. Without him, they were nothing. Everything they were was because of who he was.

The same is true of you and me. What matters most about us is to whom we belong.

And what sort of God is he? Moses has a once-in-a-millennium opportunity to see God's glory up close in Exodus 33–34. He ascends the mountain with a second set of blank stone tablets so the covenant stipulations can be reinscribed. During this mountaintop experience, Yahweh answers Moses' earnest request to *know* him. He shows himself visibly to Moses and unpacks for him what it means to be Yahweh, choosing these words to define his name and convey his character:

> What matters most about us is to whom we belong.

The LORD, the LORD, the compassionate and gracious God, slow to anger, abounding in love and faithfulness, maintaining love to thousands, and forgiving wickedness, rebellion, and sin. Yet he does not leave the guilty unpunished; he punishes the children and their children for the sin of the parents to the third and fourth generation. (Exodus 34:6-7)

Yahweh demonstrates grace for those who sin, yet he takes sin very seriously. God's grace coexists with his justice. They are both integral to his character. If holding in tension various aspects of God's character reduces anxiety and depression, then it would be worth our time to ponder this. Would God be loving if he let people get away with murder? Of course not. Yes, he forgives, but the implication is that forgiveness is available through prescribed channels—sacrifice at the tabernacle—to those who approach him with contrition. A murderer who repents is restored to a right relationship with him and with the community. On the other hand, those who disregard his means of grace merit punishment,

YAHWEH'S LONG NOSE

One of my favorite parts of Exodus 34:6-7 comes in the second line: "slow to anger" is literally "long of nose" in Hebrew. Imagine the inflamed nostrils of someone hot with anger. Their face is red, they snort with outrage. Not so with Yahweh. His nose is long enough that the heat of his anger has time to cool before he acts rashly.

My other favorite phrase is "abounding in love and faithfulness." These two words in Hebrew are *hesed* and *emet*. *Hesed* indicates Yahweh's covenant faithfulness, his loyal love expressed in action. Similarly, *emet* indicates that he is true to his word. This God who has descended to engage with the nation of Israel is by nature someone who keeps his word.[4] We can rely on him.

as we saw with Nadab and Abihu. At Sinai, Moses' picture of who Yahweh is gets a thorough upgrade.

Moses makes the most of this momentous occasion. He expresses his deepest desire, requesting Yahweh's presence to travel with them. Moses wants more than a mountaintop experience. He wants the transforming presence of God in their midst wherever they go. For Moses, it has become the only thing that matters. Yahweh agrees. He has in mind "wonders never before done in any nation in all the world" that will show the nations how awesome he is (Exodus 34:10). Yahweh is jealous, with the jealousy of a husband for his wife who is in danger (Exodus 34:14). Israel's most important task is cultivating the memory of who he is and what he has done for them.

When Moses comes down, his face is luminous. Literally.

And so are you. When you spend time in the presence of God, seeing him as he really is, you begin to see who you are as well—rather, *whose* you are. Knowing that you belong to him makes all the difference in the world.

As soon as the tabernacle is built, this same glory shown to Moses on top of the mountain descends and fills the sanctuary (Exodus 40:35).

It's the moment they've been hoping for, the sign that Yahweh will travel with them to the promised land. "The glory of the LORD appeared to all the people. . . . And when all the people saw it, they shouted for joy and fell facedown" (Leviticus 9:23-24). As well they should.

GROUP PROJECT: CENSUS OF FIGHTING MEN

Israel's sojourn at Sinai is just about over. They have met Yahweh. They have learned what it takes to be successful. They have become who they need to be. The book of Numbers describes their final preparations to march out.

We might as well be honest. These are not familiar chapters. Hardly anybody reads the book of Numbers. The multitudes who start out on a Bible read-through in January typically get through Genesis and maybe Exodus, but by Leviticus they throw in the towel, which means they never even reach Numbers. In fact, if by some great cosmic fluke, the book of Numbers disappeared from all of our Bibles, most of us would neither notice nor care that it was missing. We can do without it, right? Or can we?

There are surprises in store *even* in Numbers, if we have eyes to see.

The book begins with a census of fighting men (hence the name "Numbers"). We don't tend to find lists of names very exciting, but perhaps those of you in leadership positions can at least appreciate that God is well-organized. He takes a rag-tag bunch of slaves and whips them into shape at Sinai, leading them every step of their journey through the wilderness, even laying out exactly how to set up camp. Then he assigns jobs to various clans to make sure the whole operation works smoothly. Freedom is no castle in the sky, no philosophical concept. God's vision takes shape concretely on the pages of Numbers. It's practical. For people who have only known life as slaves and have had little practice at self-determination, God meets them where they are and makes their task straightforward. Follow me. Camp here. Eat this. Line up in this order.

But God's concrete instructions are only the first surprise. Just below the surface of these endless lists of names and numbers—lists that make our eyes glaze over—precisely here is hidden one of the most profound truths of the book. These lists are good news.

Imagine for a moment that *you* were one of those Hebrew slaves trapped in Egypt. The faint echoes of God's promises to Abraham—that his descendants would be a great nation with a great name, able to bless all nations—have all but died. The opposite is in fact true. You have become powerless and oppressed. Those who curse you are getting stronger by the day. Then, when you least expect it, help arrives. Moses ushers you out from under the strong arm of Pharaoh and you are free. You experience firsthand Yahweh's great power at Sinai and his caring provision in the wilderness. God's promises to Abraham— land, blessings, and as many offspring as the stars in the sky—are renewed for your generation and you can nearly taste their fulfillment. Gradually you learn that you can trust him. One year later—one year after the great escape—it is time to count the stars. The census lists prove that God has fulfilled the first of his great promises: you are indeed a great nation.

One man from each tribe is selected to count the eligible fighting men in his tribe. As each tribal head is named, imagine the effect on his family members—wife, siblings, children—and on the extended family that makes up his tribe:

> From Reuben, Elizur son of Shedeur,
> From Simeon, Shelumiel son of Zurishaddai,
> From Judah, Nahshon son of Amminadab . . .
> (Numbers 1:5-7)

Each man stands tall, arms crossed, nodding solemnly as his name is read. Children tug at Momma's skirts, their wide eyes seeking hers as they recognize their grandpa's name. The parade of names culminates in a parade of numbers after the counting is complete:

> From the descendants of Reuben the firstborn son of Israel: All the men twenty years old or more who were able to serve in the army were listed by name, one by one, according to the records

of their clans and families. The number from the tribe of Reuben was 46,500. (Numbers 1:20-21)

It's as if God whispers in each ear, *You no longer belong to Pharaoh. You belong to me. I know your name. You are mine. You matter. You've spent your entire life making bricks to build someone else's kingdom, making their vision a reality. But everything's different now. Your story is much older than Egypt. It stretches all the way back to a promise, and your future is bursting with possibility. Your family's name is on the roster of a new nation. You belong. You count. I will give you your own land, and you will govern yourselves.*

In Numbers 7 we're treated to another parade. This time each tribal leader gets a day to shine as he presents Moses with an identical offering for the tabernacle—a silver plate and a silver bowl filled with fine flour and olive oil (grain offering), a gold dish of incense, a bull, a ram, and a male lamb (burnt offering), a male goat (sin offering), two oxen, five rams, five male goats, and five male lambs (fellowship offering). The parade of gifts would have been each tribe's pride and joy.

We usually skip over these lists. But if our grandpa's name were listed, or if our uncle carried the silver bowl laden with fine flour, this would be our favorite part! We, too, would be participants in the worship of Yahweh!

Several years ago I had the opportunity to visit Yad Va-shem, the Holocaust museum in Jerusalem. One room contains an archive of "righteous Gentiles"—non-Jews who worked to resist the Nazi regime during World War II and rescue Jewish neighbors. I spent a few minutes in that room hunting for my grandmother's name. Oma had worked as part of the Dutch Resistance, delivering messages to Allied soldiers by rolling them up in the handlebars of her bicycle. But she didn't hide any Jews, only an American soldier who had parachuted onto their backfield after his plane was shot, so her name wasn't listed. Imagine if I had found her name listed there! These lists of archived names may seem "boring" to some, but not to those whose ancestors are honored.

For the people assembled at Sinai, these lists must have been downright exhilarating. Proof of divine election. Proof of belonging. Proof of participation in the covenant community.

The Israelites are not the same people who arrived at the mountain nearly a year before. Their dislocation and uncertainty have been replaced by clear instructions from strong leaders. Their camp is organized around the tabernacle, the concentration of God's presence in their midst. They are who they are because they belong to Yahweh. Each individual has a place in this community and a job to do, down to who carries what when it's time to move. They left Egypt as families, but they're leaving Sinai as tribes.

I have no personal military experience, but I imagine that Israel's transformation at Sinai is similar to the making of a squadron of soldiers at boot camp. Recruits arrive from various locations with diverse backgrounds and personalities. They come as individuals wanting to prove themselves. Some are too stubborn to submit to their leaders willingly at first. But by the end of their training they have become a team ready to take orders, ready to face anything together.

The Israelites are a nation now. And Yahweh has a special blessing in store for them.

#BLESSED: THE PRIESTLY BLESSING

It is here, in the midst of the census, the instructions for setting up camp, the outline of duties for the Levites and the other priestly clans, the guidelines for keeping the camp pure and fulfilling vows—here, in this unlikely place God has another surprise in store. He entrusts it first to Moses, who tells Aaron and his sons, who announce it to the entire nation. It's known as the priestly blessing—the tiny part of Numbers we've incorporated into our church services because it is beautiful. We may have heard this gospel blessing time and again. But it is more profound if we read it with Israel, against the curse of their long years of thankless toil in Egypt, in light of the freedom so newly given, as the culmination of their new vocation as Yahweh's representatives. God is so determined to bless his people that he includes it in Aaron's job description. Here is the good news:

> The LORD said to Moses, "Tell Aaron and his sons, 'This is how you are to bless the Israelites. Say to them:
> """The LORD bless you
>   and keep you;
> the LORD make his face shine on you
>   and be gracious to you;
> the LORD turn his face toward you
>   and give you peace.'"
> (Numbers 6:22-26)

And the wonder of it all is that they've done so little to deserve it. They have whined, complained, doubted, rebelled, and cowered in fear when they should have trusted. But God is unwilling to drop the promises he made to Abraham. He is committed to his plan to bless.

In the following verse, Yahweh concludes his instructions: "So they will *put my name* on the Israelites, and I will bless them" (Numbers 6:27). In blessing *by* his name, he is essentially placing his name upon his people. Yahweh had already claimed them as his own at Sinai. Now he institutes an official blessing to serve as a regular reminder. From this moment on they are identified as his.

This blessing recalls the command not to bear Yahweh's name in vain (Exodus 20:7). It is the clearest indication in Scripture of Yahweh actually putting his name on his people. In the ancient world, slaves were often tattooed with their owner's name—either on their forehead or on their hand or forearm. Temple servants were even branded with the name or symbol of the god to whom they belonged.[5] The Israelites had just been freed from forced slavery, but they had entered into another arrangement where they were not free to do anything and everything they wanted. Now they willingly belong to Yahweh. They bear *his* name, dedicating their lives to *his* service. Their new master is determined to bless. They wear his invisible tattoo.

Deuteronomy 28:9-10 reflects on this reality in reference to the next generation. It says, "Yahweh will establish you as his holy people, as he has sworn to you, if you keep the commandments of Yahweh your God and walk in his ways. All the people of the earth shall see that the name of Yahweh was invoked over you and they shall be afraid of you" (author's translation).

To have this blessing invoked over them reinforces the idea that Israel is selected for a particular purpose. As bearers of Yahweh's name, they represent him among the nations. Everyone is watching the Israelites to find out what sort of god Yahweh really is. And these nations soon discover that anyone who messes with Israel must answer to him.

Later in the book of Numbers, Balak, king of Moab, would find this out the hard way (see Numbers 22–24). Balak is afraid of the Israelites (as Yahweh had said the nations would be). He hires Balaam, a sorcerer, to call down curses on Israel. The two attempt multiple vantage points overlooking Israel's camp, hoping for curses to come. Instead, only blessings flow. No matter how much money King Balak offered the prophet Balaam, he could not entice Balaam to curse the Israelites. Balaam knew better than to cross Yahweh. Yahweh has nothing but blessing in store for his people. Even after all of their sin, Yahweh was entirely committed to blessing his people.

To bear the name of Yahweh, to bear his blessing, entails great responsibility. This explains the purpose of Israel's laws. They are to be a people set apart, a holy nation.

PROFANING YAHWEH'S NAME

Leviticus adds depth to the idea of bearing Yahweh's name by fleshing out the behaviors that profane it. Significantly, profaning the name—failing to set it apart as holy—is not just a matter of improper speech. Israel could profane the name through child sacrifice to Molek (Lev 18:21; 20:3), false swearing (19:12), participation in pagan funerary rites (21:5-6), improper handling of temple gifts (22:2), or cursing Yahweh (24:11). Leviticus 22:31-32 links profaning the name with breaking any command.[6] Israel's holiness requires distinctive behavior (Lev 11:44; 19:2; 20:24-26).

Others should be able to tell just by looking at Israel that they belong to Yahweh. What they wear, what they eat, how they treat one another, who they are intimate with, how they do business—all these reflect on Yahweh. Israel declares their covenantal status by living according to Yahweh's instructions. If they fail, Yahweh's name—his reputation—is at stake. When they do fail, the prophets charge them with profaning Yahweh's name among the nations.

LOOKING BACK: REMEMBERING SINAI

The stories we tell ourselves shape what we believe and how we behave. Steven Sample is the president of the University of Southern California. In his bestselling book, *The Contrarian's Guide to Leadership*, he suggests that one of the keys to successful leadership is to learn to tell the story of your institution.[7] Constituents need to know that they are part of something bigger than themselves and that it's headed somewhere other than bankruptcy. Left to themselves, members of our community may buy into a self-defeating narrative.

In the echo chamber of the desert, that liminal space, competing interpretations try to make sense of Israel's experience. The story can be spun any number of ways. Here are a few of the voices that ricochet off Mount Sinai:

The Sullen: "If only we had died by the LORD's hand in Egypt! There we sat around pots of meat and ate all the food we wanted, but you have brought us out into this desert to starve this entire assembly to death" (Exodus 16:3).

The Skeptic: "It was with evil intent that he brought them out, to kill them in the mountains and to wipe them off the face of the earth" (Exodus 32:12).

The Jubilant: "Praise be to the LORD, who rescued you from the hand of the Egyptians and of Pharaoh. . . . Now I know that the LORD is greater than all other gods" (Exodus 18:10-11).

> These were not wasted years. They were years of training, of becoming.

If we fast-forward to the book of Deuteronomy, we can listen in on several authorized retellings of Israel's story. In his final sermon, Moses gives us his perspective on their years in the wilderness:

> Remember how the LORD your God led you all the way in the wilderness these forty years, to humble and test you in order to know what was in your heart, whether or not you would keep his commands. . . . As a man disciplines his son, so the LORD your God disciplines you. (Deuteronomy 8:2, 5)

These were not wasted years. They were years of training, of becoming. Moses wants the people to be ready for what comes next. For that, they need to learn to tell their story. Like Steven Sample, Moses understands the importance of telling the story well. He teaches them the following grace-filled narrative—an official answer to their children's question, "What do all these laws mean?"

> We were slaves of Pharaoh in Egypt, but the LORD brought us out of Egypt with a mighty hand. Before our eyes the LORD sent signs and wonders—great and terrible—on Egypt and Pharaoh and his whole household. But he brought us out from there to bring us in and give us the land he promised on oath to our ancestors. The LORD commanded us to obey all these decrees and to fear the LORD our God, *so that we might always prosper and be kept alive,* as is the case today. And if we are careful to obey all this law before the LORD our God, as he has commanded us, *that* will be our righteousness. (Deuteronomy 6:21-25, emphasis added)

The problem with stories is that we forget them unless they are rehearsed. Several years ago I attended a conference in San Antonio, Texas. My hotel happened to be right next door to the Alamo. I racked my brain trying to recall what had happened there, but ironically, all I could come up with was the rallying cry, "Remember the Alamo!" That was precisely what I could not do, because I had not heard the story again after my elementary school history lesson.

Yahweh knows this about humans, so he comes up with a spectacular plan that will sear these memories deep into his people's consciousness: a party. Every year, the Israelites will set aside a day to reenact their last night in Egypt. This party is so important that anyone who is unable to celebrate gets a rain check—they celebrate it the following month.

For detailed party plans, we have to turn back to Exodus 12, where the nail-biting story of Israel's deliverance is awkwardly interrupted by nearly two chapters of ritual instructions. But this interruption is profound. The Passover ritual ensures that every succeeding generation of Israelites will own the exodus. It will be *their* story. The exodus makes them who they are. That's what makes this party—and its lengthy instructions—so important. The menu includes a male lamb without defect, roasted over the fire, whose blood is brushed on the doorframes of their houses, bitter herbs to remind them of the bitterness of slavery in Egypt and bread without yeast to remind them of their hasty departure. The yearly festival ensured that the exodus would be more than a distant memory. It would evoke the smell of lamb roasting, flatbread baking, and warm blood dripping. It would elicit the sight of death and family and traveling clothes. It would summon the bitter taste of slavery, the feel of soft dough and scratchy wool, the sounds of fire crackling and stories being told, the sense of Yahweh's protection over the entire household.

Traditions can be powerful, especially when they involve food. As a child, we had a somewhat unusual tradition. Each Thanksgiving Day, my entire extended family would meet at a hotel restaurant for a buffet brunch. Hours before turkey and stuffing and mashed potatoes and gravy and pumpkin pie, we would load up on waffles and syrup, fruit compote and scrambled eggs. I always thought it strange to have two giant meals in one day, but I didn't argue. Eventually I asked why and got a comical answer. As it turns out, one Thanksgiving during my Mom's childhood the oven was broken, so the family went out for a big breakfast. Somehow it became an annual tradition. Even now, some fifty years later, my cousins and their families who are scattered across North America have kept up the tradition. We don't gather the extended family anymore, but we do take our children out for breakfast on Thanksgiving Day. Something seems missing without it.

Danny and I have added to the tradition. We bring along a Bible, paper, and pen. First we read Psalm 100 and Deuteronomy 8, about the importance of remembering what God has generously given us. Then we make our annual thankful list.

If Israel forgets their story, they're in danger of forgetting who they are and to whom they belong. To help the Israelites remember the events that define them, Yahweh institutes the Passover celebration as a multisensory experience. It is a winning plan to cultivate the story and keep it alive.

MARCHING ORDERS

Sinai is framed by trumpets. Israel's arrival at Sinai is heralded by the loud blast of a ram's horn (Exodus 19:16). In Numbers 10, a trumpet blast signals that their time at Sinai has come to a close. The silver trumpet sounds. They see the cloud lift. And it's time to set out—each tribe marching in order. Each tribe under its standard.

The ark containing the covenant tablets out in front with the pillar of cloud.

Three tribes.

The tabernacle, taken apart and carried by designated clans.

Three more tribes.

The tabernacle furniture, wrapped and carried by designated clans.

Three more tribes.

Three tribes as a rear guard.

It must have been quite a parade.

If we accept current English translations, the Hebrews numbered 600,000 men plus women and children when they left Egypt (Exodus 12:37). That would total at least two million people.

It's worth mentioning, though, that there are other ways to understand the numbers in the Hebrew text. While the English text is usually very reliable, in this instance I think it's quite possible that inaccurate English translations have misled us, and the numbers may be substantially smaller. I have no desire to undermine the biblical text. My goal, first and foremost, is to translate Scripture in the most accurate way possible. To suggest that Yahweh rescued fewer Israelites from Egypt is not to undermine his power.

HOW MANY HEBREWS?

Why question the numbers given in Scripture for the Hebrew population? Two reasons: (1) Because archaeologists' best estimates of population sizes during this period of history, both in Egypt and in the land of Canaan in the decades that follow, are much lower. A much smaller group of Israelite escapees would fit the evidence we have. (2) Because this large number introduces problems with the biblical text. In the first place, it stretches credulity to suppose that the twelve sons of Jacob became a nation of two million people in only four generations (see Exodus 6:14-25 for the family tree).

Furthermore, if the total number of males over twenty years old is 603,550, then males of all ages would total over a million. Numbers 3:43 lists the total of *firstborn* males as only 22,273. If there were a million men total, then the number of firstborns compared to the total number of men would yield a ratio of fifty to one. And that's only counting males, not females. That means every Israelite mother would have averaged 100 children.[a] Obviously that's not realistic.

So what are our options?

(1) Assume that archaeologists are wrong in their population estimates of ancient Egypt and Canaan, and that vast numbers of ancient inhabitants either left no evidence of their existence in either culture or left evidence that archaeologists have either misinterpreted or not yet found.

(2) Conclude that the Bible's large numbers are rhetorical or symbolic, perhaps representing the population of a later period. Since the population of Israel under Solomon's reign is roughly comparable to the large figure, it's possible that the author is making a sophisticated literary claim that identifies Israel under the monarchy with Israel of the Exodus.[b]

(3) Translate the Hebrew differently. The Hebrew text does not contain numerals, but rather numbers spelled out with words. The entire phrase in Exodus 12:37 reads "six hundred *thousand* on foot, men without children" (author's translation), but the word *eleph* that I've rendered here as "thousand" is a homonym with several other possible translations, including military unit or clan. Both of these are reasonable possibilities.

Here are two sample passages that use *eleph* with the meaning "clan":

Judges 6:15: "'Pardon me, my lord,' Gideon replied, 'but how can I save Israel? My *eleph* is the weakest in Manasseh, and I am the least in my family.'"

Joshua 22:14: "With him they sent ten of the chief men, one from each of the tribes of Israel, each the head of a family division among the Israelite *eleph*."

In Exodus 12:37, "military units" is a smoother fit than "clans," since the whole phrase indicates that men alone are being counted: "Six hundred *eleph* on foot, men without children." The tribe of Reuben, for example, includes "forty-six *eleph* and five hundred" (Numbers 1:21, author's translation). Humphreys argues that this could be read as forty-six military units totaling 500 men. Using this as his basis, he calculates that the average Israelite military unit must have consisted of just over nine men from two families (though the actual size ranged from six to fourteen, depending on the tribe). This figure corresponds roughly to the size of military troops mentioned in the El-Amarna tablets, where on separate occasions a king requests troops of ten or twenty men each.[c] In Israel's case, Humphreys proposes a total of 5,500 men over twenty years old leaving Egypt, bringing the overall total for the Exodus to roughly 22,000 men, women, and children.[d]

Whatever your conclusion about the size of the Israelite company, the book of Numbers depicts an impressive parade of Israelite men, women, and children following the pillar of cloud as they march from

Mount Sinai. They are no longer disorganized refugees, fleeing from Pharaoh. Yahweh has brought order from chaos.

DIGGING DEEPER

Timothy R. Ashley. *The Book of Numbers.* NICOT. Grand Rapids: Eerdmans, 1993.

*Kenneth Kitchen. *On the Reliability of the Old Testament.* Grand Rapids: Eerdmans, 2003. Pages 264-65.

Austin Surls. *Making Sense of the Divine Name in Exodus: From Etymology to Literary Onomastics.* BBRSup 17. Winona Lake, IN: Eisenbrauns, 2017.

Related video from The Bible Project:
"Torah: Numbers."

INTERMISSION

WINDOW VS. PAINTING

We began this journey staring at a painting of a Narnian ship. I told you that Lewis was on to something—that reading the Bible is like looking at a moving painting that draws us in until we're part of the story. Wouldn't it be more accurate, then, to say that reading the Bible is like looking through a window? Through glass we see things as they really are. The Bible shows us what really happened, right?

Not exactly. As with any form of art, the Bible is selective. We don't know everything about Israel's time at Sinai. In fact, we know relatively little. Did they do business with Nabatean traders? Did they camp together as extended families? Did the women swap manna recipes? Did the elders sing around campfires? Did the men go on hunting expeditions? What games did the children play? We just don't know. The Bible doesn't say. Exodus is selective in its telling of the events at Sinai. We're told only what is necessary to the larger storyline. If we were watching through a window, we'd be able to see a whole lot more.

Paintings are not just selective; they also depict reality from a particular perspective. The same is true of narrative in the Bible. We don't experience Sinai through the eyes of Moses' wife or his kids. We don't know how Joshua feels about joining Moses on the mountain. We don't hear the fighting men spin stories about the battle with the Amalekites. We're on top of the mountain with Moses, engaging with Yahweh in private conversation (see Exodus 33:12-23). Later, we're at the bottom of the mountain, looking up: "When Moses came down from Mount Sinai with the two tablets of the covenant law in his hands, he was not aware that his face was radiant because he had spoken with the LORD" (Exodus 34:29). This verse is written from the perspective of the Israelites watching Moses descend.

Paintings and narratives are also interpretive. They convey the way an artist feels about the subject. They persuade us to see things the artist's way. Biblical narratives do not just report events as they can be observed with the naked eye. They often evaluate these events or give the reasons behind them. Here are a few examples:

"*Then the* LORD *relented* and did not bring on his people the disaster he had threatened" (Exodus 32:14, emphasis added).

"When Pharaoh let the people go, God did not lead them on the road through the Philistine country, though that was shorter. *For God said, 'If they face war, they might change their minds and return to Egypt'*" (Exodus 13:17, emphasis added).

"Moses heard the people of every family wailing at the entrance to their tents. *The* LORD *became exceedingly angry*, and Moses was troubled" (Numbers 11:10, emphasis added).

To say that reading biblical narrative is like viewing a painting is not to suggest that it is unhistorical. A painting has the potential to accurately and powerfully depict a historical event, inspiring generations of viewers to reflect upon and remember what was most significant about that event. Take, for example, the painting by Jacques-Louis David titled *The Death of Socrates* (see figure I.1).[1]

David depicts Socrates surrounded by his disciples, on the verge of drinking his death sentence of poison. He uses the final moments of his life as another teachable moment, remaining stoic in the face of death. Plato, from whom we learn the story of Socrates's death, was not

Figure I.1. Jacques-Louis David, *The Death of Socrates*

present in these final moments of Socrates' life, yet David paints him slouching at the foot of the bed, his back to his friend. Why include such an inaccuracy in this painting?

Because David was a genius. He knew Plato's deep grief over Socrates's death. By depicting him in the room, but looking away, the artist accurately captured Plato's disposition toward the death of his esteemed colleague without making the spurious claim that Plato witnessed it. If Plato had been missing from the painting, we would lose this central point the artist was trying to make—a point that creatively conveys the truth of history.

Authors of the biblical text have also expressed the truth using their own creative artistry. We saw this when we noted that the Sinai narratives are framed on either side with a symmetrical set of stories. The author is selective, not feeling constrained to describe each of the forty-two campsites listed in Numbers 33. The stories are told from a particular perspective, interpreting what happened rather than simply reporting events.

To say that the Bible is a painting does not make it static. Something marvelous happens when we immerse ourselves in its artistry. It becomes our own story, and we become a participant. If it hasn't happened to you yet, stay tuned for Part Two. Things are gonna get personal.

> Authors of the biblical text have also expressed the truth using their own creative artistry.

DIGGING DEEPER

*V. Philips Long. *The Art of Biblical History.* FOCI, Vol. 5. Grand Rapids: Zondervan, 1994.

Related videos from The Bible Project:
"Literary Styles" and "The Bible as Jewish Meditation Literature."

PART 2

LIVING AS THE PEOPLE WHO BEAR GOD'S NAME

6

STRIKING OUT

From Mount Sinai to Mount Zion

FULL MOUNTAIN ECLIPSE:
WHAT HAPPENED TO SINAI?

Israel's experience at Sinai was deeply formative. In the chapters ahead, we'll follow how Israel does at bearing Yahweh's name through the rest of the Bible. Before we do, I want get a bird's eye view of another motif—Sinai itself. What happens to this mountain after Israel marches away? How is it remembered? When is it revisited?

Surprisingly, we hear little of Sinai after they leave, even though "remembering" is a key theme in biblical theology. Yahweh institutes the Passover as the annual day to remember the exodus (Exodus 12:26-27; Deuteronomy 16:1-8), and the Feast of Booths to remember when Moses gave the people the law (Leviticus 23:23-43; Deuteronomy 31:10-13), but neither requires any sort of pilgrimage to Sinai. Instead, the Israelites are to remember God's deliverance in their own homes, wherever they live. Because God's presence traveled with them when they left Sinai, there's no need to go back.

But do they wish they could?

Danny and I have moved often in twenty years of marriage, fourteen times so far. Some of those moves were for a few weeks or months while waiting for a more permanent place to open up. The longest we've lived anywhere together is four-and-a-half years. In most cases, we've been able to go back later to see the old house and neighborhood, reconnect with neighbors, and visit our favorite ice cream shop. However, we've never been back to the Philippines. We lived there for two-and-a-half years as missionaries, forming friendships with fellow expats, Filipino colleagues, and Muslim street vendors. For years after we moved, I had a vivid recurring dream in which I traveled back to the Philippines to see my Muslim friends. I would go to the open market and search down every aisle, weeping as I tried to find them. The pain of losing those friendships and leaving that part of my life behind was intense.

I wonder: Do the Israelites dream of Sinai? Are they nostalgic for the place where Yahweh first called them his treasure? There are other mountains to come—Nebo, Gerazim, Ebal, Tabor, Zion—but nothing quite like Sinai. Wistfulness would be understandable. Then again, maybe the mountain held a sense of foreboding for the average Israelite that they would be happy to leave behind.

Some time elapses before Israel has a centralized place of worship. When they first enter the promised land, they head to Mount Gerazim and Mount Ebal to renew the covenant as Moses had instructed (Joshua 8:30-35). It's important that they reaffirm their commitment *inside* the land.[1] The ceremony takes place on the highest mountains, which are conveniently located at the geographic midpoint of the land (north-south as well as east-west). They build an altar on Mount Ebal and use it for a time,[2] but we don't hear about any glorious appearing of Yahweh, and the location does not remain a major part of Israel's worship. It's a bit anticlimactic, really.

At some point, the tabernacle is moved from Gilgal (Israel's military base camp just inside the promised land) to Shiloh in the central hill country. That's where it is when the boy Samuel comes into the service of Eli the priest (1 Samuel 1–2). Samuel is the prophet who

first anoints Saul as king in Israel and later David. David conquers
the ancient city of Jebus and makes it his capital, renames it Jerusalem,
and brings the ark of the covenant tablets there, presumably to take
its place in the tabernacle. The Jerusalem temple is built on a hill
proudly known as Mount Zion. Physically speaking, it is not an
impressive mountain. However, theologically speaking, Mount Zion
is the tallest mountain on earth.

I currently live in Three Hills, Alberta, but I grew up in the mountain
state of Colorado. The Rocky Mountains run through Alberta, too, with
stunning peaks of impressive height, but we can't see them from our
town. We're out on the prairies, where the most notable topographical
feature is three slight undulations to the north—our three hills. If you're
not looking for them, you'll pass right on by without noticing. They
aren't anything to write home about.

Zion is like this too. If you stand on the Mount of Olives, directly
across a narrow valley, you'll be looking *down* at Jerusalem. The way
Israel's poets speak of it, though, you'll need to remember your high-
altitude medication if you plan to visit:

> Beautiful in its loftiness, the joy of the whole earth, like the heights
> of Zaphon is Mount Zion, the city of the Great King. (Psalm 48:2)

> From Zion, perfect in beauty, God shines forth. (Psalm 50:2)

> For the LORD has chosen Zion, he has desired it for his dwelling,
> saying, "This is my resting place for ever and ever; here I will sit
> enthroned, for I have desired it." (Psalm 132:13-14)

> Many peoples will come and say, "Come, let us go up to the moun-
> tain of the LORD, to the temple of the God of Jacob. He will teach
> us his ways, so that we may walk in his paths." The law will go out
> from Zion, the word of the LORD from Jerusalem. (Isaiah 2:3)

> This is what the LORD says: "I will return to Zion and dwell in
> Jerusalem. Then Jerusalem will be called the Faithful City, and
> the mountain of the LORD Almighty will be called the Holy Moun-
> tain." (Zechariah 8:3)

Zion isn't impressive for its physical height. It's special for one reason alone: Yahweh puts his name there, claiming it as his own. His presence is somehow concentrated in the temple. It is the designated place for Israel's worship.[3]

So, for the most part, Sinai fades and is replaced by Zion.

But that's still several hundred years away from the perspective of those marching out from Sinai. We need to get back to those early days when Israel was just striking out to see how they fared in their new vocation as Yahweh's representatives.

ENEMY #1: COMPLAINTS IN THE WILDERNESS

One would hope that in light of Yahweh's dramatic deliverance, brilliant self-revelation, and clear instructions at Sinai, the road to the promised land would be a joy-filled journey. Unfortunately, it isn't. And the enemy that threatens to undo Yahweh's special representatives is not who you might expect.

We're not sure exactly how far the Israelites got before they started complaining. The narrator mentions a three-day journey before they set up camp, and then he jumps straight into the first complaint story. This and a handful of similar stories from the wilderness follow a predictable pattern: complaining results in punishment and prayer brings relief.

Before Sinai, Yahweh shows mercy. His expectations of the people are low. They don't know him well yet, and they have much to learn. After Sinai, Yahweh's expectations are higher. It's not that his character has changed. He is still "slow to anger, abounding in love" (Exodus 34:6), but they've had a whole year to learn how to honor him and one another. They know exactly what he expects. He's watching for maturity, yet he sees little. The time comes for him to express what is also true of his character: "he does not leave the guilty unpunished" (Exodus 34:7). This time, they should know better.

Whining is the bane of every parent, especially on a road trip. We're on a lengthy road trip as I write this, living out of a trailer for four weeks with two kids, one of whom gets claustrophobic in a 2,200-square-foot house, much less trapped in a vehicle. So far we've stopped at five camp-sites and a friend's property. It's not just the kids who have struggled. I've been on edge too. A road trip involves lots of liminal space—neither here nor there—settling only temporarily and relearning new routines. We've driven hundreds of miles on unfamiliar roads that wind through mountains and alongside drop-offs, past countless other cars. We've camped in wilderness areas near an active volcano, attempted to cross a swift river on foot, hiked a dozen trails, and lit fires nearly every evening. None of these were our greatest risk. The worst danger was ourselves. Maintaining cheerfulness and kindness in the midst of constant change can be an enormous challenge. Liminality exposes all our rough edges.

The Israelites' biggest challenge is not, as we might expect, maraud-ing bands or lack of food and water or scorpions or blazing sun. The single greatest threat to their survival in the wilderness is themselves. They are enemy #1. It's enough to make Moses wish he were dead. Liter-ally. He says to Yahweh, "I cannot carry all these people by myself; the burden is too heavy for me. If this is how you are going to treat me, please go ahead and kill me—if I have found favor in your eyes—and do not let me face my own ruin" (Numbers 11:14-15).

First the people complain of "hardships" (Numbers 11:1). Then they "begin to crave other food" (Numbers 11:4). Miracle manna, it seems, is getting old. Miriam and Aaron spread gossip against Moses (Num-bers 12:1-2). After the Israelite spies report on their exploration of Canaan, the whole community voices their complaint, wishing they had died in Egypt (Numbers 14:1-4). Eventually there is an insurrection against Moses and Aaron (Numbers 16:1-3).

> The single greatest threat to their survival in the wilderness is themselves. They are enemy #1.

In each of these cases, Yahweh's response is firm. He supports Moses' leadership and punishes (or elim-inates!) the rebels. These are rocky times in the wilderness.

Take, for example, when Moses commissions twelve spies to check out the promised land. As requested, they discern what the land is like and how strong the people are. "We went into the land to which you sent us, and it does flow with milk and honey! Here is its fruit. But the people who live there are powerful, and the cities are fortified and very large. We even saw descendants of Anak there. The Amalekites live in the Negev; the Hittites, Jebusites and Amorites live in the hill country: and the Canaanites live near the sea and along the Jordan" (Numbers 13:27-29).

Here's what's fascinating about the spies' report: They'd already known for a whole year that Yahweh was giving them a fruitful land populated by these particular nations. God told Moses as much at their first encounter on Mount Sinai: "And I have promised to bring you up out of your misery in Egypt into the land of the Canaanites, Hittites, Amorites, Perizzites, Hivites and Jebusites—a land flowing with milk and honey" (Exodus 3:17). Did the Israelites suppose that these residents would evacuate of their own free will? Did they think the other nations would turn out to be a bunch of wimps?

Now that they've seen the land with their own eyes, the spies fall into two camps. Caleb urges, "We should go up and take possession of the land, for we can certainly do it" (Numbers 13:30). He finds things as Yahweh had said they would be. He trusts that the same God who delivered them from Pharaoh's armies can accomplish the rest of what he's promised.

The others are not so sure: "We can't attack those people; they are stronger than we are" (Numbers 14:31). As though describing the fish that got away, they begin exaggerating, saying that the land will eat them alive and that in comparison to these other nations they are like grasshoppers. Their fear is contagious. Fear always is. By nightfall the entire community is in a panic. Enemy #1 strikes again.

Make no mistake. The problem is not the powerful nations with fortified cities, fierce as they may be. The problem is the Israelites' own refusal to believe what Yahweh has promised. By failing to trust, they have become their own worst enemy. Yahweh forgives them, but they still reap the consequences of their unfaithfulness: rather than entering the land God promised them, that generation lives out the rest of their days in the wilderness.

Israel's own tendency to sabotage itself appears in another story at the end of Numbers, one we have already discussed. In it, Yahweh prevents Balaam and the Moabite king who hired him from cursing Israel. Meanwhile, the Israelites down in the valley are oblivious to Yahweh's protection as he foils the Moabite scheme. But in the very next scene (Numbers 25), the Israelites ruin everything. Their men begin committing adultery with Moabite women in violation of the commands at Sinai. These women invite them to worship Moabite gods. Those engaged in this rebellion are put to death by sword or plague by God's initiative. Clearly, for those who bear Yahweh's name, the worst danger of all is not foreign armies, but the consequences of their own unfaithfulness. Their moral failure deserves punishment.

GENERATION NEXT: MOSES' LAST SERMON

After a thirty-eight-year "time out" in the wilderness, the consequence of Israel's failure to trust Yahweh, the first generation of faithless Israelites is dead. Only Caleb and Joshua remain, the two spies with unshakable faith. A new generation is ready to embrace the promises of Yahweh and enter the land he will give them. Aaron has also died by this point, but Moses is still at the helm. They are camped on the plains of Moab, across the Jordan from the promised land.

The book of Deuteronomy is Moses' final address to the people, preparing them for what's ahead. In it, he retells their story, reminds them who they are, and reiterates Yahweh's instructions. The book provides Moses' final overview of God's recipe for an abundant life. The opening of his sermon is unexpected:

> Hear, Israel, the decrees and laws I declare in your hearing today.
> Learn them and be sure to follow them. The LORD our God made
> a covenant *with us* at Horeb [i.e., Sinai]. *It was not with our ancestors*
> *that the LORD made this covenant, but with us, with all of us who*
> *are alive here today.* The LORD spoke to *you* face to face out of the
> fire on the mountain. (Deuteronomy 5:1-4, emphasis added)

Is Moses having a "senior moment"? Has he forgotten that the people standing before him are the next generation of Israelites? Perhaps some of them were children at Sinai, but all the adults who were there (besides Caleb and Joshua) have died. Most of them were born since.

No, Moses has not forgotten. His language is deliberate. He wants to drive home the point that these men and women are full-fledged members of the covenant. Any faithful Israelite from any period in history was there at Sinai. The covenant is not a hand-me-down. It's theirs from the beginning. Their parents disqualified themselves from its benefits, forfeiting their status as God's treasured possession by acting faithlessly. But this generation has direct access.

Moses presses his point even further as he enumerates the Ten Commandments for this new generation. This time around, rather than basing the Sabbath command on God's creative work (*you should rest because God rested on the seventh day*, see Exodus 20:11), he bases it on family history: "Remember that you were slaves in Egypt and that the LORD your God brought you out of there with a mighty hand and an outstretched arm" (Deuteronomy 5:15). They *weren't* slaves in Egypt, of course. That was their parents. But Moses wants this generation to embrace the story of the exodus from Egypt as *their* story. *They* are the slaves Yahweh delivered. *They* are the rescued ones. From Moses' vantage point, Yahweh makes a covenant with a faithful generation and their children. The faithlessness of those physically present at Sinai does not spell disaster forever. Future generations may be included in the covenant simply by embracing it with faith and responding to it with obedience.

> Moses wants this generation to embrace the story of the exodus from Egypt as *their* story.

What had been a potential in Exodus 19:5-6—they could *become* Yahweh's treasured possession—was now a reality. In Deuteronomy 26:16-19, Moses recaps the momentous day when Yahweh confirmed the covenant with this new generation on the plains of Moab:

This very day, Yahweh your God is commanding you to do these statutes and ordinances, and you shall keep them and you shall do them with all your heart and with all your soul. Today you have had Yahweh declare himself [amar] to be your God, in order that you may walk in his ways, and keep his statutes, and his commands, and his ordinances, and listen to his voice. And today Yahweh has had you declare yourself [amar] to be his treasured people (just as he promised you) in order that you may keep all his commands, and in order to set you above all the nations he has made for praise, and for a name, and for honor, in order that you may be a people holy to Yahweh your God, just as he promised. (author's translation)[4]

Each declaration of commitment is prompted by the other party, ensuring the full participation of both. These are not simply words; they put into effect the covenant relationship between Yahweh and his people. These words *do* something. A modern-day example of efficacious words—words that do something—is the statement of the officiant at a wedding, "I now pronounce you husband and wife." Before these words are spoken, the couple is not married. The statement puts into effect a new reality. In the same way, these covenant words adopt a new generation of Israelites as Yahweh's treasured possession. He becomes their God and they become his people.

ENTERING IN: JOSHUA AND THE BEGINNING OF FULFILLMENT

The book of Joshua illustrates how Yahweh's promises, declared at Sinai and reiterated in Moab, finally begin to be fulfilled. Moses has died and Joshua has taken leadership of the fledgling nation. As Moses had predicted would be the case in Deuteronomy 28:10, "Then all the peoples on earth will see that the name of Yahweh is invoked over you, and they will fear you" (author's translation). The nations were indeed watching Israel, and they were afraid. Rahab, a resident of the city of Jericho, is the first to confess this. She risks her own life to hide Israelite spies. She voices what all of Jericho's residents are thinking in the decades following Israel's escape from Egypt and their recent defeat of the two kings east of the Jordan, Sihon and Og. She admits, "When we heard of it, our hearts melted in fear and everyone's courage failed because of you, for the LORD your God is God in heaven above and on the earth below" (Joshua 2:11; cf. 4:23-24). Rahab's words echo precisely the command not to make images of anything "in heaven above or on the earth beneath" (Exodus 20:4).[5] Her profession of faith in Yahweh embodies the fulfillment of Deuteronomy 28:10. In spite of the previous generation's lack of covenant faithfulness, the nations are afraid of Israel and her God.

The encounter with the Gibeonites provides another example of fulfillment. Their fear of Yahweh and of Israel is quite evident. Since the Israelites are prohibited from making covenants with nations within the land God allotted for them, the Gibeonites pretend to have traveled a great distance (Joshua 9). They claim, "Your servants have come from a very distant country because of the fame of the LORD your God. For we have heard reports of him: all that he did in Egypt, and all that he did to the two kings of the Amorites east of the Jordan . . ." (9:9-10). Although they lie about their homeland, the Gibeonites' testimony affirms the truth of Yahweh's promise that the nations would see his deeds on Israel's behalf and tremble (see Deuteronomy 28:9-10).

Ironically, the portrait of God's covenant people does not fare well in these accounts. Rahab, the prostitute full of faith, contrasts with Achan, the faithless Israelite who endangers the entire covenant community by keeping for himself some of the plunder from Jericho that should be devoted to Yahweh (see Joshua 7). Meanwhile, the Gibeonites uncover the foolishness of the Israelites, who are taken in by their ruse.[6] Generation Next is off to a wobbly start.

The Israelites quickly lose sight of the fact that God set them apart from the nations to belong to him. They decide they'd rather be like everybody else.

THE KING'S HOUSE: DAVID'S DYNASTY

Have you ever known people who just can't stay in one place for long? Address changes, job changes, broken relationships, serial dating, even serial marriages—they keep thinking the grass will be greener somewhere else, but when they get there, the same story replays itself. There is a common denominator to each new situation: they always bring themselves. This is how it is for Israel. Settling in the promised land is not the magic solution for Israel's rebellion. They continue to be their own worst enemy. Aren't we all?

After settling in the land, the tribes of Israel are only loosely affiliated with one another, ruled by local "judges" for hundreds of years. Many of these judges have major character flaws and as a whole, the Israelites spiral downward into serious moral failure. The Israelite priests after the time of the judges are scoundrels. They disregard the sacrificial instructions and take whatever they want from the people (1 Samuel 2:17; 3:13). The priests—the guys whose job it is to make sure Yahweh is honored and the covenant maintained—are the very people who are cutting corners and acting like they run the show. For this reason, Yahweh declares that he will cut off the current priesthood and raise up a "faithful priest" and an "anointed one" to lead the people (1 Samuel 2:35). Samuel, clearly the fulfillment of that priestly promise, proves himself "trustworthy as a prophet" (1 Samuel 3:20 NJPS).

Eventually, in spite of the appointment of Samuel as a worthy leader, Israel demands to have a king like other nations. Yahweh had intended to give them a king, but the timing of Israel's request is a symptom of their lack of faith in him (1 Samuel 8:7-9, 19-20).[7] Rather than being distinct, they want to blend in with the nations around them, each of which has a king. Samuel warns the people of the dangers of kingship and exhorts them to follow Yahweh alone wholeheartedly (1 Samuel 12:20-21). But they demand and get their king. Samuel reassures them, "*For the sake of his great name* the LORD will not reject his people, because the LORD was pleased to make you his own" (1 Samuel 12:22, emphasis added). Yahweh's reputation is still explicitly tied to Israel. The task of his anointed ruler—whether king, prophet, or priest—is to call the people back to covenant faithfulness, to model how a name bearer ought to live.

Perhaps you can think of a time when someone was chosen as captain of your sports team or class president not because they demonstrated leadership skills, but because they were good looking or the life of the party. Saul is tall, dark, and handsome—fitting the bill of what the people think they want—but as Israel's first king he proves himself to be cowardly, paranoid, and susceptible to fits of rage. His failure to follow Yahweh's simple instructions results in his forfeiture of the kingship (1 Samuel 13:13-14; 15:26) as well as the departure of Yahweh's presence (1 Samuel 16:14). So much for a king helping Israel fulfill her vocation as name bearers!

The book of Samuel is a literary masterpiece designed to show us who *Yahweh* chooses as king. Saul keeps sinking lower and lower. Meanwhile, Yahweh directs Samuel to anoint David as king (1 Samuel 16:13, 18). The famous story of David's fight with Goliath reveals the stark contrast between David and Saul. Saul, we just noted, is really tall. He stands head and shoulders above everyone else. Yet when a tall Philistine challenges the Israelites to a duel, Saul cowers at a safe distance from the battle lines and tries to persuade someone else to do what he ought to be doing. He even offers rewards, including the hand of his daughter in marriage.

David, on the other hand, seems unfazed by Goliath's size and refuses to be lured by Saul's reward or impressed by Saul's armor. For him, the pertinent issue is God's reputation. By defying Israel's armies, Goliath is insulting Israel's God. David's blood boils. He calls out to Goliath, "You come against me with sword and spear and javelin, but I come against you in the name of the LORD Almighty, the God of the armies of Israel, whom you have defied" (1 Sam 17:45).[8] David's victory over Goliath ensures that "This day the LORD will deliver you into my hands . . . and the whole world will know that there is a God in Israel"

(1 Samuel 17:46). David clearly grasps the mission of God's covenant people, and he takes it upon himself to carry it out, even when Israel's anointed ruler is chicken.

Yahweh's selection of David as his anointed ruler becomes more and more obvious as the narrative unfolds (2 Samuel 3:18; 5:10, 12). Finally, he is enthroned. In one of his first acts as king, David brings the ark of the covenant tablets to Jerusalem (2 Samuel 6:1-23). It had been captured by the Philistines some time earlier, who returned it to Israel within months to avoid Yahweh's wrath (1 Samuel 5–6). For twenty years the ark was kept in a home in Kiriath Jearim (1 Samuel 7:2), but David's priority was to bring it to the center of Israel's political life. With the ark in Israel's possession in the capital city, David's kingship is secure. His enemies are vanquished. His own palace is built. It's a golden time. Then he has an idea: I should build a temple for Yahweh in Jerusalem!

David's conversation with Yahweh about this project revolves around the words "name" and "house," playing with their various meanings. David proposes to build a "house" (i.e., a temple) for Yahweh's "name" (that is, a place where he will be honored). Yahweh sends the prophet Nathan to respond to David's idea, saying that instead Yahweh will build David's "house" (that is, his dynasty) and give him a "name" or reputation (2 Samuel 7:9).[9] David recognizes the uniqueness of Israel's election: "And who is like your people Israel—the one nation on earth that God went out to redeem as a people for himself, and to make a name for himself, and to perform great and awesome wonders by driving out nations and their gods from before your people, whom you redeemed from Egypt?" (2 Samuel 7:23).

God's promise to build David's dynasty, as positive as it is, serves as a gentle rebuke. Temples are not the prerogative of kings but are built by divine initiative. David has blood on his hands, so his son must be the one to "build a house for my [Yahweh's] Name" (2 Samuel 7:13). That son is Solomon, the fruit of David's union with another man's wife—just one more proof that God redeems our epic failures.

RIBBON CUTTING: SOLOMON'S TEMPLE

Solomon's primary positive accomplishment is the construction of the temple David desired on Mount Zion. The temple is repeatedly associated with Yahweh's name.[10] When it is built, a special "ribbon-cutting" ceremony dedicates it to the worship of Yahweh. Yahweh reaffirms his covenant with Solomon, promising his presence and blessing as long as Solomon walks in his ways (6:11-13; cf. 8:23-26). Solomon dedicates the temple with a prayer that beautifully encapsulates the biblical-theological theme of bearing Yahweh's name to the nations. He prays:

> As for the foreigner who does not belong to your people Israel but has come from a distant land *because of your name*—for they will hear of your great name and your mighty hand and your outstretched arm—when they come and pray toward this temple, then hear from heaven, your dwelling place. Do whatever the foreigner asks of you, *so that all the peoples of the earth may know your name and fear you,* as do your own people Israel, and may know that this house I have built bears your Name. (1 Kings 8:41-43, emphasis added)

Solomon recognizes the missional significance of Yahweh's acts on Israel's behalf. The election of Israel as Yahweh's special people and Jerusalem as the special place for his house motivates God to act on their behalf (1 Kings 8:53; 11:13, 32, 36; cf. 14:21). Yahweh's fame provides the sole basis for Solomon's appeal for blessing, "so that all the peoples of the earth may know that the LORD is God and that there is no other" (1 Kings 8:60).

Not only does Solomon's temple dedication feature the name of Yahweh, but it also echoes the dedication of the tabernacle at Sinai. Sinai, referred to here as Horeb, is specifically mentioned as the ark is brought into the inner sanctuary: "There was nothing in the ark except the two stone tablets that Moses had placed in it at Horeb, where the LORD made a covenant with the Israelites after they came out of Egypt" (1 Kings 8:9). Just as "Moses could not enter the tent of meeting because the cloud had settled on it, and the glory of the LORD filled the tabernacle"

(Exodus 40:35), so at Solomon's temple dedication "the priests could not perform their service because of the cloud, for the glory of the LORD filled his temple" (1 Kings 8:11).[11] The presence of Yahweh filling this new temple was a tremendous affirmation of Yahweh's ongoing covenant commitment to Israel. Centuries had already passed since Sinai, years punctuated by faithlessness and rebellion on the part of the Israelites. Still, Yahweh keeps his promise and offers more grace.

Solomon's wisdom has a magnetic effect on the surrounding nations. First, all Israel marvels at his wisdom (1 Kings 3:28); then the nations begin to notice (1 Kings 4:29-34). King Hiram of Tyre blesses Yahweh on account of Solomon's wisdom (1 Kings 5:7). The Queen of Sheba travels a great distance to hear his wisdom personally and blessed Yahweh (1 Kings 10:1-10). Indeed, the "whole world" seeks Solomon's wisdom (1 Kings 10:24). This sounds like the fulfillment of the Abrahamic promise to bring blessing to the nations. But it doesn't last.

Yahweh's standard remains clear. If Israel fails to keep the covenant, Yahweh will destroy the temple and make Israel the object of mockery in the sight of the nations (1 Kings 9:6-9). In spite of Solomon's wisdom, he proves himself to be easily swayed from covenant faithfulness, marrying hundreds of wives for the sake of political alliances, and providing ways for them to continue to worship gods other than Yahweh. Solomon takes his place among the majority of Israel's leaders who tolerated blatant disregard for the covenant.

After Solomon, the kingdom is split in two. His son Rehoboam rules the southern kingdom, which comes to be known as Judah. Jeroboam rules the northern kingdom, known as Israel. Jeroboam's first act as king is to set up golden calves in Dan and Bethel, marking the northern and southern boundaries of his territory. This ensures that the Israelites will *not* travel further south to worship Yahweh at the temple Solomon built in Jerusalem. It seals the demise of the ten northern tribes, none of whose subsequent eighteen kings worship Yahweh. Eventually, the Assyrians drag the heart of this kingdom into exile, just as Moses predicted.

Judah fares moderately better. Of her twenty kings, eight attempt to stay true to the covenant with Yahweh. Hundreds of years later, as the Assyrian king Sennacherib threatens to destroy Jerusalem, King Hezekiah prays for mercy, grounding his plea on Yahweh's reputation: "Now, LORD our God, deliver us from his hand, so that all the kingdoms of the earth may know that you alone, LORD, are God" (2 Kings 19:19). Judah is being mocked by the nations (2 Kings 19:21-22) and Yahweh responds through the prophet Isaiah, promising to defend her for his own sake (2 Kings 19:34). However, his rescue does not turn Israel from its path. God's own people are too persistent in their rebellion.

Moses had looked ahead to this day. He saw what was coming. In his song in Deuteronomy 32, he called the people "a nation without sense" (v. 28) who "abandoned the God who made them" (v. 15). It would only be a matter of time before the curses announced in Deuteronomy 28 would come to rest on them because of their unfaithfulness. Finally, on the basis of Judah's untiring wickedness, Yahweh announces that he will reject his people, his city, and even his temple (2 Kings 23:27). The threatened exile of the southern kingdom becomes a reality.

Enough is enough.

Through those dark days, when the light of the covenant is almost snuffed out, the prophets are the single voice of reason, calling God's people back to their true vocation as worshipers of Yahweh and bearers of his name. They look at the mess from God's perspective, providing a view from 30,000 feet.

DIGGING DEEPER

*Daniel I. Block. *Deuteronomy.* NIVAC. Grand Rapids: Zondervan, 2012.

*David M. Howard Jr. *An Introduction to the Old Testament Historical Books.* Chicago: Moody, 1993.

Sandra L. Richter. *The Deuteronomistic History and the Name Theology: Lᵉšakkēn Šᵉmô Šām in the Bible and the Ancient Near East.* BATW 318. Berlin: de Gruyter, 2002.

*Christopher J. H. Wright. *The Mission of God: Unlocking the Bible's Grand Narrative.* Downers Grove, IL: IVP Academic, 2006.

Related video from The Bible Project: "Torah: Deuteronomy."

7

WHAT YAHWEH SEES

The Faithful Few

ONE MAN SHOW? ELIJAH AT SINAI

Through the centuries, God sent prophets to announce his word to his people, calling them back to covenant faithfulness. Most ignored their message, but their words were preserved by the faithful few for future generations. The first significant prophet we meet during Israel's monarchy is Elijah, who ministered after the Israelite kingdom had split in two, with Israel in the north and Judah in the south. At that time, the northern kingdom of Israel was led by two devout worshipers of the Canaanite god, Baal. Not only is worshiping other gods a direct violation of the covenant, but King Ahab and Queen Jezebel become obsessed with eliminating Yahweh-worship altogether. They kill any prophets of Yahweh they can find, but they have a terrible time tracking down Elijah. Elijah, whose name means "My God is Yahweh," announces a drought lasting several years, earning him the nickname "Troubler of Israel" (1 Kings 18:17). His threat isn't random. Lack of rain is a curse prescribed at Sinai in the event that Israel disregards the covenant:

> If you follow my decrees and are careful to obey my commands,
> I will send you rain in its season, and the ground will yield its
> crops and the trees their fruit. . . . But if you will not listen to me
> and carry out all these commands, and if you reject my decrees
> and abhor my laws and fail to carry out all my commands and so
> violate my covenant . . . I will break down your stubborn pride
> and make the sky above you like iron and the ground beneath
> you like bronze. Your strength will be spent in vain, because your
> soil will not yield its crops, nor will the trees of your land yield
> their fruit. (Leviticus 26:3-4, 14-15, 19-20)

Lack of rain should be the first clue that the Israelites have gone off the rails, but their perspective has been skewed.

Lack of rain is also a source of deep embarrassment for Baal, as he is supposedly the storm god, responsible for thunder, lightning, and rain.[1] An ancient story known as "The 'Aqhatu Legend" illustrates Baal's inability to bring rain under similar circumstances. Here his name is spelled *Ba'lu*:

> Thereupon *Dani'ilu* the man of *Rapa'u*, uttered a spell upon clouds
> in the heat of the season, upon the rain that the clouds pour down
> on the summer fruits, upon the dew that falls on the grapes. Seven
> years has *Ba'lu* failed, eight (years) he who rides upon the clouds:
> no dew, no showers, no upsurging (of water) from the deeps, no
> goodly voice of *Ba'lu*.[2]

Baal is directly blamed for the lack of rain.

Drought is also an embarrassment to King Ahab, who depends on Baal's endorsement of his kingship. Shrewdly, Elijah plans to beat Baal at his own game. He arranges a contest with the prophets of Baal in which the god who sends lightning will be recognized as God. He gives Baal the home turf advantage, holding the contest on sacred Mount Carmel. After a whole day of desperate prayer, Baal's prophets give up. Baal is silent and so are the skies. Elijah prays a single, simple prayer and Yahweh sends a dramatic answer: the lightning he sends from a cloudless sky burns up not only the sacrifice on the altar but the stone altar itself. Instantly, everyone present recognizes that Yahweh is God. The rains soon follow, removing any remaining doubt about who caused the drought. Yahweh's victory vindicates the prophet who bears his name.

When Queen Jezebel hears what happened, she vows to kill Elijah within twenty-four hours. Elijah immediately heads south, outside of Jezebel's territory, traveling as far as Beersheba, the southernmost city of Judah. From there he walks into the wilderness, curls up under a bush, and prays to die. Elijah's death wish is likely more than personal despondency. He feels acutely the ineffectiveness of his prophetic ministry. If King Ahab can reject Yahweh after Mount Carmel, then the covenant is doomed.

This time, instead of answering his prayer as requested, Yahweh sends hope. An angel bakes him a loaf of bread (how practical!) and brings him water twice, restoring his strength. Elijah sets out for Horeb, "the mountain of God" (1 Kings 19:8). Commentator Peter Leithart notes that in this story, Elijah retraces Israel's steps and relives Israel's story. Elijah's confrontation with the king and his gods mirrors Moses' confrontation of Pharaoh in Egypt. Elijah's journey into the wilderness and miraculous provision of food mirrors Israel's experience in that same wilderness. Finally, Elijah returns to Sinai to meet with Yahweh regarding the broken covenant.[3]

Why did he go? What was he hoping to accomplish? Yahweh asks Elijah this very question. Elijah answers: "I have been very zealous for the LORD, God Almighty. The Israelites have rejected your covenant, torn down your altars, and put your prophets to death with the sword. I am the only one left, and now they are trying to kill me too" (1 Kings 19:10).

From Elijah's prophetic vantage point, the covenant seems to have come to an end. Has he come to Mount Sinai to begin the covenant again? It would be an appropriate place to do so. Like Moses, he stays in a cave on the mountain. Like Moses, he converses with Yahweh. Like Moses, Elijah has the opportunity to see Yahweh pass by. Elijah shows himself to be a model prophet in the tradition of Moses, performing miracles and meeting Yahweh personally as only Moses had done (Deuteronomy 34:10-12). Elijah's concern over the breech of the Sinai covenant is front and center.

Yahweh responds to Elijah's despondency by assigning him a task. Elijah is to anoint the next king of Israel as well as his own successor. Yahweh also reassures Elijah, "I reserve seven thousand in Israel—all whose knees have not bowed down to Baal and whose mouths have not kissed him" (1 Kings 19:18). Elijah is not alone. His ministry has not been in vain. At Sinai, Yahweh again reveals himself and reassures his prophet that the covenant is still in effect. Although most have failed to bear the name well, a faithful remnant endures. Other prophets were part of this remnant, and among the most prominent stand Jeremiah and Ezekiel.

ROBBER'S DEN: JEREMIAH'S TEMPLE SERMON

Perhaps you've heard the story of Ali Baba and the Forty Thieves, from the tales of the *Arabian Nights*. Ali Baba is a poor woodcutter who stumbles upon a group of thieves in the forest. He watches as they approach a hidden cave with a magic door and pronounce the secret password to gain entrance: "Open Sesame!" Once inside, they cry "Close Sesame!" and the door shuts behind them, ensuring their safety while they count their stolen treasures. Or so they think. Now that Ali Baba has heard the password, their secrets are no longer safe. As the story unfolds, the thieves lose everything and Ali Baba becomes fabulously rich.

The prophet Jeremiah tells a similar tale. He stands at the gateway into Yahweh's temple in Jerusalem, announcing Yahweh's message for the southern kingdom of Judah. He calls them out by mocking their own secret password—"the temple of the LORD, the temple of the LORD, the temple of the LORD!" (Jeremiah 7:4). They rely solely on these "magic" words, thinking that because Yahweh dwells among them in the Jerusalem temple, they are immune from his judgment. Jeremiah exposes their hypocrisy:

Will you steal and murder, commit adultery and perjury, burn incense to Baal and follow other gods you have not known, and then come and stand before me in this house, which bears my Name, and say, 'We are safe'—safe to do all these detestable things? Has this house, which bears my Name, become a den of robbers [or robber's den][4] to you? But I have been watching! declares the LORD. (Jeremiah 7:9-11)

Like Ali Baba in the forest, Yahweh has had his eye on the people of Judah. He is alarmed that they are treating the temple as a secret hideout, safe from all harm, when they are guilty of highway robbery. Breaking the covenant is a family affair for the people of Judah. Yahweh laments, "The children gather wood, the fathers light the fire, and the women knead the dough and make cakes to offer to the Queen of Heaven. They pour out drink offerings to other gods to arouse my anger" (Jeremiah 7:18).

They have forgotten the commands of Sinai, yet they still expect their temple sacrifices to be effective. Yahweh suggests they go on a field trip to Shiloh in the north, where the tabernacle once stood in the days of the prophet Samuel. Not only had the tabernacle been removed, but by this point the northern kingdom of Israel had already been conquered by the Assyrians and scattered to the four winds. If it could happen to God's people in the north, it could happen to Judah. The temple would not save them.

Sure enough, as Jeremiah announced would happen, Yahweh intervened by allowing the Babylonians to destroy Jerusalem and Judah. Thousands of Judeans were dragged away from their homeland. God raised up another prophet, Ezekiel, to address his people with a message similar to Jeremiah's. Writing from Babylon during the exile of Judah, Ezekiel describes the effect Judah's sin has on God's reputation. In graphic language, he paints a picture of how bad things became. The idolatry of the people of Judah (a violation of the first commandment) defiled the land Yahweh gave them. Their behavior is as detestable as a pile of bloody menstrual cloths sitting out in the open. Talk about vivid imagery! The natural consequence is that God had to clean house. He swept his people into other nations. If they cannot manage to live according to his covenantal terms, then they can no longer enjoy the covenantal benefits.

But here's the kicker: "Wherever they went among the nations they profaned my holy name, for it was said of them, 'These are the LORD's people, and yet they had to leave his land'" (Ezekiel 36:20). God's people didn't need to say a word. Just by going into exile, Judah casts Yahweh in a negative light because he appears to be powerless to protect them. Never mind that Yahweh himself is sending them into exile. From the perspective of the nations, Yahweh isn't much of a match for the gods of Babylon. His reputation is on the line because he's chosen to claim these people as his. For better or for worse, they bear his name.

Perhaps you've had a leadership role in your community and felt the pressure that comes when everyone is watching your kids to see how well behaved they are. Your sermon holds little weight when your kids are fighting in the front pew. God knows just how you feel.

So Yahweh plans to do something about his people's plight. He can't have the nations thinking he is impotent. He's got to set the record straight, and he speaks plainly with his people. He's about to put into effect a dramatic rescue plan, gathering his people from the nations, bringing them home, cleansing them, and bringing abundance. But he's very blunt: "I want you to know that I am not doing this for your sake, declares the Sovereign LORD" (Ezekiel 36:32). The point of God's rescue plan is clear: to "'show the holiness of my great name, which has been profaned among the nations, the name you have profaned among them. Then the nations will know that I am the LORD,' declares the Sovereign LORD, 'when I am proved holy through you before their eyes'" (Ezekiel 36:23).

It is not the people's predicament that merits God's action. Yahweh's own reputation is at stake.

SINAI RE-IMAGINED: PROPHETIC
VISIONS OF RESTORATION

Although the prophets speak out strongly against Israel's unfaithfulness, with the help of the Spirit of God they're able to see beyond sin and judgment to the deliverance God has planned—and what a deliverance it is! They look at the devastation around them, and by faith, imagine full restoration. It's possible to disqualify oneself from covenant blessings, but the covenant itself is unstoppable. Yahweh has pledged himself to bless the world through the offspring of Abraham. He's not going to let a rotten generation or two (or ten) derail his plans.

> It's possible to disqualify oneself from covenant blessings, but the covenant itself is unstoppable.

He gives the prophets glimpses of a day when restoration will be possible, along with all the glorious promises God intended from the beginning. Take the book of Isaiah, for example. This prophet of Judah announces certain judgment, but as soon as covenant rebellion is dealt with, God has great things in store.

> But now listen, Jacob, my servant,
>   Israel, whom I have chosen.
> This is what the LORD says—
>   he who made you, who formed you in the womb,
>   and who will help you:
> Do not be afraid, Jacob, my servant,
>   Jeshurun, whom I have chosen.
> For I will pour water on the thirsty land,
>   and streams on the dry ground;
> I will pour out my Spirit on your offspring,
>   and my blessing on your descendants.
> They will spring up like grass in a meadow,
>   like poplar trees by flowing streams.
> (Isaiah 44:1-4)

It's not unusual to see the language of agricultural abundance paired with the outpouring of the Spirit in the prophets: Both are evidence of covenant renewal.[5] In Elijah's day, drought was the direct consequence of covenant unfaithfulness. Here, the reverse is true. Faithfulness brings fruitfulness. In that day of spiritual renewal, Isaiah says something truly remarkable will occur:

> Some will say, "I belong to the LORD";
>   others will call themselves by the name of Jacob;
> still others will write on their hand, "The LORD's,"
>   and will take the name Israel.
> (Isaiah 44:5)

Unlike the days of Ahab and Jezebel, when worshipers of Yahweh had to go into hiding, or the days of Jeremiah, when the prophet's life was in danger, in the future envisioned by Isaiah, the nations will flock to join the people of Yahweh. Instead of a people reluctant to identify themselves as Yahweh's while other nations run them out of town, Isaiah 44:5 speaks of a great spiritual awakening, when people will clamor to belong to him. Some will even make their allegiance to Yahweh physically evident, with a tattoo that says *layahweh*, "Belonging to Yahweh." These are the same words engraved on the high priest's forehead ornament. He was a symbol of the status of the entire nation. The prophet can see it now, tattooed on the hands of those joining Yahweh's people.

This is what the prophet sees far in the distance. First, there are still hard hearts to win.

Isaiah 58–62 contains a whole cluster of passages in which Israel is called by a new name. For this prophet, the work of redemption and transformation is an occasion for renaming, a change in identity. Conversely, rebellion reverses progress, reverting to old titles.[6] Then, in a deeply emotional lament poem, the prophet expresses his wish to return to Sinai for a do-over. Beginning in Isaiah 63:7-8, the prophet recalls Yahweh's election of Israel using covenant terms derived from Deuteronomy such as covenant faithfulness (*hesed*), goodness (*tov*), and "my people," an expression that never refers to other nations.[7] But the recital of history turns sour as he describes their rebellion (Isaiah 63:10). Their disobedience is so acute that Israel's own ancestors would not have recognized them (Isaiah 63:16). Israel's enemies have overrun her holy place because Israel's moral and spiritual deterioration has resulted in the complete loss of Yahweh's protection (Isaiah 63:18-19).

Yahweh's name has been all but lost along with their memory of his saving acts: "No one calls on your name" (Isaiah 64:4-7). It is no wonder that the prophet pleads with God for another dramatic self-revelation. He longs to turn back the clock to the moment when Israel was first brought into a covenant relationship with Yahweh, to hit the reset button on their election.

The key passage for our purposes is Isaiah 63:19–64:1, where the prophet's lament breaks into a plea. Although these two verses are divided by a chapter break in English, they constitute a single verse in Hebrew, linked by poetic sound patterns.[8]

> We have become as those who from ages past you did not rule over,
> those over whom your name was not invoked.
> Oh that you would split the heavens—
> that you would come down and the mountains would quake
>   before you.[9]

The dramatic intervention envisioned by the prophet is reminiscent of Sinai. God's appearance before his people then was staggering: "Mount Sinai was covered with smoke, because Yahweh descended on it in fire. The smoke billowed up from it like smoke from a furnace, and the whole mountain trembled violently" (Exodus 19:18). Now the prophet wants Yahweh to return to the mountain.

We know that the prophet is thinking of Moses because he has already explicitly retold the story of the exodus in Isaiah 63:11-14. Of special interest to us is the mention of the *purpose* of Yahweh's great acts of redemption: "to make for himself an everlasting name" (Isaiah 63:12, ESV) and "to make for [himself] a glorious name" (Isaiah 63:14). Israel's election as the people of Yahweh was designed to magnify his reputation among all nations. While the prophet maintains that Israel is the people of God, there is no longer a basis in Israel's behavior to claim superiority over the nations. She has reverted back to her pre-election status—"like those not called by your name"—in need of a fresh revelation of Yahweh's power and forgiveness.

The prophet is ready to return to Sinai.

Like Isaiah, the prophet Hosea also envisions a redo of Israel's wilderness experience. He likens Israel to an unfaithful wife who turns to prostitution in spite of her husband's love for her. The metaphor is fitting. Israel's worship of other gods is a violation of the covenant commitment made with Yahweh—a covenant for which marriage is our closest analogy. Rather than gratitude for all Yahweh has provided, Israel attributes her blessings to other gods, such as Baal, praying to *him* for rain and thanking *him* for fruitful crops.

Through Hosea, Yahweh announces his plan: "Therefore I am now going to allure her; I will lead her into the wilderness and speak tenderly to her. . . . There she will respond as in the days of her youth, as in the day she came up out of Egypt" (Hosea 2:14-15). Israel needs another encounter with God in the wilderness—one that will show her once and for all that she belongs to Yahweh and that he deserves her complete devotion. The result is a beautiful reaffirmation of the covenant formula that echoes the first two commandments: "I will say to those called 'Not my people,' 'You are my people'; and they will say, 'You are my God'" (Hosea 2:23).

The wilderness is worth it for such a result.

Do these prophetic imaginations ever take shape on the pages of history? And if they do, what happens to the Sinai covenant?

REBOOT: THE RENEWED COVENANT

My friend Shannon had a rough childhood. From ages twelve to eighteen she was sullen and rude to her parents. Her outlook was entirely negative. She tells me that even when she wanted to change, wanted to break from the script, the words would come out with the wrong tone. She was stuck, and so were her parents. Change finally came when Shannon went off to college. Being away from home gave her the freedom to start fresh. When her parents came to visit her several months after she started, they were shocked at how much she had changed. They were able to begin again too. Now, years later, they are very close as a family.

Sometimes things are so terrible that a reboot is the best way forward. That's what the prophet asked for in Isaiah 63, a return to Sinai. Jeremiah had the privilege of announcing to the people of Jerusalem Yahweh's answer to that prayer. He spoke of a future day when the exile would come to an end, God's people would serve him faithfully, and the Davidic dynasty would be restored (Jeremiah 30:3, 9). He says, "Their children will be as in days of old, and their community will be established before me," with the result that "you will be my people, and I will be your God" (Jeremiah 30:20, 22). Covenant renewal! As we would expect, spiritual restoration is accompanied by agricultural fruitfulness (Jeremiah 31:5).

Let's zero in on a well-known passage in Jeremiah 31, the new covenant text. Interpreters have often assumed that this passage announces a radical break from the old covenant at Sinai—that Jeremiah is foretelling the end of covenant law and the beginning of grace in Jesus, an entirely new arrangement. But look closely:

> "The days are coming," declares the LORD, "when I will make *a new covenant* with the people of Israel and with the people of Judah. *It will not be like the covenant I made with their ancestors* when I took them by the hand to lead them out of Egypt, *because they broke my covenant*, though I was a husband to them," declares the LORD. (Jeremiah 31:31-32, emphasis added)

Yes, the prophet announces a new covenant, one unlike the covenant at Sinai, but *how* is it new? A different covenant partner? No, this one is also with Israel and Judah, signifying the restoration of the original twelve tribes. Why do they need a new covenant? The reason is clear. Not because there was something wrong with the Sinai covenant. Simply *"because they broke my covenant."* The problem was with the people.[10] We'll see in a moment that the law hasn't changed. What changes is the mode of delivery.

As the prophet explains,

> *"This is the covenant* I will make with the people of Israel after that time," declares the LORD. *"I will put my law in their minds and write it on their hearts.* I will be their God, and they will be my people. No longer will they teach their neighbor, or say to one another, 'Know the LORD,' because *they will all know me,* from the least of them to the greatest," declares the LORD. "For I will forgive their wickedness and remember their sins no more." (Jeremiah 31:33-34, emphasis added)

No, the covenant hasn't changed. It involves the same partners and the same law. The difference is that God will enable every Israelite to internalize it. Yahweh said earlier that "Judah's sin is engraved with an iron tool . . . on the tablets of their hearts" (Jeremiah 17:1). Their sin occupies the center of their thinking, feeling, and decision making. When the covenant is renewed, their center of gravity will be the Torah instead: It will be written on their hearts. Ezekiel 11:17-20 echoes this idea, too, when it says that God will "remove from them their heart of stone and give them a heart of flesh," enabling them "to follow my decrees and be careful to keep my laws."

As he's done before, Yahweh extends forgiveness. This time he offers Israel a new opportunity. Forgiveness has always been available through the sacrificial system (note the constant refrain through Leviticus 4–6, "and they will be forgiven"). However, this time he plans to offer something more permanent and transformative so that they won't need to keep bringing animal sacrifices.

It's a "new" covenant in the same way that the prophet says Yahweh's mercies are "new every morning" (Lamentations 3:23). Yahweh's mercies

HOW NEW IS THE NEW COVENANT?

To understand what Jeremiah means by "new" in his discussion of the new covenant, we can turn to other prophetic passages where the word "new" appears. Ezekiel 11:17-20 announces that Yahweh will put a "new spirit" in his people after their return from exile. He talks about a "new heart" and "new spirit" again in Ezekiel 18:31 and Ezekiel 36:24-28. Both are for the purpose of removing their stubborn rebellion and animating their obedience to Yahweh. We might say that God plans to restore their heart and spirit to his original design, responsive to their Creator.

Lamentations describes Yahweh's compassions as "new every morning" (Lamentations 3:23). Obviously here "new" cannot mean entirely new or different. Yahweh's mercies are not radically different each day; they are renewed, made freshly available in spite of Israel's sin. The verbal form of the word "new" is used in Lamentations 5:21, asking God to "renew our days as of old." Here the context makes clear that restoration rather than a decisive break is in view.

are not radically different each day; they are renewed, made freshly available. This is what Yahweh announces he will do with the covenant. He's reformatting their hard drive. All the programs are the same as before, but the messes they've made of things will be wiped away for a fresh start. That's good news indeed!

Hebrews 8:13 is the biggest challenge to my contention that the new covenant is continuous with the old one.[11] Hebrews says explicitly that "by calling this covenant 'new,' he has made the first one obsolete; and what is obsolete and outdated will soon disappear." But the author goes on to describe what exactly will disappear: namely, the sacrificial system. Sacrifices brought forgiveness, but they could never cleanse guilty consciences because people kept sinning. The first system of sacrifice, instituted at Sinai, was only temporary. Now that Jesus has given himself once for all, the earthly temple is not necessary. Sacrifices are redundant.

WAS THE SINAI COVENANT CONDITIONAL?

Some have described the Sinai covenant as "conditional," saying that because God required Israel's obedience, their failure brought an end to the covenant. However, to say that the covenant has ended is misleading. How could God punish them for their disobedience to a covenant that has been called off? No, the covenant itself was not conditional. Rather, the enjoyment of covenant blessings was contingent upon loyalty to Yahweh. In order to benefit from the covenant, the Israelites had to keep up their end of the agreement. Unfaithfulness did not spell the end of the covenant; it simply meant that they came under the jurisdiction of its curses rather than its blessings. The covenant itself endured.

The laws were good laws. They just didn't have the power to transform hearts. The covenant was a good covenant. The administration of that covenant (temple, priests, and sacrifices) was just temporary.

Israel's covenant wasn't a complete disaster. Despite failing as a nation, a few faithful men and women keep alive the possibility of renewal for the rest of the people who bear Yahweh's name. They are the people with hearts wide open.

HEARTS WIDE OPEN: THE FAITHFUL FEW

There's always a remnant. Even when everyone else seems to have abandoned the faith, there are always a few who stay the course and remember whose they are.

Elijah felt lonely. He thought he was the only one left who followed Yahweh, but 7,000 others had refused to bow to Baal. Every generation has its faithful who resist being lured by the world. These men and women are in a unique position to see what Yahweh sees and to call on him to act. They have not been blinded by disobedience or numbed by going along with the crowd.

They are the ordinary faithful.

Meet Joanne. She lives away from the public eye, alone in a suburban neighborhood of Charlotte, North Carolina. She has no cable TV, no internet, and no smartphone. Her husband, Ron, died several years ago. He had suffered a stroke, leaving him unable to drive and in need of extra care. Joanne spent most of her adult life as a missionary in Africa and never learned to drive, so the two of them were housebound, dependent on others to take them to the grocery store, to medical appointments, or to church. Joanne is not a likely candidate for a book illustration. Hardly anyone sees her. But I did.

> Every generation has its faithful who resist being lured by the world.

We lived around the corner from Ron and Joanne for almost five years. I watched as her circle of activity grew ever smaller. Her active involvement in church was the first to be curtailed. Then her daily walks. Ron could not be left alone for long. Joanne never complained. She looked to Jesus for her strength. Once I asked if she was able to manage caring for Ron on her own. She paused, trying to find the right words. "Able? I don't suppose that's the best word. No, I'm not able. But I'm *en*abled. God gives us everything we need, doesn't he?"

Joanne is a living example of faithfulness. She may seem ordinary, but she's battling the demons of apathy and self-centeredness, fear and worry, day after day. She simply glows when she talks about how Jesus is her everything. Joanne doesn't pretend things are easy, but she renews her trust in God daily. From that unshakable confidence in Jesus flows a wellspring of life into those around her. Joanne leads a Bible study in her home and mentors several women. She encourages her children and grandchildren by phone and writes letters that showcase the grace of God in her life. Joanne's life and heart are wide open.

The Psalms offer us a glimpse of other hearts open to God—not pretending that all is well, but bringing every hurt to the throne. When we've run out of words, we can pray with Old Testament saints, "Not to us, LORD, not to us but *to your name be the glory*, because of your love and faithfulness" (Psalm 115:1, emphasis added).

Listen to the heartfelt words of those distressed by the world's brokenness and those who recognize their own complicity with evil:

"*For the sake of your name*, LORD, forgive my iniquity, though it is great" (Psalm 25:11, emphasis added).

"Help us, God our Savior, *for the glory of your name*; deliver us and forgive our sins for your name's sake. Why should the nations say, 'Where is their God?'" (Psalm 79:9-10, emphasis added).

"But you, Sovereign LORD, help me *for your name's sake*; out of the goodness of your love, deliver me. For I am poor and needy, and my heart is wounded within me" (Psalm 109:21-22, emphasis added).

These passages from the Psalms have in common a concern for Yahweh's reputation, his name. Men and women through the ages have prayed these words. They have committed themselves to bear his name with honor. They have kept the faith when others have thrown in the towel. Wouldn't you love to know their stories? I sure would.

We can read the story behind one biblical prayer during the exile. Daniel is among the Israelites who feel the full brunt of negative consequences for covenant unfaithfulness. He and his companions are taken to Babylon after the fall of Jerusalem. He is a shining example of one who remained steadfast in his devotion to Yahweh even in an environment hostile to his faith. A beautiful prayer is recorded in Daniel 9 that shows us his heart wide open to God, fully aware of Israel's failed vocation. It's worth quoting at length, now that we have a firm grasp on the covenant theme of bearing Yahweh's name. (Better yet, read the entire prayer in verses 4-19!)

> Lord, the great and awesome God, who keeps his covenant of love with those who love him and keep his commandments, we have sinned and done wrong. We have been wicked and have rebelled; we have turned away from your commands and laws. We have not listened to your servants the prophets, who spoke in your

name to our kings, our princes and our ancestors, and to all the people of the land. . . . Therefore the curses and sworn judgments written in the Law of Moses, the servant of God, have been poured out on us, because we have sinned against you. . . . Now, our God, hear the prayers and petitions of your servant. *For your sake,* Lord, look with favor on your desolate sanctuary. Give ear, our God, and hear; open your eyes and see the desolation of the city *that bears your Name.* We do not make requests of you because we are righteous, but because of your great mercy. Lord, listen! Lord, forgive! Lord, hear and act! *For your sake, my God,* do not delay, *because your city and your people bear your Name."* (Daniel 9:4-6, 11, 17-19, emphasis added)

Daniel is aware of the sin problem. He knows that Israel has failed to uphold the covenant and that they deserve God's wrath. But he also knows that Yahweh's reputation is at stake. He grounds his prayer in Israel's vocation as God's representatives, crying out for God to act on behalf of his people.

Even in the anguish of these prayers, what Yahweh sees is beautiful. Every heartfelt prayer is proof that the covenant lives on among the faithful. Perfection is not necessary. The sacrificial system in Leviticus demonstrates God's willingness to forgive. All that's required is that we keep coming back with hearts wide open, committing ourselves to the most important work of all—honoring the one whose name we bear.

DIGGING DEEPER

Daniel I. Block. *The Book of Ezekiel: Chapters 24–48.* NICOT.
Grand Rapids: Eerdmans, 1998.

*Walter Brueggemann. *The Prophetic Imagination.* 2nd ed. Minneapolis: Fortress, 2001.

*Aaron Chalmers. *Interpreting the Prophets: Reading, Under-
standing and Preaching from the Worlds of the Prophets.*
Downers Grove, IL: IVP Academic, 2015.

*J. Clinton McCann Jr. *A Theological Introduction to the Book of
Psalms: The Psalms as Torah.* Nashville: Abingdon, 1993.

Jeffrey J. Niehaus. *God at Sinai: Covenant and Theophany in the
Bible and Ancient Near East.* SOTBT. Grand Rapids: Zondervan,
1995.

*Christopher J. H. Wright. *The Mission of God: Unlocking the
Bible's Grand Narrative.* Downers Grove, IL: IVP Academic,
2006.

Related videos from The Bible Project: "Prophets," "Holy Spirit,"
and "The Way of the Exile."

8

JUST GIVE ME JESUS

The Gospel Witness

SIGN ME UP! JESUS AS NAME BEARER

Is all this talk about the Sinai covenant and the theme of "bearing Yahweh's name" just an Old Testament thing? Is it relevant to Christians today? Or is it merely something of historical interest? To answer these questions, we need to look carefully at how the New Testament interacts

WHERE'S YAHWEH IN THE NEW TESTAMENT?

One thing becomes clear right away when we turn the page from Malachi to Matthew. A remarkable shift occurs. The name "Yahweh" disappears completely. Two factors play into this. The first is the change in language from Hebrew and Aramaic to Greek. ("Yahweh" is very hard to say because Greek lacks both "y" and "w." Come to think of it, there's not really a letter "h" either.) A second factor that explains the disappearance of Yahweh's name is Jewish reverence. Jews by the time of Jesus decided that it's best not to say the divine name at all to avoid the risk of profaning it.[1] However, these reasons do not entirely explain the shift.

with these questions. Is it "out with the old, in with the new"? Or is the Sinai covenant still in effect?

Let's first look at how Jesus interacts with God's name. During his earthly ministry, Jesus prays for the sanctification of his Father's name, and he makes that name known. But after his death, the name "Jesus" comes to the forefront of the church's expression of faith, becoming the only name "by which we must be saved" (Acts 4:12). In some way, the divine name is transferred to Jesus. Let's find out how.

When Jesus is born, Matthew emphasizes the significance of the event by highlighting his name. The infant is *called* the Messiah, or anointed one (Matthew 1:16), but he is *named* Jesus, which means "Yahweh saves" (Matthew 1:21, 25). Messiah is his title. Jesus is his name. This name will mean more to us if we recall a bit of history. At Sinai, Moses had a right-hand man named Hoshea, which means (rather ambiguously) "he saves" (see Numbers 13:8). Who saves? The name doesn't specify, though the man himself is never given credit for saving Israel. Hoshea was a military hero and one of the twelve spies that Moses sent to scope out the land of Canaan. We encountered the story already: ten of the spies come back terrified, claiming that the residents are too strong to confront. Hoshea is one of the two who insist that Yahweh is able to conquer the land of Canaan. He and Caleb put their confidence in God's strength. It is then that Moses changes Hoshea's name to Yeshua, in English Joshua, a name which means "*Yahweh* saves" (Numbers 14:6).[2] There can no longer be any doubt about the source of salvation.

The Greek name Jesus (*Iesou*) is a translation of the Hebrew *Yeshua*— *Yahweh* saves.[3] Just like Joshua, Jesus' own name announces that Yahweh has come to save his people. Unlike Joshua, Jesus' name says something about its bearer. His birth signifies the return of Yahweh to his people, recalling the name prophesied by Isaiah: "Immanuel," God with us (Matthew 1:23). Through the incarnation, Yahweh has come to be with his people and save them. The name "Immanuel" implies not only that God's presence is evident in the events surrounding Jesus' birth, but that Jesus is Yahweh himself, come to be with his people.[4]

That's what makes it all the more striking that Jesus does not focus on his own name. Instead, he magnifies the name of his Father. When he teaches his disciples to pray, approaching God with hearts wide open, he prays that the Father's name would be sanctified, reversing centuries of its desecration through Israel's unfaithfulness to the covenant (Matthew 6:9; Luke 11:2). Jesus' prayer, "hallowed be your name," is not just wishful thinking, as though Jesus is hoping that Yahweh is doing well up there. His prayer implies a personal commitment to honoring that name through a life of faithful obedience. He fulfills Israel's vocation to bear Yahweh's name with honor.

For Jesus, *calling* on God's name is not enough, nor is prophecy, exorcism, or miracles done in his name. The key disposition of one who truly belongs to God is a commitment to action—to doing his will rather than one's own (Matthew 7:21-22; cf. Luke 6:46). The name of God is not a charm to be used at will. It is not a magic amulet to guarantee protection. Those who fail to carry out God's will bear his name in vain. Jesus has no patience for those whose verbal proclamations do not match their agenda. He condemns the Pharisees and scribes for having lips and hearts that contradict each other, saying that they "worship [God] in vain" (Mark 7:5-7). They walk around wearing official religious titles, but their hearts are haughty and self-reliant.

> Jesus' prayer, "hallowed be your name," is not just wishful thinking, as though Jesus is hoping that Yahweh is doing well up there. His prayer implies a personal commitment to honoring that name through a life of faithful obedience.

Jesus takes his vocation as Yahweh's representative so seriously that others can see Yahweh by looking at him. John repeatedly highlights this, noting that Jesus had been sent by the Father to carry out his work in the world. "The works that the Father has given me to finish—the very works that I am doing—testify that the Father has sent me" (John 5:36). He goes on, "I have come in my Father's name" (5:43). Jesus is the *segullah*, the treasured one appointed to represent Yahweh. He even tells his disciples, "The one who looks at me is seeing the one who sent me" (John 12:45). This is not just because he is God incarnate. It's also because his behavior and his character reflect God's the way every covenant member's character should. He wants his disciples to imitate him. He explains, "I have set you an example that you should do as I have done for you" (John 13:15).[5]

Jesus can tell his disciples, "If you really know me, you will know my Father as well" (John 14:7). He even claims to have been "marked . . . with [the Father's] seal" (John 6:27). I have already described the ancient practice of using engraved gemstones, or seals, to stamp documents as a signature or to make an impression on a lump of clay over a jar opening in order to authorize its contents. I also mentioned the discovery of divine

> By bearing God's name, Jesus lives out Israel's vocation, showing us how it ought to be done.

seals, bearing the name of a god, used to authorize temple documents or lay claim to temple property. Jesus' awareness of having been marked by his Father's seal fits this concept well. While not all stamp seals were inscribed with a name, most Israelite seals were. Jesus' claim to have been marked with a divine seal indicates that he sees himself as wearing an invisible tattoo with Yahweh's name on his person. His highest goal is to bring that name glory (John 12:28).

By bearing God's name, Jesus lives out Israel's vocation, showing us how it ought to be done. We'll look next at how Matthew portrays him as a human who embodies all that Israel was supposed to be and do, while at the same time showing us he is greater than Moses because he is the lawgiver himself.

DÉJÀ VU: JESUS AS THE TRUE ISRAEL

Matthew does far more than simply record what happened to Jesus. His gospel is creatively structured and brilliantly written. Mount Sinai looms large in his gospel! Here's how:

Matthew's gospel breaks neatly into five blocks of teaching, mimicking the five books of the Torah (Genesis, Exodus, Leviticus, Numbers, Deuteronomy). These five blocks of teaching are preceded by an introductory story in which Jesus' life is in danger because King Herod, like Pharaoh, is killing Jewish babies. To escape, his parents take him to Egypt. It's an inside-out exodus story! When the coast is clear, they return to Palestine, retracing Israel's journey from Egypt to the promised land. Next we fast-forward to Jesus' adulthood, where he passes through the waters of baptism in the Jordan, reminding us of Israel's crossing both the Reed (Red) Sea and the Jordan.

After this, Jesus is sent by the Spirit into the wilderness for forty days, where he reenacts Israel's wilderness wanderings (Matthew 4:1-11). The tempter comes to him three times, calling Jesus' true identity into question: "If you are the Son of God . . ." Each time, Jesus responds by quoting Scripture. His choice of passages is not random. Jesus chooses precisely those chapters of Deuteronomy where Moses is reminding the Israelites of the lessons they ought to have learned in the wilderness, lessons Jesus knows by heart. Let's take a closer look.

First, the devil tries to entice Jesus to provide bread for himself. After forty days without food, Jesus is understandably hungry. Unlike the Israelites of old, Jesus does not complain or fall into despair. He trusts his Father, responding to the devil with the last line of Deuteronomy 8:3, "Man does not live on bread alone, but on every word that comes from the mouth of the LORD." Makes sense, right? But to get the full impact of Jesus' quotation, we need the previous verse for context:

> *Remember how the LORD your God led you all the way in the wilderness these forty years, to humble and test you in order to know what was in your heart, whether or not you would keep his commands.* He humbled you, causing you to hunger and then feeding you with manna, which neither you nor your ancestors had known, to teach you that man does not live on bread alone but on every word that comes from the mouth of the LORD." (Deuteronomy 8:2-3)

Jesus knew exactly what he was doing. He was reliving Israel's story. And he was demonstrating his dependence on the Father's provision, resisting the urge to rely on his own strength. Yahweh had called Israel his firstborn son (Exodus 4:22), and he provided for their needs in the wilderness. Jesus knows that his needs will be met, too.

Next, the devil takes Jesus to the holy city (on Mount Zion!), bringing him to the pinnacle of the temple. He tries to beat Jesus at his own game by quoting Scripture: "'If you are the Son of God,' he said, 'throw yourself down. For it is written: "He will command his angels concerning you, and they will lift you up in their hands, so that you will not strike your foot against a stone"'" (Matthew 4:6). Satan wants Jesus to force God's hand, testing his identity by demanding a dramatic rescue.

Jesus won't budge. He quotes the first part of Deuteronomy 6:16, "Do not put the Lord your God to the test." The rest reads, "as you did at Massah." We can read the story of Massah in Exodus 17. The people are quarrelsome, demanding that Moses give them water to drink. They whine, "Why did you bring us up out of Egypt to make us and our children and livestock die of thirst?" (Exodus 17:3). They test Yahweh, saying, "Is the Lord among us or not?" (Exodus 17:7). If the demand for water to prove God's presence is inappropriate, how much more so is a risky jump from the peak of the temple? Jesus will not manipulate God's hand to rescue him. He will not repeat Israel's mistake.

The devil makes a final attempt, this time appealing to human lust for power. He takes Jesus to "a very high mountain" (reminiscent of Sinai?), where he can see all the kingdoms of the world (Matthew 4:8). "All this I will give you," he promises, "if you will bow down and worship me" (Matthew 4:9). Satan offers Jesus a shortcut to power. If Jesus is the Messiah, all nations will eventually bow at his feet (see Psalm 2). The end result is what God has already planned, but the devil's shortcut to that end is a direct violation of the first commandment.

Without hesitation, Jesus paraphrases Deuteronomy 6:13, "Worship the Lord your God and serve him only." No path to success is the right path if it violates the covenant. The end does not justify the means.

With this, the devil leaves Jesus. The Messiah has passed the test that Israel failed. Matthew wants us to see Jesus as the new Israel. He is walking the same paths, reliving Israel's story, but maintaining covenant faithfulness all the way. All this sets the stage for the heart of Matthew's gospel—the five sermons given by Jesus during his ministry. Other gospel writers focus more on his miracles or his signs or his suffering. For Matthew, the core of Jesus' ministry is his words.

I've already demonstrated the centrality of the Sinai narratives to the Torah. Everything from Exodus 19 to Numbers 10 (fifty-nine chapters of material!) happens at Sinai. It's no wonder that the core of Matthew's Torah-shaped account is Jesus' teaching on a mountain.

DEAD GIVEAWAY: JESUS AS GREATER THAN MOSES

Matthew's first block of Jesus' teaching is known as the Sermon on the Mount. That alone should be a dead giveaway. Jesus chooses a mountainside as the context for his instructions. Not only that, he starts in on the law almost immediately: "Do not think that I have come to abolish the Law or the Prophets: I have not come to abolish them but to fulfill them" (Matthew 5:17). If anyone was hoping to be done with Sinai now that Jesus is here, this is the moment of truth. He upholds the law, telling the crowds that every commandment matters and that entrance to God's kingdom requires a righteousness even greater than that of the current Jewish religious leaders. *Uh-oh.*

Then he begins to get uncomfortably specific, pointing out areas in which his contemporaries have let things slide. "You have heard that it was said . . ." he begins, addressing murder, adultery, divorce, oaths, judgment, and loving their neighbor. If they've tried to dodge their responsibility ("I haven't killed anyone, so I'm basically okay"), Jesus asks them to take a closer look. He raises the bar by returning to the original intent of the Sinai instructions. "You have heard that it was said . . . but I tell you." *I tell you not even to be angry; not ever to let conflict go unreconciled; not even to look with lust; not to divorce except in extreme circumstances;*

JUST GIVE ME JESUS

*not to swear oaths at all; not to resist an evil person; not to hate your enemy,
but rather to love them.* Jesus does not do away with the Old Testament
law. He calls people back to it. And he holds them to it.

Jesus is also clear about what covenant faithfulness should look like
to others. Bearing Yahweh's name does not mean that we are to make
our religious observances publicly con-
spicuous. Jesus warns his disciples not to
pray on the street corners or make it obvious that they're fasting in order to be seen
(Matthew 6:5, 16).

> Jesus does not
> do away with the
> Old Testament law.
> He calls people
> back to it.

He defines discipleship around obedi-
ence. It's not enough to claim allegiance to Jesus; one must also do God's
will. Lip service to Jesus without action that flows out of an intimate
relationship is falsely bearing his name (Matthew 7:21-23).

So there's Jesus, on a mountain, teaching with authority about
the Jewish law. Are we supposed to see him as Moses? I've lost count
of the number of times I've heard or read that when Jesus climbed up on
the mountain to teach his disciples that he's acting like a "new Moses"
or perhaps the "prophet like Moses" described in Deuteronomy 18:9-22.
In that passage, Moses had announced, "The LORD your God will raise
up for you a prophet like me from among you, from your fellow Israelites. You must listen to him" (Deuteronomy 18:15).

However, the point of Deuteronomy 18:9-22 is to contrast the ways
that other nations seek divine guidance (e.g., sorcery and witchcraft)
with the way Israel is to hear from Yahweh—through the prophets he
sends them—as well as to warn them to watch for false prophets.
Moses does not anticipate a single prophet at the end of the ages, but
rather a succession of prophets: Yahweh's ongoing provision for them
to know what he expects of them. New Testament passages that refer
back to Deuteronomy 18 do so in reference to the line of prophets
rejected by the Israelites (see Acts 3:22-23 and 7:37). If there is an
expectation of an end-times prophet, the New Testament clearly
identifies that prophet as John the Baptist, announcing the coming of

Jesus.[6] While Jesus shares some similarities with the prophets, he clearly supersedes them.

Here's the bottom line: Jesus is not simply a conduit of God's teachings the way Moses was. He is the *source* of those teachings. He possesses authority that Moses and the other prophets never had. Moses was only a messenger. Jesus is both the sender and deliverer of the message. Jesus is Yahweh in the flesh. He doesn't say "thus says the Lord." His teaching comes from within: "*I* tell you."

The crowds are amazed at his authority (Matthew 7:29). As they should be.

SABBATH SHOWDOWN: JESUS AS ONE WITH AUTHORITY

Jesus demonstrates this authority in other ways, too. A story will help us understand the relationship between Jesus and the Sinai instructions. In Matthew 12, we join Jesus and his disciples as they walk through a field of grain on the Sabbath. The Pharisees, the self-appointed Jewish lawyers of the day, watch on the sidelines with narrowed eyes as the hungry disciples rub stalks of wheat between their hands to remove grain and then pop it in their mouths to chew on. The Pharisees toss their penalty flags on the field and spring into action, "Look! Your disciples are breaking Sabbath law!"

The crux of the Pharisees' objection to the disciples is not the behavior itself. The law clearly gave permission to eat grain from a neighbor's field as long as it was picked by hand, not using harvest tools (see Deuteronomy 23:25). No, their objection was not to the eating of grain, it was an issue of breaking the Sabbath, a serious offense worthy of the death penalty (see Exodus 31:14). It was not unlawful to eat on the Sabbath, but harvesting grain was out of bounds according to Jewish leaders, and in the Pharisees' narrow view of the law, the disciples were engaged in harvesting. In other words, the law they had broken is not explicit in the Torah but falls in the category of law-breaking behavior as defined by the current religious administration.

Jesus is unruffled. He easily beats them at their own game, shrewdly citing three Old Testament texts as justification for their actions. First, he brings up David: "Haven't you read what David did when he and his companions were hungry? He entered the house of God, and he and his companions ate the consecrated bread—which was not lawful for them to do, but only for the priests" (Matthew 12:3-4). Of course the Pharisees had read the story of David, Israel's rightful, anointed king on the run from the ruler whom Yahweh had rejected, King Saul.[7]

Matthew has already made clear in the early chapters of his book that Jesus is the son of David (Matthew 1:1, 20), anointed by God's Spirit (Matthew 3:16-17), who is experiencing increasing opposition from Jewish leaders (Matthew 9:3, 11, 34; 10:16-31). Surely Jesus had in mind the analogy to his own situation. The statement Jesus makes through the use of this story is subtle but radical. He seems to be suggesting that the same legal exemptions that applied in the case of David—Israel's true king in exile—also apply to him and his disciples. No wonder the Pharisees were incensed!

Jesus' second example also relates to temple worship: "Or haven't you read in the Law that the priests on Sabbath duty in the temple desecrate the Sabbath and yet are innocent?" (Matthew 12:5). Obviously, priests must work on the Sabbath because their work is necessary for proper worship to take place. Therefore, they are innocent. Jesus follows this observation with an oblique claim: "I tell you that something [or someone] greater than the temple is here" (Matthew 12:6). Jesus does not merely equate his ministry with the priesthood, which in itself would have been seen as blasphemous. More than that, he claims directly that he and/or his ministry is greater than the temple![8]

Then, as if he had not insulted them enough already, Jesus insinuates that they have not understood the Old Testament at all: "If you had known what these words mean, 'I desire mercy, not sacrifice,' you would not have condemned the innocent" (Matthew 12:7). His quotation about mercy points to a section of Hosea in which God judges Judah for breaking their covenant with Him, especially the priests (Hosea 6:6).

In fact, Hosea accuses the priests of murder (6:9)! Is Jesus implying that the Pharisees' failure to understand Hosea's message puts them in the same category as these seditious Jewish leaders?

Jesus concludes his argument with a rapid one-two punch. First, he claims directly the innocence of his disciples (Matthew 12:7). Then, in case the Pharisees have missed his subtle allusions, he states that "the Son of Man is Lord of the Sabbath" (Matthew 12:8). "Son of Man" is Jesus' favorite self-designation, a veiled way of pointing to his divinely delegated authority. The plain meaning of the phrase is simply "human," but it carries greater connotations because in Daniel's vision (Daniel 7:13) "one like a son of man" is given an everlasting dominion and an indestructible kingdom. In the vision, this figure represents God's holy people who will rule on his behalf (see Daniel 7:27). It is no surprise that the Pharisees are enraged and later seek to destroy him. By calling himself the "Son of Man," Jesus' claims are enormous: authority to set aside Sabbath laws, correctly interpret the Hebrew Scriptures, and even to reign over God's kingdom! He is greater than the law. He is the lawgiver.

From there he enters the synagogue where the Jewish leaders try to trap him again, asking him if it's lawful to heal on the Sabbath. Jesus cleverly heals a man with just a word—something that cannot be construed as lawless behavior, even on the Sabbath. Again the situation is a slap in the face to Israel's leaders. The man he healed had a shriveled hand, evoking the story of Israel's ancient king, Jeroboam. Jeroboam's hand had shriveled when he stretched it out against the true prophet of Yahweh, giving orders to seize him (1 Kings 13:4). The prophet then prayed and the king's hand was restored. Jesus doesn't pray. He simply tells the man with a shriveled hand to stretch it out and be restored. The incident confirms Jesus as one even greater than a prophet while exposing Israel's leaders as the enemies of Yahweh.

Matthew follows this story with a lengthy quotation from Isaiah 42, identifying Jesus as the servant that the prophet had announced would come. However, instead of following the Hebrew Old Testament, which reads, "in his *torah* the islands will put their hope," Matthew follows the

Greek Old Testament, which reads, "in his *name* the nations will put their hope" (Matthew 12:21, quoting Isaiah 42:4). Jesus does not set aside the Torah, but he is so much greater. It all points to him.

The Sermon on the Mount shows that Jesus understands himself as one who possesses authority to interpret the law and give fresh revelation. His Sabbath interchange portrays him as Lord of the Sabbath, one greater than the temple, with power to heal. If his divine identity is still veiled to some, it won't be for much longer. The mountain of transfiguration makes it obvious.

SHINING FACES: THE TRANSFIGURATION

This lesson concerning Jesus' identity is confirmed in a dramatic way. He brings Peter, James, and John, his closest disciples, up a high mountain. Time after time, Jesus + mountain = something interesting. This time is no exception. When they reached the pinnacle, Jesus' "face shone like the sun, and his clothes became as white as the light" (Matthew 17:2). It was a glorious revelation. This event has Sinai written all over it—the cloud, the glory, the divine voice. Moments later, they have company— Moses and Elijah. Both men are back from the dead, conversing with Jesus on the mountain. In different eras, both had conversed with Yahweh at Mount Sinai. Both had witnessed Yahweh's glory before their very eyes, but they had only been allowed to see God's back. Now they see his face—the face of Jesus. And it shines gloriously.

Moses had seen Yahweh when he revealed himself to the exodus generation and entered into the covenant with them, appointing them as his special representatives to bear his name among the nations. Elijah had seen Yahweh when it looked like that covenant was in tatters, with only a small remnant of faithful Israelites. Moses witnessed the failure of the golden calf within days of the covenant's beginning. Likewise, most in Elijah's day had fallen into the worship of other gods and failed to represent Yahweh well. Like Jesus, both men "suffered rejection and hostility from the people to whom they were sent."[9] Jesus has already explained that his glory would come through suffering. Moses and

Elijah could both testify to the truth of this in their own ministries. Because both men passed from this earth in supernatural fashion—Moses buried by God on Mount Nebo and Elijah transported to heaven in a flaming chariot—they came to represent the messianic age, igniting the hopes of Israel for God's intervention.[10] Now the disciples witness Jesus' glory, God-made-flesh, as the covenant is being renewed through his ministry. Jesus is also the one who models covenant faithfulness for Israel by representing the Father perfectly.

Peter thinks he has a bright idea: let's put up shelters for each of you! Like King David, he takes the initiative, wanting to build a house for God, wanting to make this moment endure. Glory is a bit more of what he had in mind for Jesus rather than the suffering Jesus had predicted. But before Peter can finish speaking, God the Father answers, surrounding them with a bright cloud: "This is my son, whom I love; with him I am well pleased. Listen to him!" (Matthew 17:5)

The divine voice puts Peter in his place: your job is to listen to Jesus, not to try to manage my glory. "Listen to him" (Matthew 17:5) echoes Deuteronomy 18:15-19, where the people are told to pay attention to the "prophet like Moses" who will arise.[11] Jesus inherits the legacy of the prophets who reveal God's word to the people of faith, but this particular prophet is even greater than Moses. The glory is his own. Jesus trumps both Moses and Elijah because they disappear, leaving him to carry out deliverance for Israel.[12]

And then it's over. As quickly as it started, Moses and Elijah are gone. Jesus rouses his disciples from their trembling face plant and they return down the mountain. But what they saw they will not soon forget.

Before we leave this mountain, we must ask what it means for followers of Jesus today. New Testament scholar Michael Kibbe recently wrote that the story of the transfiguration is not just about a revelation of Jesus' divine identity, it's also about us. The key to this connection is Jesus' shining face. Perhaps you remember Moses' experience on the mountain: "When Moses came down from Mount Sinai with the two tablets of the covenant law in his hands, he was not aware that his face was radiant because he had spoken with the LORD" (Exodus 34:29). Each time Moses meets with Yahweh, his face glows as he relays Yahweh's message to the people.

Paul reflects on this in his second letter to the church in Corinth. He says, "He anointed us, set his seal of ownership on us, and put his Spirit in our hearts as a deposit, guaranteeing what is to come" (2 Corinthians 1:21-22). Paul goes on to compare his ministry with the ministry of Moses in chapter three. Moses' radiance gradually faded and needed constant renewal. For that reason, the glory Moses experienced pales in comparison with Jesus' glory, which never fades. But here's the payoff: "And we all, who with unveiled faces contemplate the Lord's glory, are being transformed into his image with ever-increasing glory, which comes from the Lord, who is the Spirit" (2 Corinthians 3:18). Instead of fading, our glory gets brighter and brighter.

Moses' face shone when he saw Yahweh, but he veiled it because the Israelites could not bear to look at it (Exodus 34:29-35). Our faces also reflect God's glory, and we experience transformation so that we look more and more like him. Jesus' transfiguration offers us a preview of our own transfiguration: It points to the new creation.

Jesus' resurrection is the first glimpse we get of new creation. He's called the "firstborn from among the dead" (Colossians 1:18). He is not simply resuscitated, as Lazarus and Talitha and others are, for those others will die again. Not Jesus. Jesus is raised to a different kind of life. He can eat and drink, but he's also able to walk through walls. His body will no longer decay. He will never die. Jesus is the first to enter the renewed creation. His bodily resurrection is our assurance—proof positive—that we will be raised to that kind of life as well. As we gaze at him, we begin to reflect that new creation glory.

Kibbe explains, "If the light of the gospel has shone in our hearts, we are responsible to make that light as visible as possible to those around us."[13] Jesus shines, not so that we can soak it in for ourselves, but so that we can reflect the glory to others.

DIGGING DEEPER

*Richard Bauckham. *Jesus and the God of Israel:* God Crucified and Other Studies on the New Testament's Christology of Divine Identity. Grand Rapids: Eerdmans, 2008.

R. T. France. *The Gospel of Matthew.* NICNT. Grand Rapids: Eerdmans, 2007.

Richard B. Hays. *Echoes of Scripture in the Gospels.* Waco, TX: Baylor University Press, 2016.

*Michael Harrison Kibbe. "Our Future in the Face of Jesus." *Christianity Today.* July/August 2017, 66-69.

Related videos from The Bible Project: "God," "Messiah," and "Heaven and Earth."

9

BLOB TAG

The Mission of Jesus

NO OTHER NAME: JESUS, NAME ABOVE ALL NAMES

I once babysat a four-year-old boy who refused to answer to his given name, Steven. If I wanted his attention, I had to call him "Darkwing Duck." So complete was his obsession with Darkwing Duck that he learned how to read a clock and memorized the TV schedule. Missing an episode would have been worse than missing dessert. He loved to "fly" around the house in a cape, jumping off couches and announcing, "I am the terror that flaps in the night. I am Darkwing Duck!" Coming from a kid who was not yet fully potty trained, this was even more amusing than his cartoon hero's notoriously lame entrances. Although he insisted on the name Darkwing Duck, he didn't fool anyone. He was still Steven.

Names are important. To change a name indicates a change of identity. Although we've seen evidence of Jesus' self-understanding as one who bears *Yahweh's* name, the early church elevated the name of *Jesus*. From its earliest days, the church uses Jesus' name in ways reminiscent of the Old Testament's use of Yahweh's name. Reverence transferred seamlessly from Yahweh to Jesus, without explanation or apology. Here's a prime example: on the day of Pentecost, Peter declares that the outpouring of the Holy Spirit witnessed by the crowds fulfills Joel's prophecy and signals that the "latter days" have arrived. Peter's extended quotation from Joel 2 concludes with the words, "everyone who calls on the name of the Lord (*kyrios*) will be saved" (Acts 2:21; cf. Joel 2:32). In Joel, that name is *Yahweh*, signified in our English translations by "the LORD" in all caps. For Joel, *Yahweh* brings salvation to the remnant. Since *kyrios* is the Greek word that normally translates Yahweh in the Old Testament but also designates the "Lord" (or "master") Jesus in the NT, the significance of Peter's quotation is not immediately evident. Is Peter saying that those who call on *Yahweh* will be saved? Or those who call on *Jesus*?

Later in the narrative Peter clarifies by healing a lame man "in the name of Jesus Christ" (Acts 3:6) and declaring, "Salvation is found in no one else, for there is *no other name* under heaven given to mankind by which we must be saved" (Acts 4:12). Appearing so soon after his quotation of Joel, Peter's statement presents a paradox: no other name but Yahweh and no other name but Jesus. The salvation available only to those who called on Joel's *kyrios*, Yahweh, is now found exclusively in Peter's *kyrios, Jesus.* Peter is convinced that Jesus of Nazareth is Yahweh in the flesh, "God with us."[1]

Elsewhere in the book of Acts people call on Jesus' name (9:14, 21; 22:16), are baptized in his name (2:38; 8:16; 10:48; 19:5; cf. Matthew 28:19), perform healing in his name (4:7-10), teach in his name (4:18; 5:28), do signs and wonders in his name (4:30), proclaim his name (8:12), have faith in his name (3:16), and receive forgiveness in his name (10:43). The shift in focus from the name of Yahweh to the name of Jesus is maintained through the rest of the New Testament. Remarkably, none of the New Testament apostles teach otherwise. Let's look at three sample texts—from Philippians, Hebrews, and Revelation—to show the pervasiveness of the practice of elevating Jesus' name in the early church. Later we'll consider how it relates to the theme of bearing Yahweh's name.

The hymn of Philippians 2 ascribes to Jesus the "the name that is above every name" (v. 9).[2] Significantly, it also echoes Isaiah 45:23, one of the most important monotheistic texts in the Hebrew Bible. Yahweh had announced, "I am God and there is no other" (Isaiah 45:22), adding, "Before me every knee will bow; by me every tongue will swear" (45:23). In Philippians 2:9-11, Paul applies these words to Jesus (emphasis added):

> Therefore God exalted him to the highest place
>   and gave him the name that is above every name,
> that *at the name of Jesus* every knee should bow,
>   in heaven and on earth and under the earth,
> and every tongue acknowledge *that Jesus Christ is Lord*,
>   to the glory of God the Father.

Here Jesus is drawn into a role that Yahweh himself was expected to fulfill. Bearing Yahweh's name (the "name above every name"), Jesus receives worship that belongs to God alone, and yet somehow God the Father is still glorified. As explained earlier, *kyrios* stands for the proper divine name, Yahweh, throughout the Greek Old Testament and into the New Testament. Therefore, the "name above every name" is not "Jesus." Rather, he is given "the name" LORD (*kyrios*), which is Yahweh. Knees will bow at the name that *belongs to* Jesus, that is, Yahweh.[3]

The author of Hebrews applies a string of Old Testament quotations to Jesus to attest his superiority to the angels, explicitly because of his superior name (1:4), a name he subsequently proclaims (2:12). Hebrews 1:8-9 quotes Psalm 45:6-7, where the king is called *elohim*, or god, meaning that he is considered a resident of the divine realm. The king governs on God's behalf, so his rule has other-worldly implications. Speaking to the anointed human king, the psalmist says in verse 6,

> Your throne, O god, will last for ever and ever;
>   a scepter of justice will be the scepter of your kingdom.

However, the Psalm also attributes blessing and anointing to the king's God in verse 7:

> You love righteousness and hate wickedness;
>   therefore God, your God, has set you above your companions
>   by anointing you with the oil of joy.

Quoting this psalm is an ideal way for the author of Hebrews to emphasize Jesus' divine status without implying Yahweh's replacement.[4] Hebrews highlights Jesus' exalted messianic kingship (1:5), the call to worship him (1:6), his dominion (1:8-9), and his status as creator (1:10-12).

Finally, John's visions in the book of Revelation reveal a man called "Faithful and True" (Revelation 19:11) and "Word of God" (19:13). His thigh is inscribed "King of Kings and Lord of Lords" (19:16) and he exercises the dominion of Yahweh (19:15; cf. Psalm 2:9). The man wore many crowns inscribed with a secret name (Revelation 19:12), reminiscent of the high priestly diadem inscribed with Yahweh's name (Exodus 28:36-37).[5] Thus John's vision presents a vibrant image of Jesus as one whose character and reputation were identical to Yahweh's, who bore the unique name of the Father, and carried out his will among the nations.

The New Testament clearly and consistently portrays Jesus as bearing the name above all names. Jesus, wearing the invisible tattoo of a covenant member that marks him as belonging to Yahweh, models for his followers what it means for them to bear Yahweh's name as well. But he alone receives the worship due Yahweh because he is Yahweh in the flesh.

The early church arrived at this conclusion for a variety of reasons. We saw some of them in the previous chapter, with his authority as paramount. Jesus' authority is most clearly seen in his instructions to his disciples. Believers are sent in his name into all the world to do God's will.

SENT: SAUL'S COMMISSION

Last year I was asked to organize onsite registration for a conference. We were expecting as many as 1,000 people in attendance, so I could not do it on my own. Although it was my responsibility to ensure a smooth check-in process, I would need the help of several other volunteers. I decided to recruit more people than was strictly necessary so that I would not need to sit at the registration table myself. This freed me up to oversee the process, visit with participants, and count how many were in attendance. When the volunteers arrived, I gave them a brief orientation as to their duties and then released them to carry out our mission.

Jesus understands that he has a job to do. He commits himself to bring honor to the Father's name. But he is not under the impression that it is all up to him to accomplish this. As my pastor, Alvin Beuchert, said in a recent sermon, "Jesus finished all the work God gave him to do, but he did not finish all the work."[6] Just as he was sent to do the Father's will, so he sends his disciples into the world. They are commissioned to carry out his mission (Matthew 10:1-20; John 13:20).

Acts 9 contains one of the most explicit and surprising references to bearing the name in the New Testament. Saul is a Jewish leader committed to stamping out the worship of Jesus.[7] In fact, when we join his story, he's on his way to Syria to find followers of Jesus and take them as prisoners. Along the road, Jesus appears to him in a blinding vision, knocking him to the ground. Meanwhile, the Lord tells a disciple of Jesus in Damascus named Ananias, one of those in Saul's crosshairs, to seek him out and pray for his eyesight to be restored. Ananias is understandably nervous (Acts 9:13-14). However, the Lord assures him, "Go! This man is my chosen instrument to *bear my name* to the Gentiles and their kings and to the people of Israel" (Acts 9:15).[8] Saul's destiny is to suffer for the sake of Jesus' name (Acts 9:16). As Jesus had predicted before the transfiguration, his disciples must take up their cross (Matthew 16:24-25). That's exactly what Saul goes on to do—experiencing persecution, and ultimately expressing a willingness to die for Jesus' name (Acts 21:13; see 9:29). Saul is sent.

IN JESUS' NAME

Jesus calls on his followers to lose their lives for his sake (Matthew 16:25) and to leave home for the sake of his name (Matthew 19:29; Mark 10:29). He delegates authority to them over sickness, demons, and even death (Matthew 10:8; 28:18-19; Mark 3:13-15; 6:7; Luke 9:1; 10:17-20; 22:28-30), promising to do what they asked in his name (John 14:13-14; 15:16; 16:23-26). As a result of their obedience, they suffer for his name (Acts 5:41; 9:16), just like he did. He has passed the baton.

However surprising this is, Saul's commission as Christ's ambassador is not unique. He expects believers to imitate him the way he imitates Jesus (1 Corinthians 11:1; Ephesians 5:1), saying that they are children of God (Romans 1:6-7). Belonging to Christ is expected to result in behavior consistent with a profession of faith (2 Timothy 2:19).

Why would there be any connection at all between believers' behavior and Jesus' name? Because they bear his name. Christ's coming had ushered in a new era of redemption, but the mission was the same: while

BLASPHEMING GOD'S NAME

Paul is not alone in teaching that believers represent Jesus. Other New Testament writers also highlight this. James, for example, reminds believers that those exploiting them blaspheme "the noble name of him to whom you belong" (James 2:7). The awkward Greek sentence ("the noble name which is invoked over you") mirrors the Hebrew phrase so often used to describe the Israelites as those called by his name (see Deuteronomy 28:10).[9]

When Christians fail to live uprightly, it has the same effect as Israel's disobedience in the Old Testament—the name is blasphemed. Paul urges his Jewish listeners in Rome not to boast that they possess the Torah while breaking it and causing the name to be blasphemed (Romans 2:24). Similarly, he warned those who participated in communion "unworthily" (1 Corinthians 11:27), or who failed to persevere in their faith (1 Corinthians 15:2; 10:36; 2 Corinthians 6:1). Christians were not even to associate with a so-called "brother" who acted rebelliously (1 Corinthians 5:11). Instead, they were to represent God through their testimony (1 Corinthians 15:15) and through their behavior (2 Corinthians 4:11), shining like stars in an ungodly generation (Philippians 2:14-15). Paul prays that the Thessalonians will walk worthy of their calling so that Jesus' name may be glorified (2 Thessalonians 1:11-12). Throughout the New Testament, believers' behavior affects Jesus' reputation.

Israel's task had been to bear Yahweh's name among the nations, the church is now to bear Jesus' name among the nations.

Jesus' last words to his disciples underscore his own authority to send them as his emissaries. They also sound a lot like Moses' commission of Joshua (see Deuteronomy 31:23 and Joshua 1:1-9).[10]

> All authority in heaven and on earth has been given to me. Therefore go and make disciples of all nations, baptizing them *in the name of the Father and of the Son and of the Holy Spirit*, and teaching them to obey everything I have commanded you. And surely I am with you always, to the very end of the age. (Matthew 28:18-20, emphasis added)

> Israel's task had been to bear Yahweh's name among the nations, the church is now to bear Jesus' name among the nations.

What are they sent to do? Make more disciples by baptizing others *in the name* and teaching them to obey. Faithful obedience, as always, is key to the mission. Once baptized, these new followers will also bear his name, and they will also be watched. As Jesus' representatives, they are promised his presence ("with you always") while they live out their vocation. New Testament scholar Richard Hays points out, "In Matthew's concluding commissioning scene, Jesus assumes the roles *both* of Moses (authoritative teacher departing) *and* of God (continuing divine presence)."[11]

Jesus finished all the work God gave him to do, but he did not finish all the work. He sent his disciples to do it, and he never promised it would be easy.

TOUGH GOING: SUFFERING FOR JESUS' NAME

It should come as no surprise that Peter tells followers of Jesus to expect suffering. He's the one who opposed the idea so fiercely in the first place and was rebuked by Jesus for it (Matthew 16:21-28). On that occasion, Jesus explained, "Whoever wants to be my disciple must deny themselves and take up their cross and follow me" (Matthew 16:24). Belonging to God does not guarantee that things will be easy. In fact, it guarantees the opposite. The logic is simple: Jesus suffered. We follow Jesus' example. Therefore we'll suffer. Suffering is part of the pathway to glory.

Peter encourages us in spite of the pain:

> Dear friends, do not be surprised at the fiery ordeal that has come on you to test you, as though something strange were happening to you. But rejoice inasmuch as you participate in the sufferings of Christ, so that you may be overjoyed when his glory is revealed. If you are insulted *because of the name of Christ*, you are blessed, for the Spirit of glory and of God rests on you. (1 Peter 4:12-14, emphasis added)

But don't be an idiot, Peter warns:

> If you suffer, it should not be as a murderer or thief or any other kind of criminal, or even as a meddler. However, if you suffer as a Christian, do not be ashamed, but praise God *that you bear that name.* (1 Peter 4:15-16, emphasis added)

We can't be a jerk and then claim that we're suffering for Jesus when consequences come. Those to whom Peter was writing suffered in part due to the radically countercultural nature of Christianity at that time. Believers living faithfully for Christ today in cultures that have had a Christian presence for many centuries may not encounter suffering for their faith in the same ways.[12] But if we do, we're in good company.

John's vision in Revelation 2:3 also mentions the enduring of hardship for the sake of Jesus' name. If you're suffering, it does not mean you've been disobedient. Jesus was the only perfect human who ever lived, and yet he suffered to the point of death.

I attended a Christian school from preschool through high school, an unlikely place to experience persecution for my Christian faith, right? I wish I could tell you that it was a thriving faith community. Unfortunately, I felt a lot of pressure to stop taking my faith so seriously.

I was never beaten up physically, but I was teased a lot. "God" was a topic reserved for Sunday school and Bible classes, but was unwelcome on the playground. I was called a "goody two shoes" when I talked about following Jesus the rest of the week. No doubt I didn't always handle some of these interactions as well as I could; I suspect that even some of my teachers felt I was giving God too much air time. (My fourth-grade teacher made me choose something other than the Bible to read during free reading time.) Many of my former classmates are now mature Christians who have devoted their lives to ministry, but that was not the case during our childhood. It made friendships difficult and awkward.

There's another legitimate kind of suffering we may experience. Not just persecution or rejection, but prolonged waiting for God to answer our prayers. All is not well in the world. Things don't go as they should. We don't always know what we ought to do. We go through liminal seasons. It's human nature to try to make sense of our experience, to wonder *why*. And to question who we are and where we belong. Just as a variety of narratives battled for Israel's attention, our hardships can be spun any number of ways: *Is this trial a mark of failure? A spiritual attack? A punishment from God? Do I have what it takes to overcome this? Does God even care if I do?*

In those seasons of waiting, we are faced with many questions. We may no longer be certain about who we are. We are not sure how God is leading, or even *if* he's leading. In our desperation to restore a sense of order to our lives, we're always in danger of adopting the wrong narrative. But God has lessons to teach us that can only be learned in a state of dislocation. Lessons about who we are. About who he is. And how he's calling us to *be* in the world. Wrapped in liminality are gifts such as perseverance, perspective, rest, creativity, empathy, gratitude, and most of all, faithfulness. Rushing on to the next thing may prevent us from becoming who he wants us to be when we get there. In this place of upheaval and instability, we must let him shape us. We serve a God whose primary purpose is not to make us comfortable or successful in the eyes of the world, but to transform us. Liminality—that unsettled and unsettling place that reveals our deepest fears and longings—is his workshop.

Israel's failure to trust God's goodness in the wilderness was fatal for an entire generation. But liminality is not unique to Israel. As we move in and out of liminal seasons, we are invited to exercise a trust in God that leads to *life*. The key to cultivating that trust is to remember what God has done on our behalf, to keep telling the story. He is faithful! When we take time to remember the victories, we'll have strength for the in-betweens. God has gifts for us in this uncomfortable place if we can stick it out.

> God has lessons to teach us that can only be learned in a state of dislocation.

We sometimes assume that following Jesus would eliminate struggle, even if we should know better. The good news is that Jesus promises his presence with us. And he promises a future day when all that's wrong will be made right:

> Strength for today and bright hope for tomorrow,
> Blessings all mine, and 10,000 besides.[13]

Sinai is a paradigm of God's revelation and our vocation, but it is not the climax of the story. The New Testament authors are ready to move beyond Sinai. Let's see what they have in mind.

SINAI 2.0: THE HEAVENLY MOUNT ZION

So far it has not been difficult to demonstrate the continuity between the Sinai covenant and the New Testament. Jesus saw himself as bearing Yahweh's name. He commissioned his disciples to bear that name among the nations, carrying out God's mission in the world. Matters are more complicated when we come to the apostle Paul. I've claimed that Yahweh's law at Sinai is a gift. Paul, on the other hand, has very negative things to say about the law, equating it with slavery. As Daniel Block states, "Taking Paul's statements about the law at face value creates an intolerable opposition to the Torah."[14] How can we reconcile my understanding of Sinai with Paul's apparent lack of enthusiasm for it?

Galatians especially seems to complicate matters:

> Before the coming of this faith we were held in custody under the law, locked up until the faith that was to come would be revealed. So the law was our guardian until Christ came that we might be justified by faith. Now that this faith has come, we are no longer under a guardian. . . . When the set time had fully come, God sent his Son, born of a woman, born under the law, to redeem those under the law. (Galatians 3:23-25; 4:4-5)

Paul even goes on to associate Sinai and its laws with Hagar and her son Ishmael, the rejected son of Abraham, calling readers to come out from under the Jewish establishment in Jerusalem and live in freedom (Galatians 4:21-31). What are we to make of this?

Our problem comes when we try to read Paul back into Exodus, as though Paul is saying that the law was bad from the beginning. Paul certainly opposes the way the Torah is being interpreted and applied in his own day, but Moses would have shared his opinion. Both insisted that circumcision of the heart was what truly mattered (Deuteronomy 10:16; Romans 2:29).[15]

At the time of the exodus, the law was considered a gift, showing the Israelites how to live as God's people. Even Paul calls the law "holy, righteous, and good" in his letter to the Romans (7:12). But it was only ever a means to an end: relationship with Yahweh. In Christ a new pathway to that relationship opened for us, based on his own faithful obedience to the law. To continue to live under the law ourselves, ignoring Jesus' faithfulness, would be a form of slavery not unlike slavery in Egypt. The reason is this: God set aside the tabernacle system, providing a perfect sacrifice in Jesus. He destroyed the dividing wall between Jew and Gentile, making a way for anyone to become part of his family, without circumcision. Laws regarding sacrifice and laws regarding ethnic separation were no longer appropriate. They had become a form of slavery to *how things were*. The law was never meant to offer salvation. It was merely the means of maintaining what had been given. Redemption was always made possible by God's gracious gift. To reject that gracious gift offered in Jesus would be a return to Egypt.

Think back before the exodus, when Joseph went to Egypt. He went as a slave against his will, but God blessed him in Egypt so that he rose to a position of power and was able to save his entire family from the famine that ravaged the region. When Jacob and his sons joined Joseph in Egypt, it was God's gracious provision for their needs. In time, Egypt became a prison for their descendants. We must continue to look to God for redemption. A gift to one generation can become shackles for the next, if we fail to see what God is up to.

Mount St. Helens is part of the Cascade mountain range in the Western United States, a long-time favorite for residents of the region. Just north of the mountain was a pristine vacation spot, Spirit Lake, around which camps, resorts, and cabins became the destination for generations of Washingtonians in the 50s, 60s, and 70s. In March of 1980, the mountain started to rumble, emitting smoke and ash. Volcanologists from all over the world gathered to watch, measure, and wait to see what St. Helens would do. Within a week, earthquakes, plumes of volcanic ash, and steam had become so frequent (up to thirty volcanic events per day!) that residents and vacationers in the surrounding area were forced to evacuate. All except one. Harry R. Truman (not the US president) lived for over 50 years on the shores of Spirit Lake. For decades, vacationers had enjoyed their holidays at his lodge. Harry, in his eighties by then, was unwilling to leave. He was skeptical about the possibility of an eruption, but if the mountain blew, he wanted to be there. If it buried him, that's where he wanted to die.

In the days preceding May 18, 1980, the mountain grew calmer. Though earthquakes continued, the eruptive activity paused. After several uneventful days, forest rangers escorted residents back to the lake on May 17 to retrieve personal belongings. On the morning of May 18, the mountain awoke with no advance warning. An earthquake measuring 5.1 on the Richter scale caused an explosion on its western slopes, triggering a massive landslide, the largest in recorded history. Ash combined with melted glaciers and boiling groundwater to produce a thick river of mud that flowed seventeen miles downriver, destroying forests, bridges, and homes. Trees covering 230 square miles were strewn like matchsticks, stripped and toppled by the force of the blast. Spirit Lake was deluged with 60 meters of debris from the avalanche, swallowing empty buildings and burying Truman. The mountain had been his life. To him, it was the only thing worth living for. On it he staked his entire existence. With the eruption, it became his tomb.[16]

If we're not careful, Sinai could become like Mount St. Helens for believers in Jesus. This was precisely Paul's concern. He told the church in Galatia that if they clung to the law as a means of salvation it would be death for them. Sinai was critically important in its day—unveiling God's gracious covenant. It remains critically important for us as we seek to know the God who revealed himself there and as we wrestle with what it means to be his people. However, if we try to set up shop in its shadow, hanging our hopes on the law rather than the lawgiver, and ignoring the seismic shift that comes with the fuller revelation of Jesus Christ, Sinai will become our death.

Hebrews 12 has a similar message. The author contrasts Sinai with the heavenly prototype of Mount Zion. Yahweh's visit at Sinai provoked fear and trembling. The people refused to hear more from God because they feared what his presence would do to them. In contrast, the assembly of God's people at the heavenly Mount Zion is full of joy. They are receiving a "kingdom that cannot be shaken" (12:28), with Jesus as the mediator of a renewed covenant. While the joy of Mount Zion outpaces that of Sinai, it does not replace it altogether. God's people enjoy the same covenant status—worshiping the one, true God and bearing his name among the nations. The difference is that in this new era, God's people have internalized his law with the help of the Spirit. They can celebrate the once-for-all sacrifice of Jesus, with no more need for the daily sacrifice of bulls and goats.

For the author of Hebrews, the first covenant is insufficient for two reasons. As Michael Kibbe explains, "that covenant would inevitably fail because Israel refused to keep it and because those appointed to sustain Israel's obedience were unable to do so."[17] The problem was not the covenant itself. The problem was sinful people, relying on other sinful people whose ministries were only temporary. Jesus brings the covenant relationship into a new era, providing a perfect sacrifice—himself, offered by a perfect and eternal priest—himself, so that the benefits would never fade. Jesus provided "perpetual access to the presence of God that enables continued obedience and life."[18] Rather than mediate between Yahweh and the people, as Moses did, Jesus ushers God's people into his very presence.

That can't be topped.

IMAGE CONSCIOUS:
ELECTED REPRESENTATIVES

Jesus is greater than Moses and what he offers us is even greater than God's gracious gift at Sinai. According to Colossians 1:15, Jesus is "the image of the invisible God." He represents the Father perfectly, but he is not the first image of God. The first humans were designated as God's image in Genesis 1:26-27. Scholars have suggested a variety of possibilities for what this might imply. Rather than an indication that they looked like God or shared some of his characteristics (e.g., creativity or relationality or eternal nature), I read Genesis as saying that humans *function* as the image. Humans are not *like* God's image, they *are* his image.[19]

In the ancient world, an "image" or *tselem* was something concrete. Every deity had a temple, and every temple had an image. The image was a physical representation of the deity, a visible sign of his or her dominion. John Walton argues that the creation account in Genesis is meant to remind us of a temple dedication.[20] Yahweh has built the cosmos as the temple in which he resides and the domain over which he presides. Rather than setting up a statue of himself, he makes men and women. We function as the sign of his rule to the rest of creation.

This sounds quite similar to bearing Yahweh's name: Covenant members are also representatives of God to the nations. However, there's an important difference between the concepts of *being the image* and *bearing the name*. Discussing it here will help to clarify the implications of each and offer a fuller picture of biblical theology.

Both *being the image* and *bearing the name* relate to the concept of election. God has chosen people and given them a job to do.

Too often we think of "election" as a matter of "being picked to be saved." But in Scripture, election is more like a game of blob tag, where if I'm "it," and I tag you, then we're both it. We run around together and try to tag as many others as we can, who join hands with us and continue tagging others until everyone has been tagged. In this game, the essence of "it-ness" is to tag others. So, too, the essence of election, and therefore the essence of the believer's vocation, is to represent God by mediating his blessing to others. Once we are "it" we don't lean back in our recliners, glad that someone picked us. No, to be "it" is to tag others. And to be elect—to be his—is to bear his name among the nations, to demonstrate by our lives that he is king and to mediate his blessing to others. That is the whole point of being the elect. Theologian Suzanne McDonald coins the phrase "election to representation," insisting that "this approach considers election to be the means through which God's purpose of blessing is enacted, *not* the way in which the parameters of that blessing are defined."[21]

Every human being is an image bearer, whether conscious of it or not. As the crown of creation, humans bear witness to the majesty of our creator God. We extend his rule over creation by caring for it and bringing order to it.

Name-bearing, on the other hand, is restricted to those in covenant relationship with Yahweh. It's a second dimension of election involving only a subset of humanity. The purpose of covenant election is to provide a visual model of people rightly related to the creator God, Yahweh.

Jesus fulfills both dimensions of election by perfectly imaging God *and* bearing his name with honor. He is the human *par excellence* as well as the faithful covenant member through whom others can be reconciled to God.

Jesus alluded to these two dimensions of election in a fascinating conversation with the Pharisees. In Matthew 22, they set out to trap him, asking whether Jews should pay taxes to Caesar. He saw right through their scheme, employing a clever tactic of his own. Requesting a coin as an object lesson, he asked,

> "Whose image is this? And whose inscription?"
>
> "Caesar's," they replied.
>
> Then he said to them, "So give back to Caesar what is Caesar's and to God what is God's." (Matthew 22:20-22)

The coin had a physical imprint of Caesar's head; it bore his image. It was also inscribed with his name. The covenant people share the twin distinction of being God's image and bearing his name. Jesus evades the tricky political question (shall we pay taxes?) by turning attention to the more important one. Sure, pay your taxes, but devote your entire lives to God's service. Live out your vocation as his representatives.

With all this in mind, we have a final issue to address. So far, we've skirted a key question (though I assumed it in this chapter). I've saved it for last. What is the relationship between Jewish covenant members who follow Jesus and those of us who are Gentiles? How is it that Sinai becomes our covenant too?

DIGGING DEEPER

*Richard Bauckham. *Jesus and the God of Israel:* God Crucified and Other Studies on the New Testament's Christology of Divine Identity. Grand Rapids: Eerdmans, 2008.

Daniel I. Block. *The Triumph of Grace: Literary and Theological Studies in Deuteronomy and Deuteronomic Themes.* Eugene, OR: Cascade, 2017. Chapter 17 (Deuteronomy 18) and chapter 18 (Galatians).

Richard B. Hays. *Echoes of Scripture in the Letters of Paul.* New Haven: Yale University Press, 1989.

Michael Kibbe. *Godly Fear or Ungodly Failure?: Hebrews 12 and the Sinai Theophanies.* ZNTW 216. Berlin: de Gruyter, 2016.

*Suzanne McDonald. *Re-imaging Election*: *Divine Election as Representing God to Others and Others to God.* Grand Rapids: Eerdmans, 2010.

Catherine L. McDowell. *The Image of God in the Garden of Eden: The Creation of Humankind in Genesis 2:5–3:24 in Light of mīs pî pīt pî and wpt-r Rituals of Mesopotamia and Ancient Egypt.* Siphrut 15. Winona Lake, IN: Eisenbrauns, 2015.

*Richard J. Middleton. *A New Heaven and A New Earth: Reclaiming Biblical Eschatology.* Grand Rapids: Baker, 2014.

Francis Watson. *Paul and the Hermeneutics of Faith.* New York: T&T Clark, 2004.

*Christopher J. H. Wright. *The Mission of God: Unlocking the Bible's Grand Narrative.* Downers Grove, IL: IVP Academic, 2006.

Related videos from The Bible Project: "Reading Biblical Law" and "Image of God."

10

WHO LET YOU IN?

Gentiles and the Mission of God

PROFILE UPDATE: PETER AND THE GENTILES

It would be rather odd to write a book all about Sinai for Christians if Sinai has nothing to do with us. I hope it has become clear how Jesus intentionally connects himself with the Sinai covenant—by fulfilling its laws and showing himself to be the lawgiver, by living out his vocation as a name bearer, and by commissioning his disciples to do the same. But as we've discussed the theme of God's people bearing his name, our focus has been solely on the Jews as the name bearers. They're the ones at Sinai. They're even the ones chosen as Jesus' disciples. Even Paul's letter to the Galatians was aimed at those who were tempted to convert to Judaism and live as Jews. Obviously Sinai would have been of great interest to them. But what about the rest of us? Is Sinai for us, too?

Peter answers that question without much fanfare. If we're just reading along, minding our own business, we might miss it entirely. What he does is audacious, but he is matter-of-fact about it. Writing to Gentile believers scattered throughout Asia Minor, he contrasts unbelievers with these non-Jewish followers of Jesus, saying "But you are a chosen people, a royal priesthood, a holy nation, God's treasured possession, that you may declare the praises of him who called you out of darkness into his wonderful light. Once you were not a people, but now you are the people of God; once you had not received mercy, but now you have received mercy" (1 Peter 2:9-10). The language should, by now, be quite familiar.

Included in his list are covenant titles given to Israel at Sinai—royal priesthood, holy nation, treasured possession (Exodus 19:5-6). On top of that, he adds another—chosen people—that is also historically reserved for the Jewish nation. "Chosen people" (or "chosen race") comes from Isaiah 43:20-21, which tells us the *reason* for their election, "that they may proclaim my praise." Peter's only acknowledgment that these titles did not formerly apply to Gentiles is the statement "once you were not a people, but now you are the people of God." You were outsiders, unchosen, but now you're in. Even this statement is remarkable. Peter is clearly alluding to the Old Testament prophet Hosea, whose children are given names to serve as prophetic words to the nation of Israel. He names a son Lo-Ammi ("not my people") as an indication that God had rejected his own people (Hosea 1:9), later announcing that he would readopt Israel and renew the covenant (Hosea 2:23). Now Peter applies these same designations to the Gentiles. If God can restore his rebel children after all they've done, why not adopt Gentiles, too?

> You were outsiders, unchosen, but now you're in.

"Race" or "people" and "nation" are ironic ways to refer to Peter's audience, made up of a variety of ethnic groups and scattered throughout an entire region. The gospel has made possible something impossible in the physical realm. It's also audacious in another sense: Before Peter's letter, the word "people" (*'am* in Hebrew or *laos* in Greek) was used only to designate Jews.

Peter doesn't just slap these titles on his audience without thinking about what they entail. He has a clear picture of the responsibilities of those who bear Yahweh's name. He tells them, "Live such good lives among the pagans that, though they accuse you of doing wrong, they may see your good deeds and glorify God on the day he visits us" (1 Peter 2:12). The job of covenant members is to live in a way that shows they belong to Yahweh. He warns them, "If you are insulted *because of the name of Christ*, you are blessed, for the Spirit of glory and of God rests on you. . . . If you suffer as a Christian, do not be ashamed, but praise God that you *bear that name*" (1 Peter 4:14, 16).

Peter has a well-developed understanding of the roles and responsibilities of covenant members. When he applies the special titles from Sinai, he has the rest in mind as well. Believers, who are lavishly loved by their heavenly Father, have been given work to do—not so they can earn God's favor, but so they can bring him glory among the nations. The Spirit's presence in our lives is proof that we belong.

So if Gentiles are now covenant members, what about the Jews? Peter makes no move to reject the Jews or indicate that they've been replaced by Gentiles. Instead, by using these familiar titles with Gentiles in view, he indicates that he no longer sees any distinction between the two groups. Just as the nation of Israel was uniquely selected to bear Yahweh's name among the nations, Gentiles have become name bearers too, through their belief in Christ.

It's worth lingering here to take a closer look at Peter's masterful use of the Old Testament to help us with the mystery of how Peter arrived at this conclusion. I told you that he uses three titles from Sinai—royal priesthood, holy nation, treasured possession. The first two of these are taken verbatim. Peter's Greek phrases match exactly the Greek translation of Exodus 19:5-6. Not so with "treasured possession." Here we have a puzzling departure: Peter doesn't use the Greek word that translates the Hebrew *segullah* in every other passage (*periousios*), which would highlight the uniqueness of the treasure itself. Instead, Peter emphasizes the process of becoming Yahweh's possession by using a slightly different phrase (*eis peripoiēsin*) found only in Malachi 3:17. This slight shift in phrasing opens up a profound theological possibility.

Peter's citation of Malachi is significant because it is the only Old Testament passage where the term *segullah* refers to a righteous remnant,

rather than the entire nation of Israel. In light of Israel's covenant unfaithfulness, the prophet Malachi had envisioned a future day when Yahweh
would select a new *segullah* made up only of those who fear his name.
Malachi had said, "'They will become mine,' says Yahweh of Armies,
'On the day when I prepare a *segullah*'" (3:17, author's translation). By
quoting Malachi directly, Peter shows us that he sees this very promise
as having been fulfilled in the believing community made up of both
Jews and Gentiles.

Peter doesn't directly defend his inclusion of Gentiles in this letter,
so we're left wondering what gave him the audacity to make such a move.
To find answers, we need to look back at his own story.

ANATOMY OF A PARADIGM
SHIFT: PETER'S VISION

Peter's deviation from typical readings of the Old Testament in his own
day is noteworthy. His application of Old Testament titles to a multi-
ethnic church must reflect his perspective that the age of fulfillment has
come, the time when Gentiles are on equal footing with Jews in the
kingdom of God. Where, then, does this revelation come from? What
is the basis for his confidence in proclaiming Gentile inclusion? It's not
the earthly ministry of Jesus. Jesus had very little interaction with Gentiles and very little to say about them.

If we take seriously the letter's claim to be written by the apostle Peter,
then we don't have far to look for an explanation for his paradigm shift.
Acts 10–11 recounts his startling vision in the port city of Joppa. While
waiting for dinner, he sees a triple vision: A sheet filled with unclean
animals is lowered from the sky three times, and a voice declares,
"Dinner's ready!"

Peter is as nauseated as he is confused, "No way! I wouldn't dream
of eating that for dinner!" Peter is a good, torah-abiding Jew. He's lived
his entire life according to the kosher food laws in Leviticus 11 that mark
certain foods off-limits. The purpose of these laws is to set Israel apart
as distinct from the nations (see Leviticus 20:25-26). When the vision

returns a second and third time, Peter finally realizes that God is trying to get through to him: "Do not call anything impure that God has made clean" (Acts 10:15). Peter's vision served as a divine object lesson: *the Gentiles are no longer to be considered unclean.* This is the first step in Peter's paradigm shift.

While he's upstairs dreaming, three men sent by a Gentile Centurion named Cornelius are on their way to see him. It's a remarkable divine appointment. Cornelius' vision tells him to seek a man named Peter who is staying in Joppa. Peter's vision tells him to go with the men seeking him. When he arrives at Cornelius' house, Peter dives right into a sermon: "I now realize how true it is that *God does not show favoritism* but accepts from every nation the one who fears him and does what is right" (Acts 10:34-35). Peter wastes no time in sharing the good news of forgiveness for Gentiles on the basis of Jesus' death and resurrection.

God has another surprise in store. As Peter is speaking, the Holy Spirit falls on his Gentile audience. Peter's companions are astonished (Acts 10:44-46). The outpouring of the Spirit has always been a sign of God's favor and of covenant renewal (see Isaiah 44:3). Since the Spirit has already fallen on them, Peter has them baptized in the name of Jesus. He later explained to the skeptics: "If God gave them the same gift he gave us who believed in the Lord Jesus Christ, who was I to think that I could stand in God's way?" (Acts 11:17).

We can speculate about how Peter envisions the relationship between Israel and the church, but the fact is that he leaves the question unaddressed in his first epistle. For Peter the decisive shift seems to have happened at Joppa, though he does not mention it in his letter. If the Holy Spirit is poured out on Gentiles, then they *are* the people of God. Period. There is no need to talk separately about the Jews, for there is no longer any distinction. The only distinction now is the one described in the verse following Malachi 3:17 regarding the *segullah*. Malachi 3:18 goes on to make a distinction between the righteous and the wicked. The *segullah* is no longer everyone in the community. God's future *segullah* includes only the righteous.

Peter shows evidence that he believes this to be true in 1 Peter 2:12 and 4:3, where he talks to his readers as if they are no longer Gentiles. A new distinction has been made, not on ethnic terms, but with regard to righteousness.

Are there broader implications for Peter's application to the Gentiles of God's promises to the Jews? Indeed, there are. His pattern of using the Old Testament suggests that not just the titles of Israel but also her vocation is true of the church. If Gentiles have been incorporated into the people of God, included in the righteous remnant without distinction, then our inheritance is

> If the Holy Spirit is poured out on Gentiles, then they *are* the people of God. Period.

one and the same. As we follow in the footsteps of Israel's Messiah, we too take on the responsibilities of God's "treasured possession." This involves both proclamation of the gospel message and good deeds consistent with biblical expectations for those who bear his name. Peter does not leave to our imagination or creativity the task of figuring out what this entails. The rest of his letter makes clear what kind of behavior is required.

Peter opens his letter by saying that his readers are "chosen . . . to be obedient" (1 Peter 1:2). This obedience includes sober-mindedness (1:13; 4:7; 5:8), holiness (1:15), a deep love for others (1:22; 4:8), absence of malice, deceit, hypocrisy, envy, and slander (2:1), self-denial of sinful desires (2:11), submission to authority (2:13-14; 3:1-6; 5:5), endurance of unjust suffering without retaliation (2:20-23), treatment of wives with respect (3:7), harmonious living that practices sympathy, love, compassion, and humility (3:8), repayment of evil with blessing (3:9), turning from evil to seek peace (3:11), answering with gentleness and respect (3:15), offering genuine hospitality (4:9), using one's gifts to serve others (4:10-11; 5:2), rejoicing in suffering (4:12), humility (5:5-6), and resistance to the devil (5:9). Peter's letter cannot be said to lack practical life application!

The moral conduct required of believers is grounded in our new identity as Yahweh's treasured possession. We are not simply given a list of rules for godly living; we are invited to become part of his covenant community. He has called us out of darkness into his marvelous light, made us a people, his own treasured possession, and has given us a significant role in his kingdom as priests set apart for his purposes. In order for all he has planned for us to be realized, we must live like we truly are his treasured possession—like we belong to him.

TEAM MEETING: THE JERUSALEM COUNCIL

Peter's paradigm shift gets him in trouble. Before too long, conflict erupts. Some Jewish Christians insist that Gentiles need to convert to Judaism first in order to follow Jesus. This would involve circumcision, a kosher diet, and obedience to the rest of the Torah. Others say Gentiles can follow Jesus as Gentiles, without converting first. Church leaders call for a meeting in Jerusalem in Acts 15, known as the Jerusalem Council. It's difficult to overestimate the importance of this meeting for the church. These men are deciding the direction the entire church will go. No doubt, emotions run high.

Peter speaks first. For Peter, the outpouring of the Holy Spirit on Gentile believers at Cornelius' house offered all the evidence needed to show that God had accepted them as members of the covenant community *without* circumcision. Peter cannot deny what he saw with his own eyes. He says,

> Brothers, you know that some time ago God made a choice among you that the Gentiles might hear from my lips the message of the gospel and believe. God, who knows the heart, showed that he accepted them by giving the Holy Spirit to them, just as he did to us. *He did not discriminate between us and them,* for he purified their hearts by faith. Now then, why do you try to test God by putting on the necks of Gentiles a yoke that neither we nor our ancestors have been able to bear? No! *We believe it is through the grace of our Lord Jesus that we are saved, just as they are.* (Acts 15:7-11, emphasis added)

James gets up next. His introduction is fascinating. Using Peter's Aramaic name, he says: "Simon has described to us how God first intervened to choose *a people for his name* from the Gentiles" (Acts 15:14, emphasis added). The phrase "a *people* . . . from the Gentiles" must have surprised his listeners. These terms are always contrasted in the Old Testament: One is either a part of Yahweh's people or one of the Gentiles, and the two are never confused.[1] Using such a thoroughly Jewish title as "people" for Gentiles was radical.[2] In fact, Peter had said nothing about God's name. He had simply pointed to the gift of the Spirit to Gentiles. However, for the apostles the Holy Spirit's presence functioned as a seal, stamping believers with the name of Yahweh and showing that they belonged to his covenant people. James' statement alludes to this. Then, lest he be accused of theological innovation, James appeals to the prophets to lend support to his idea.

In Amos 9:12, Yahweh speaks of Israel's future restoration, mentioning the role of "all the nations that bear my name."[3] James found it the ideal place to anchor his argument about Gentile inclusion in the covenant. The Old Testament had designated four entities as bearing Yahweh's name: the high priest (on his forehead), the people of Israel (via the priestly blessing), Jerusalem (because Yahweh chose it as the site for the temple), and the temple or ark (because they signify Yahweh's presence among his people). James quotes the single clear exception. Amos 9:12 is not the only text in the Old Testament that predicts Gentiles turning to Yahweh, but only here are they said to have had his name "invoked upon them" (author's translation). This is the only Old Testament passage that suggests Gentile inclusion without prior conversion to Judaism.[4]

Together, Peter and James sound the death knell for the old way of thinking about who's in and who's out. The experience of the Holy Spirit along with the testimony of the Old Testament Scriptures make an insurmountable argument. The council agrees. Gentiles can follow the Jewish Messiah. Gentiles who follow Jesus bear Yahweh's name. Note that they are not setting aside Sinai. They are simply setting aside laws whose purpose was to separate the Israelites ethnically from other nations so that those nations may join the covenant community.

When I applied for a faculty position at Prairie College in Alberta, Canada, I did so with a measure of hesitancy. At first, I figured there was no harm in applying because they would likely try to hire a Canadian, while I was born and raised in the United States. Within just a few weeks, Prairie invited me for a campus interview, the last step before a job offer. Danny and I wrestled over the decision, learning all we could about the school and its history. It seemed so random to move to the prairies of Canada—a place we had never lived nor dreamed of living! We agreed to fly up for the interview, but we took with us a long list of reasons why we didn't think the position was a good fit. From the moment we landed, our resistance began to melt. One by one, the items on our list disappeared. We loved the town, found houses we could afford, enjoyed the faculty and staff, and figured out a budget that could work. Still, the move felt random, until the last morning of our visit, when God gave us a completely unexpected surprise: We found out that I was already a citizen of Canada.

How could I be a Canadian citizen without knowing it? My dad was born in Canada to Dutch immigrants. He later immigrated to the States, where he met and married my mom. I was born two years later. As it turns out, the Canadian government is very generous with its citizenship. Whether I claimed it or not, I'd been a citizen all along. Suddenly a move to Canada did not feel so random. It was as if God handed me a gift he'd had wrapped and ready for forty years, just waiting for the moment I needed it. We felt it was his way of saying, "You think this is random? I've had it in the works for a long, long time." It's hard to describe the feeling evoked by this news. For weeks, I kept shaking my head, treasuring the gift of this discovery.

My surprise Canadian citizenship gave me a glimpse of how Gentile believers in the early church must have felt when they heard the result of the Jerusalem Council. *You're invited! You can follow Jesus just as you are. We discovered that hundreds of years ago the prophets looked ahead to this day, speaking of you who bear Yahweh's name—Gentiles who belong. Welcome to the family!*

With this major paradigm shift in mind, it's easier to see the myriad ways that God prepared his people for this. His promise to bless the nations through the line of Abraham was not meant to be patronizing. Gentiles were included in the lineage of Jesus, hinting at the possibility of a future full-scale incorporation (Matthew 1:5-6). Gentiles were to be part of the family. When Jesus sent out his disciples he said they would testify before Gentiles (Matthew 10:18). The risen Christ announced that "repentance for the forgiveness of sins will be preached in his name to all nations" (Luke 24:47; cf. Acts 1:18). I wonder if his disciples had any idea the surprises God had in store!

PLAYING AN OLD SONG: PAUL AND THE SONG OF MOSES

Paul is solidly on board with Peter's bold new initiative to take the gospel to Gentiles. In his letter to the Romans, he zeroes in on the idea that believers in Jesus, even Gentile believers, are ushered into the new covenant because of their faith in the faithfulness of Jesus. Reading Romans is like driving down the road and suddenly hearing a childhood favorite on the radio. Even when he is not quoting Moses directly, Paul is wrestling with the very heart of Moses' teaching. Paul's application of these truths in his own day is surprising at times, even shocking, but we cannot escape the fact that Moses provides the grid through which Paul seeks to understand the gospel.

In Deuteronomy, Moses calls the people of Israel to renew the covenant with the Lord before they enter the land he had promised. Moses reminds them of the law and then spells out the blessings for those who obey and the curses for those who disobey. Interestingly, Moses leaves no doubt in his listeners' minds: they *will* disobey and be cursed. Their track record has proved them faithless. In the final chapters of the book, Moses explains that after judgment, restoration would be possible, if they listened and obeyed (Deuteronomy 30:1-10).

Moses insists that God's law is accessible to them, a point which Paul picks up and applies creatively to the accessibility of Christ's righteousness

to those who believe (Deuteronomy 30:11-14; cf. Romans 10:5-10). Then
Moses presents Israel with a choice: if they love and obey God, they will
experience life and blessing; if they fail to listen and instead worship
other gods, they will be cursed and die (Deuteronomy 30:16-20). God
gives Moses a prophetic song to sing publicly before his death. Deuteronomy 32 records that song, which bears remarkable parallels to the
book of Romans.[5] Here we will discover a key feature of Paul's theology.
Let's work our way through the song to see how.

Moses' song in Deuteronomy 32 develops as follows:[6] Yahweh's righteousness and faithfulness are the starting point (vv. 3-4), in contrast to
Israel's sin (v. 5). Moses recites a narrative of God's election, care and
provision for Israel (vv. 6-14), which is followed by idolatry and ungrate-
fulness (vv. 15-18), provoking punishment (vv. 19-27). Divine wrath is
only checked by the pride of Israel's enemies, who lack understanding
(vv. 28-34). Yahweh's judgment is based on his character (vv. 35-42) and
will conclude with a celebration when he gets the final word and destroys
his enemies (v. 43). With this the song is ended, but not the chapter. Not
incidentally, the chapter closes with Yahweh's explanation to Moses of
why he will not enter the land with his people: "Because you did not
uphold my holiness among the Israelites" (Deuteronomy 32:51). Even
Moses himself has failed to fully honor Yahweh's character—to represent
him well—and he forfeits entrance into the promised land.

A striking contrast emerges in Deuteronomy between Yahweh and
his people. God is described this way: "He is the Rock, his works are
perfect, and all his ways are just. A faithful God who does no wrong,
upright and just is he" (Deuteronomy 32:4). The next verse describes
Israel: "They are corrupt and not his children; to their shame they are
a warped and crooked generation" (32:5). So we see the contrast: while
God is faithful, Israel is faithless. Moses has already made clear in Deuteronomy 30:15-20 what the end result of such faithlessness will be,
namely, death. The life that was to be marked by the blessing of God
and long life in the land of promise is forfeited for the folly of idolatry.
With this contrast in mind, we turn to Paul's letter to the Romans.

Paul unveils the goal of his ministry in the first few verses of Romans, "to call all the Gentiles to the obedience that comes from faith for [Jesus Christ's] name's sake" (Romans 1:5). He writes to Christians in Rome who "also are among those Gentiles who are called to belong to Jesus Christ" and "called to be his holy people" (Romans 1:6-7). So many Old Testament echoes reverberate in these verses! For Paul, Gentiles who believe are Gentiles who belong. They are part of the "holy people" who were set apart at Sinai to enter into covenant with Yahweh, so that their faith enhances God's reputation. It's all "for his name's sake."

The phrase "obedience that comes from faith" has been a matter of debate. The Greek reads simply "obedience of faith." What does this mean? Is the act of faith the obedience that God requires? Or is it faith that results in obedience? If we keep in mind the message of Deuteronomy and the theme of name-bearing that we've explored throughout this book, the relationship between the two is not so mysterious. For Moses, those who obey God's commands and worship him alone are considered "faith-full," those who do not are "faith-less." Obedience and faith could almost be considered synonyms. To claim belief in God without obeying him—to bear his name in vain—would be an unthinkable contradiction for Moses.

In Romans 5:10, as he works out the implications of his bold claims in chapter one, Paul drops a bomb. Echoing Deuteronomy 32:41, he says, "For if, while we were God's enemies, we were reconciled to him through the death of his Son, how much more, having been reconciled, shall we be saved through his life!"[7] Paul includes himself and his readers in the category of "enemies" once destined to receive the judgment of God.

Against that backdrop he introduces his readers to Jesus. Jesus, who is repeatedly called God's Son, has done what Israel (God's "firstborn son" in Exodus 4:22) could not do—namely, maintain faithful obedience to God. By taking upon himself the death penalty promised in Deuteronomy to those who disobey, he cancels death and ushers us into life if we have faith in his faithfulness, even if we are Gentiles.

Christ is the faithful son standing in for faithless Israel. His obedience in life and in death provides a way from death to life for those who believe. He is the covenant keeper who ushers in the new covenant!

YOUR INVISIBLE TATTOO

It should be obvious by now that you have a tattoo.

If you follow Jesus, you've been marked with his name.

Remember Jesus' words in John 6:27, saying that he wore God's "seal of approval"? In what was likely Paul's earliest letter, he describes himself as carrying Jesus' marks or brand (*stigmata*) on his body (Galatians 6:17).[8] The Greek word *stigmata* is used outside the Bible to refer to the brands of slaves as well as religious tattoos.[9] Paul declares that God "anointed us, *set his seal of ownership on us*, and put his Spirit in our hearts as a deposit, guaranteeing what is to come" (2 Corinthians 1:21-22). Spirit-filling is the evidence that believers belong to God and bear the stamp of his name. Paul reiterates this truth in Ephesians 1:13: "When you believed, you were marked in him with a seal, the promised Holy Spirit."

This spiritual tattoo becomes visible in John's visions in the book of Revelation. In John's vision, the seal is carried by an angel who has been commissioned to mark the foreheads of "the servants," that is, the redeemed community, to protect them from God's judgment (Revelation 7:2-3).[10] What follows is a parade of tribes, reminding us of the book of Numbers. Twelve thousand from each tribe are sealed (Revelation 7:4-8). Because the name inscribed on the high priestly headdress was Yahweh, to say that the name belonging to Jesus is written on their foreheads signals that Jesus shares the divine identity. Furthermore, the designation of God as "Father" in this passage echoes the Lord's Prayer ("our Father, who is in heaven") and signifies the fulfillment of Jesus' plea that God's name be made holy (Matthew 6:9).

Invisible no more, this spiritual tattoo of the divine name is also manifest in a later vision: "Then I looked, and there before me was the

Lamb, standing on Mount Zion, and with him 144,000 who had his name and his Father's name written on their foreheads" (Revelation 14:1). The vision draws on both Old and New Testaments for its imagery, depicting the name that belongs to both Jesus and his Father inscribed on believers' foreheads, that is, the name Yahweh.[11] The symbolic branding of the Israelites at Sinai becomes legible on Mount Zion. How appropriate!

Those who are not part of the redeemed community still have a tattoo, but it bears a different name. John's vision depicts a beast that spoke blasphemy, bearing blasphemous names on its heads (13:1, 6; cf. 17:3). A second beast marked the hands and foreheads of the nonelect with his name, persecuting all those who refused the brand (13:16-17; cf. 17:5). Like the beast, those branded by the beast cursed God's name (16:9, 11, 21). In so doing they violated the first two commandments of the covenant—worshiping one other than Yahweh and receiving another name. An angel describes these enemies of God as "those who worship the beast and its image," or "anyone who receives the mark of its name"; such a person will have "no *rest* day or night" (Revelation 14:11). The allusions to the Ten Commandments are unmistakable: apostate *worship* of other *images*, and *bearing* another *name*, resulting in a lack of *rest*. Those so marked were eventually judged along with the beast (15:2; 16:2; 19:20).

Thus the vision of Revelation presents vivid, concrete images of election. No one is neutral; people either bear the divine name or the name of the beast on their foreheads, indicating the object of their worship and allegiance. When Christ is ultimately victorious, only those who did not receive the mark of the beast will reign with him and behold his face (20:4; 22:4). The vision issues an urgent warning to those who have yet to submit to God's rule. The choice is ours. Surrender before it's too late! We have a standing invitation to join the covenant family. The Father waits with arms wide open. Because of the faithfulness of Jesus, we can be marked with God's name and participate in his mission to bring blessing to all nations.

From time to time people ask me what to do with the Old Testament law. That question is easier to answer now that we've taken this journey through Scripture together. Rather than asking if we have to obey Old Testament law, we need to ask what our relationship is to Israel's covenant. Our answer to this question will determine the way in which we appropriate all the instructions of the Old Testament.

Because of the life, death, and resurrection of Jesus, Israel's Messiah, we have been granted membership in the covenant. We have been incorporated into his renewed covenant community. His sacrifice ushered in a new era. That reality, paired with our changed cultural situation, means that many of the Old Testament laws no longer function for us as they did for Israel. Obeying them by the letter would not uphold the purpose for which they were given.

> Because of the faithfulness of Jesus, we can be marked with God's name and participate in his mission to bring blessing to all nations.

The need for a temple has disappeared, fulfilled in Christ, and therefore sacrifices are no longer necessary. Still, the laws of sacrifice teach us about how seriously God takes sin and the thoughtfulness with which we must honor him by admitting our failures and trusting in his mercy.

Laws that were designed to keep Israel separate as an ethnic group have also been set aside. This includes laws relating to ritual purity, diet, and clothing. Other categories of laws will need to be thoughtfully considered in relation to Israel's cultural context and our own. Like Israel, we are to express the character of Christ by the way we live. We *get* to obey his commands.

As members of his new covenant community, we have the privilege— the *grace*—of living as his treasured people. James insists that our faith must be a faith that works, a faith that sets us apart from those who have not experienced deliverance in Christ. Our faith is proved genuine by our obedience—expressed in love for the God who rescued us from sin and death and in love for others. Love for God and love for neighbor embody everything the law requires. The fact that God has revealed to us what pleases him is one of his most gracious gifts—it's an invitation to know him, to become like him, and therefore to be part of his mission.

OLD TESTAMENT LAWS TODAY

Here's an example of how a Christian might use the Old Testament law as the basis for ethical reflection. In Deuteronomy 22:8, Moses instructs the people, "When you build a new house, make a parapet around your roof so that you may not bring the guilt of bloodshed on your house if someone falls from the roof." A parapet is an extension of the exterior wall above roof level, resulting in a solid protective wall for anyone standing on the roof. In ancient Israel the typical home had a flat roof on which lots of living took place. Occupants might sleep on the roof during the summer months, worship there, separate grain from chaff, or socialize.[12] The practical function of a parapet is obvious, given the architecture and lifestyle of the Israelites.

In North America, we typically do not hang out on the rooftops. Most homes do not have flat roofs, and the only occasions on which we climb our peaked roofs are to clean out the gutters (or eaves troughs, for my Canadian readers), or to replace the shingles, in which cases a parapet would merely get in the way. However, the principle of God's instruction is clear: the safety of the family and visitors to the home is the responsibility of a homeowner. Modern-day equivalents might include railings for our staircases, covers for our electrical outlets (if we have small children), and bracing for furniture such as dressers or bookcases so that they do not tip over. We could even extend our application of this command to clearing snow from our sidewalks so that passersby do not slip and fall on the ice. The point is that as members of the covenant community, it is our duty to look out for the well-being of those around us.

DIGGING DEEPER

Richard Bauckham. "James and the Gentiles (Acts 15:13-21)." Pages 154-84 in *History, Literature, and Society in the Book of Acts.* Edited by Ben Witherington. New York: Cambridge University Press, 1996.

*Roy Gane. *Old Testament Law for Christians: Original Context and Enduring Application.* Grand Rapids: Baker, 2017.

Carmen Joy Imes. "'Treasured Possession': Peter's Use of the Old Testament in 1 Peter 2:9-10." MA Thesis, Gordon-Conwell Theological Seminary, 2011.

*N. T. Wright. *Justification: God's Plan and Paul's Vision.* Downers Grove, IL: IVP Academic, 2009.

Related videos from The Bible Project: "Acts 8–12," "Gospel of the Kingdom," and "Son of Man."

CONCLUSION

ALL WE WERE MEANT TO BE

John's vision in Revelation makes visible and explicit what until then was spiritual and implicit. "Then I looked, and there before me was the Lamb, standing on Mount Zion, and with him 144,000 who had his name and his Father's name written on their foreheads" (Revelation 14:1). His vision also speaks of those who worship the beast and receive the mark of *his* name on their foreheads. We must choose where our allegiance lies. For those who persevere, John said, "They will see his face, and his name will be on their foreheads" (Revelation 22:4).

One afternoon several years ago, when we lived in North Carolina, I was grocery shopping with the kids. We made it back out to the car, and I was trying to get everything loaded up. I had asked the kids to get in their seats and get buckled, but they were moving as slow as molasses and bickering with each other. I went to put the shopping cart away and when I came back they *still* weren't in their seats. I completely lost it. "What is wrong with you? Did you not hear me? Get in your seats this instant! This is ridiculous!" I slammed the van door and turned around just in time to see the secretary from the kids' public school walking past.

A big reason we enrolled our kids in public school was so that our family could share Christ with unbelievers. I volunteered every week, my husband ate regularly with the kids in the lunchroom, and we were present at as many activities as possible. Then in one moment of anger all we had worked for was tarnished by my temper. I thought I was in an anonymous place where I could "let it all out" with no consequences. I learned that we don't get to pick and choose when we bear his name.

The Bible tells us the story of a God who is determined to keep his promise to bless his people, even when they forfeit their right to receive it. That's good news for all of us. By the grace of God in Christ, those "parking lot moments" don't erase our name from his roster. Instead, they prompt us to repent and receive his forgiveness. Because of the perfect faithfulness of Jesus, the blessings of protection, grace, and peace can still be ours.

We talk about the idea of "bearing God's name" a lot at our house. We talk about it because I spent five years writing a three-hundred-page dissertation on the command not to bear Yahweh's name in vain and another year and a half getting it published. One day, pretty early on in my studies, the clock struck 5:30 and it was time to start dinnertime chores. I sent the kids off to do theirs while I got dinner ready. After a few minutes, I noticed that the girls seemed especially cheerful and attentive. I can assure you—this was not normal. I glanced over to see what they were doing and was tickled to see that both of them had slapped a masking tape label on their foreheads that read "Yahweh." I grinned as they explained. "We're bearing the name of Yahweh by doing our chores cheerfully today!"

They got it! As believers we've been branded with his name, and that reality should change the way we do everything. As Paul said to the Colossians, "Whatever you do, whether in word or deed, do it all in the name of the Lord Jesus, giving thanks to God the Father through him" (Colossians 3:17). Or as the New Living Translation puts it, "Whatever you do or say, do it as a representative of the Lord Jesus."

Sinai is a big surprise. The surprise is the grace of God to a bedraggled company of former slaves of Egypt who have done nothing to deserve his attention. The surprise is an invitation to a long-term committed relationship. The surprise is that they are counted as his and he is determined to bless them, in spite of their ingratitude. The biggest surprise is God's inconceivable plan to link his own reputation with theirs—to put his name on them and charge them with the task of international public relations.

I told you there were surprises in store at Sinai!

The New Testament does not detach itself from this story. Jesus shows up to model for us how to bear Yahweh's name by obeying perfectly the law given at Sinai—loving God and loving others. After his death and resurrection, the invitation goes out to everybody else—to the Gentiles!—to join the family. We get the invisible tattoo along with all the Jews who follow Jesus. Together we get to join the mission of God.

As we pay attention to Sinai and its ripple effects through the rest of the biblical story, we discover that faith is not just private and salvation is not just personal. The benefits of our salvation are not only interior; they are conspicuous and corporate. Yahweh does not transform individuals at Sinai and send them their separate ways. He creates a nation. He does it with us, too. As Peter says, "You are . . . a holy nation" (1 Peter 2:9). We belong to God and to each other. We'll never fully experience all the blessings God has in store for us if we try to go solo.

> You become your truest self as part of this extraordinary community of men and women who are being transformed from the inside out— who are becoming and living as his people.

You are who you are because of who he is and who he says you are. You become your truest self as part of this extraordinary community of men and women who are being transformed from the inside out— who are becoming and living as his people.

Far from irrelevant or obsolete, the Old Testament story tells us who we are. It tells us *whose* we are. And that changes everything.

ask Christianif she wants to read it!

ACKNOWLEDGMENTS

Israel became a nation at Sinai in the liminal space of the wilderness. Books are produced in liminal space as well; they gradually take on more definite shape as scattered insights become paragraphs and chapters. Many walked with me on the journey of learning and writing and revising. For each one I am grateful.

Daniel Block first inspired me to study the concept of "bearing God's name," inviting me to do so as his doctoral student at Wheaton College from 2011 to 2016. I'm so grateful he told me to keep the dissertation chapter that hit the cutting floor. Much of it reappeared here. I also had the privilege of input from Sandy Richter, Karen Jobes, Marc Cortez, and Richard Averbeck on the dissertation, and while none of them was involved in the production of this book, their influence will be felt by those who know them. Rollin Grams will see evidence of my MA thesis here too, which he so ably supervised at Gordon-Conwell Theological Seminary in 2011. Many friends—too many to name here—urged me to turn these academic projects into a book for the wider church. Thanks for spurring me on!

Dan Reid first entertained my book proposal and helped me strengthen it before his retirement. In the meantime IVP hired my dear friend from seminary, Anna Moseley Gissing, who has skillfully guided the rest of the process. I'm thrilled for the opportunity to participate in

IVP's mission "to provide thoughtful books that encourage readers to believe, and to bring their whole lives under Christ's leadership—heart, soul, mind and strength."[1]

I wrote most of this book at Prairie College in the summer of 2018, with a sign taped to my door to minimize interruptions. My generous colleagues (I'm looking at you, James Enns) helped to protect my writing time and cheer me on, praying for me as I wrote. Phil Callaway offered great advice about the process from one writer to another, and my editorial team at Prairie caught many mistakes and clarified fuzzy thinking before I submitted the manuscript: Pat Massey, Abigail Guthrie, Amelia Fehr, and Danny Imes. It was extra special to get editorial feedback from our eldest daughter, Eliana, who is a fantastic writer herself and whose no-nonsense approach spared you many of my idiosyncrasies ("Mom, you can't say that!"). Eliana is my sharpest critic and my biggest fan. I relished several days of uninterrupted writing at Dave and Jean Neville's guest cottage, which was a true gift.

People often ask me how I get it all done. The answer is Danny Imes. I am forever grateful for his partnership. His gifts of administration and helps are in full operation at home so that I am free to write and teach. I had no idea what a treasure I was getting when I said "yes" twenty-one years ago!

Finally, a very special thank you to Chris Wright, who agreed to write the foreword to this book. His books have been a huge influence in the development of my thinking. I'm grateful for his scholarship and dedicated participation in God's mission. Readers who have not yet read *The Mission of God* or *The God I Don't Understand* should run out and buy them right this minute. You'll thank me later.

This book is dedicated to my parents, Dan and Verna Camfferman; to my husband, Danny; and to our children, Eliana, Emma, and Easton. As I began my doctoral studies, I wanted a dissertation topic that my family could appreciate. You have lived this adventure of study with me for over a decade through thick and thin. Now we can share it with the world!

APPENDIX: RESOURCES FROM THE BIBLE PROJECT

INTRODUCTION

"What is the Bible?"

The Bible Project

www.ivpress.com/imes1

"The Story of the Bible"

The Bible Project

www.ivpress.com/imes2

"Tanak" (Advanced)

The Bible Project

www.ivpress.com/imes3

1 LEAVING EGYPT

"Torah: Exodus 1–18"

The Bible Project

www.ivpress.com/imes4

2 SURPRISED AT SINAI

"Reading Biblical Law"

The Bible Project

www.ivpress.com/imes5

"Shema: YHWH"

The Bible Project

www.ivpress.com/imes6

"Sacrifice and Atonement"

The Bible Project

www.ivpress.com/imes7

"Torah: Exodus 19–40"
The Bible Project
www.ivpress.com/imes8

3 MAJOR DEAL

"Law"
The Bible Project
www.ivpress.com/imes9

4 NOW WHAT?

"Covenants"
The Bible Project
www.ivpress.com/imes10

"Exodus, part 1"
The Bible Project
www.ivpress.com/imes11

"Exodus, part 2"
The Bible Project
www.ivpress.com/imes12

"Holiness"
The Bible Project
www.ivpress.com/imes13

"Torah: Leviticus"
The Bible Project
www.ivpress.com/imes14

5 READY TO ROLL

"Torah: Numbers"
The Bible Project
www.ivpress.com/imes15

INTERMISSION

"Literary Styles"

The Bible Project

www.ivpress.com/imes16

"The Bible as Jewish Meditation Literature"

The Bible Project

www.ivpress.com/imes17

6 STRIKING OUT

"Torah: Deuteronomy"

The Bible Project

www.ivpress.com/imes18

7 WHAT YAHWEH SEES

"Prophets"

The Bible Project

www.ivpress.com/imes19

"Holy Spirit"

The Bible Project

www.ivpress.com/imes20

"The Way of the Exile"

The Bible Project

www.ivpress.com/imes21

8 JUST GIVE ME JESUS

"God"

The Bible Project

www.ivpress.com/imes22

"Messiah"

The Bible Project

www.ivpress.com/imes23

"Heaven and Earth"

The Bible Project

www.ivpress.com/imes24

9 BLOB TAG

"Reading Biblical Law"

The Bible Project

www.ivpress.com/imes25

"Image of God"

The Bible Project

www.ivpress.com/imes26

10 WHO LET YOU IN?

"Acts 8–12"

The Bible Project

www.ivpress.com/imes27

"Gospel of the Kingdom"

The Bible Project

www.ivpress.com/imes28

"Son of Man"

The Bible Project

www.ivpress.com/imes29

DISCUSSION QUESTIONS

INTRODUCTION

1. The author suggests that the Bible is like the picture of Narnia in *The Voyage of the Dawn Treader*. How are they similar?

2. Have you ever had the experience of being drawn into the biblical story? What was it like?

3. In your opinion, do laws take away freedom?

4. What are some differences between laws in the Bible and laws today?

5. What parts of the Old Testament do you find most difficult to swallow?

1 LEAVING EGYPT

Read Exodus 13–18.

1. According to the author, why is it important for us to pay attention to where the Old Testament laws appear in the overall story?

2. How does da Vinci's painting *The Last Supper* relate to the Sinai narratives?

3. Do you think Maslow's hierarchy of needs is a helpful way to think about Israel's wilderness journey? Why or why not?

4. Have you had a time when you've experienced liminality—lingering (or languishing!) between one stage of life and another? If so, what was it like for you?

5. How has God proved himself by providing for your needs?

2 SURPRISED AT SINAI

Read Exodus 19; Psalm 19.

1. Why would the law given at Sinai be good news for the Israelites? How is it an expression of grace?

2. According to this chapter, what qualifications for leadership does Moses have?

3. What does the title *segullah* imply about Israel's identity and vocation?

4. The author claims that "true freedom requires clearly communicated boundaries." Can you think of examples of how this is still true today?

5. Is there a healthy boundary or law that you've been resisting?

6. The author tells about a time when a mentor expressed confidence that she would graduate. Share about a time when someone said something about you, good or bad, that changed your trajectory.

3 MAJOR DEAL

Read Exodus 20.

1. According to the author, why are the Ten Commandments inscribed on two tablets?

2. Are other nations expected to obey the law given at Sinai? Why or why not?

3. How does the "preamble" to the Ten Commandments (Exodus 20:2) affect our understanding of the commands?

4. Before reading this book, what did you think the command "not to take the LORD's name in vain" (Exodus 20:7) prohibited?

5. If the author is right that the Name Command has to do with bearing the name and not just speaking it, can you give examples of how Christians in your society violate this command?

6. In your opinion, what might be the benefits and pitfalls of Christians today observing the Sabbath?

4 NOW WHAT?

Read Exodus 24–30, 32; Leviticus 1–9.

1. The author suggests that "the law is not the be all and end all for Israel." How did God anticipate Israel's need for ongoing guidance?

2. Why is the sprinkling of blood a profound symbol for the Israelites?

3. Like Aaron with the golden calf, it's tempting to minimize our own participation in rebellion. In your opinion, what motivates us to do this?

4. Why are the tabernacle instructions "a matter of national security"?

5. How are the tabernacle blueprints an expression of God's grace?

6. If you lived in ancient Israel, which role in the building or operating of the tabernacle would you most enjoy (artistic design, weaving, engraving, building, carrying, lighting the lamps, offering sacrifices)?

7. Does your current job require strict adherence to procedure, like the Israelite priests, or innovation and creativity? Would you find the sacrificial system reassuring or constrictive?

5 READY TO ROLL

Read Exodus 12, 33–34; Numbers 1–2, 6–7; Deuteronomy 8.

1. According to the author, why would the lists of names in Numbers have been exhilarating to the ancient Israelites?

2. How does the blessing the priests pronounce over the people in Numbers 6:24-27 relate to the command not to bear Yahweh's name in vain?

3. What makes a family tradition memorable?

4. The author mentioned several different ways to understand the number of Israelites who left Egypt. Which explanation do you find most plausible?

5. As a group, spend a few moments in quiet reflection considering this question: What picture comes to your mind when you think about God? Share what you see and how it has changed over time.

6. How does your picture of God compare with the way God reveals himself at Sinai?

INTERMISSION

1. The author claims that a painting is not necessarily less historical than a photograph. How can this be true?

2. How can the Bible present reliable history as well as transcend history by becoming part of our own story?

3. What truths from Part One of the book have been most thought provoking or revolutionary for you?

6 STRIKING OUT

Read Numbers 11–14, 16; Deuteronomy 5, 26; Joshua 1–2, 2 Samuel 7; 1 Kings 8.

1. According to the author, what makes Mount Zion impressive?

2. What is the significance of Moses' statement in Deuteronomy 5:1-4?

3. How are Rahab and the Gibeonites the beginning fulfillment of God's promise to Abraham?

4. Why do you think the Israelites and their leaders had such a hard time remaining faithful to Yahweh?

5. In what ways have you been your own worst enemy?

7 WHAT YAHWEH SEES

Read 1 Kings 18–19; Jeremiah 7, 31; Daniel 9.

1. In what way is Elijah's victory at Mount Carmel an affront to Baal as well as to King Ahab?

2. What problem does the exile cause for Yahweh and what is his solution?

3. Why do you think God uses agricultural imagery to depict the consequences of rebellion as well as the blessings of obedience?

4. Ancient Israel is not the only religious community guilty of hypocrisy. If Jeremiah showed up at your church this Sunday and preached in the doorway as he did in Israel's temple, what forms of hypocrisy do you think he would call to account?

5. Have you known someone like Joanne who lives a life of ordinary faithfulness?

6. Share about a time when you felt stuck and needed a fresh start.

8 JUST GIVE ME JESUS

Read Matthew 4–7, 12, 17.

1. What does it mean when Jesus prays "hallowed be your name"?

2. How can Jesus' temptation in the wilderness serve as a model for us today?

3. In what ways is Jesus greater than Moses?

4. What did you find most surprising in this chapter?

5. According to the author, why do Moses and Elijah appear with Jesus on the Mount of Transfiguration?

9 BLOB TAG

Read Acts 9; Galatians 3–4; Philippians 2; Hebrews 1, 12; 1 Peter 4.

1. Explain the significance of Peter's quote of Joel 2 in reference to Jesus.

2. How is the biblical concept of election like a game of blob tag?

3. How can we reconcile Paul's negative statements about the law with the author's claim that the law is a gift?

4. Pastor Alvin Beuchert claims, "Jesus finished all the work God gave him to do, but he did not finish all the work." From your perspective, what work remains to be done?

5. Is glory always preceded by suffering?

6. Have you experienced suffering for your faith?

10 WHO LET YOU IN?

Read Deuteronomy 30, 32; Acts 10–11, 15; Romans 1, 5; 1 Peter 2; Revelation 7, 14.

1. Why is it audacious for Peter to call his readers "a chosen people, a royal priesthood, a holy nation, God's treasured possession" (1 Peter 2:9-10)?

2. On what two criteria does James base his conclusion that Gentiles who follow Jesus are now included in the covenant?

3. Israel is called God's "firstborn son" and King David is called God's "son" as well. How does this covenant background of the concept of "sonship" shape our understanding of what it means for Jesus to be the "Son of God"?

4. Many people think of religion as a private matter. How does the concept of bearing Yahweh's name or bearing Jesus' name challenge that notion?

5. Which of the practical applications from Peter's letter listed in this chapter do you find most challenging?

6. Choose a law given at Sinai and discuss how you could express its wisdom in your current cultural context (e.g., Exodus 21:33; 22:29; or 23:4-5).

CONCLUSION

1. The author claims, "Faith is not just private and salvation is not just personal." What evidence can you give for this from your experience?

2. Can you think of a recent example of when Christianity got a bad name because of the way that a single Christian behaved?

3. What area of your life needs to change because you bear the name of Yahweh?

4. How can you take more seriously your identity as a member of a whole community of those who belong to Jesus? What would it look like to participate more fully?

5. What truths from Part Two of the book have been most thought provoking for you?

NOTES

INTRODUCTION

[1] "Aftermath, Part 3: Not Difficult," YouTube, 39:44, "Andy Stanley," April 30, 2018, www.youtube.com/watch?v=pShxFTNRCWI.

[2] "Dr. Brown Interviews Pastor Andy Stanley," YouTube, 50:19, "ASK DrBrown," July 2, 2018, www.youtube.com/watch?v=C7Jcu03lJso.

1 LEAVING EGYPT

[1] This momentous event has similarities with the salvation we have in Jesus. We are invited to dine with him at the Lord's table, with his blood as a sign that we are part of the renewed covenant and enjoy God's protection. When plagues of judgment fall on all those who have rejected his rule, we will be kept safe to enter God's kingdom in the new creation.

[2] David J. A. Clines, ed., *The Dictionary of Classical Hebrew* (Sheffield: Sheffield Academic, 1993), 6:723.

[3] With gratitude to Karl Kutz for this insight, from class notes to his Pentateuch class at Multnomah University.

[4] For a helpful discussion of chiasm or ring structure with examples, see J. P. Fokkelman, *Reading Biblical Narrative: An Introductory Guide* (Louisville: Westminster John Knox, 1999), 97-122.

[5] Gordon J. Wenham, *Genesis 1–15*, WBC (Dallas: Word, 1987), 1:156-58.

[6] This instance of literary symmetry and those that follow are taken from Frank Moore Cross, *Canaanite Myth and Hebrew Epic: Essays in the History of the Religion of Israel* (Cambridge, MA: Harvard University Press, 1973), 308-16; Robert L. Cohn, *The Shape of Sacred Space: Four Biblical Studies*, AAR Studies in Religion 23 (Chico, CA: Scholars Press, 1981), 18; Mark S. Smith, *The Pilgrimage Pattern in Exodus*, Journal for the Study of the Old Testament Supplement Series 239 (Sheffield: Sheffield Academic, 1997), 289.

[7]Victor Turner, "Liminality and *communitas*," 74-84 in Paul Bradshaw and John Melloh, eds., *Foundations in Ritual Studies: A Reader for Students of Christian Worship* (Grand Rapids: Baker Academic, 2007).

[8]Information about Maslow's work can be found in many sources. See, for example, Calvin S. Hall, Gardner Lindzey, and John B. Campbell, *Theories of Personality*, 4th ed. (New York: John Wiley & Sons, 1998), 444-54.

[9]Terence E. Fretheim, "The Plagues as Ecological Signs of Historical Disaster," in *What Kind of God? Collected Essays of Terence E. Fretheim*, ed. Michael J. Chan and Brent A. Strawn, Siphrut 14 (Winona Lake, IN: Eisenbrauns, 2015), 225-35.

[10]Terence E. Fretheim, *Exodus*, Interpretation (Louisville: Westminster John Knox, 2010), 175.

[11]Fretheim, *Exodus*, 175.

2 SURPRISED AT SINAI

[1]"Legend of Isis and the Name of Re," translated by Robert K. Ritner in William Hallo and K. Lawson Younger, eds., *Context of Scripture* (Leiden: Brill, 2003), I.22:33-34. "Re" is an alternative spelling of Egyptian sun god, Ra.

[2]Herbert Huffmon and Simon Parker, "A Further Note on the Treaty Background of Hebrew Yada," *BASOR* 184 (1966): 37n12; Moshe Weinfeld, *Deuteronomy and the Deuteronomic School* (Oxford: Oxford University Press, 1972), 69n1, 226n2; Moshe Greenberg, "Hebrew S^egullā : Akkadian Sikiltu," *JAOS.*71 (1951): 172–74. For more bibliography and fuller discussion see Carmen Joy Imes, *"Treasured Possession": Peter's Use of the Old Testament in 1 Peter 2:9-10* (MA thesis, Gordon-Conwell Theological Seminary, 2011), 37-40.

[3]Bernard Grossfeld, trans., *Targum Onqelos to Exodus*, Aramaic Bible 7 (Wilmington, DE: Glazier, 1988), 52-53.

[4]Christopher J. H. Wright, *The Mission of God: Unlocking the Bible's Grand Narrative* (Downers Grove, IL: IVP Academic, 2006), 256.

[5]As translated by Benjamin R. Foster, *Before the Muses: An Anthology of Akkadian Literature*, 3rd ed. (Bethesda, MD: CDL Press, 2005), III.56, 763. Used by permission.

[6]Foster, *Before the Muses*, 763-65. Emphasis mine.

[7]Raymond Westbrook, ed., *A History of Ancient Near Eastern Law*, 2 vols. (Leiden: Brill, 2003), 1:17, 20, 98; John H. Walton, *Ancient Near Eastern Thought and the Old Testament: Introducing the Conceptual World of the Hebrew Bible* (Grand Rapids: Baker Academic, 2006), 287-302; Michael LeFebvre,

Collections, Codes, and Torah: The Re-Characterization of Israel's Written Law, LHB/OTS 451 (New York: T&T Clark, 2006), 36, 90-91, 259, 261.

[8]By the time we get to the New Testament, the Pharisees are quite fastidious about law enforcement, but they reflect a Hellenistic understanding of the function of law which is quite different than the approach of their Jewish ancestors. For a full defense of this claim, see LeFebvre, *Collections, Codes, and Torah*.

3 MAJOR DEAL

[1]The Akkadian word is *ade*. Simo Parpola and Kazuko Watanabe, *Neo-Assyrian Treaties and Loyalty Oaths*, State Archives of Assyria 2 (Helsinki: Helsinki University Press, 1988), xv; Paul Kalluveettil, *Declaration and Covenant: A Comprehensive Review of Covenant Formulae from the Old Testament and the Ancient Near East*, Analecta Biblica 88 (Rome: Biblical Institute Press, 1982), 31. For a more recent discussion, see Daniel I. Block, "For Whose Eyes? The Divine Origins and Function of the Two Tablets of the Israelite Covenant," in *Write That They May Read: Studies in Literacy and Textualization in the Ancient Near East and in the Hebrew Scriptures: Essays in Honour of Professor Alan R. Millard*, edited by Daniel I. Block, C. John Collins, David C. Deuel, and Paul J. Lawrence (forthcoming).

[2]Jacob Lauinger, "Some Preliminary Thoughts on the Tablet Collection in Building XVI from Tell Tayinat," *Journal of the Canadian Society for Mesopotamian Studies* 6 (2011), 10–11.

[3]"No. 56A Shattiwaza of Mitanni & Suppiluliuma I of Hatti," in Kenneth A. Kitchen and Paul J. N. Lawrence, *Treaty, Law and Covenant in the Ancient Near East* (Wiesbaden: Harrassowitz, 2012), 1:391. Words in brackets are either assumed in the original text or are damaged or missing. Ancient tablets of clay or stone were susceptible to chips or wear over time.

[4]"Heidelberg Catechism: Lord's Day 34," Resources, Reformed Church of America, www.rca.org/resources/heidelbergcatechism.

[5]We'll talk later about how (or if) they relate to us today.

[6]For a discussion of the difficulty of counting the commands of the Decalogue, see Mordechai Breuer, "Dividing the Decalogue into Verses and Commandments," in *The Ten Commandments in History and Tradition*, ed. Ben-Zion Segal, trans. Gerson Levi (Jerusalem: Magnes, 1990), 291-330; Daniel I. Block, *How I Love Your Torah, O LORD!: Studies in the Book of Deuteronomy* (Eugene, OR: Cascade, 2011), 56-60; DeRouchie, "Counting the Ten: An Investigation into the Numbering of the Decalogue," in *For Our Good Always: Studies on*

the Message and Influence of Deuteronomy in Honor of Daniel I. Block, ed. Jason S. DeRouchie, Jason Gile, and Kenneth J. Turner (Winona Lake, IN: Eisenbrauns, 2013), 93-125; Carmen Joy Imes, *Bearing YHWH's Name at Sinai*, 132-35.

[7]Edward L. Greenstein, "The Rhetoric of the Ten Commandments," in *The Decalogue in Jewish and Christian Tradition*, ed. Henning Graf Reventlow and Yair Hoffman, Library of Hebrew Bible/Old Testament Studies 509 (New York: T&T Clark, 2011), 9; Carmen Joy Imes, *Bearing YHWH's Name at Sinai: A Reexamination of the Name Command of the Decalogue*, Bulletin for Biblical Research, Supplements 19 (University Park, PA: Eisenbrauns, 2018), 133.

[8]Jeremiah 7:23; 11:4; 13:11; 24:7; 30:22; 31:1, 33; 32:38; Ezekiel 11:20; 14:11; 36:28; 37:23, 27.

[9]Block, *How I Love Your Torah*, 32-33.

[10]He has written about his adventure in Charlie Trimm, "Honor Your Parents: A Command for Adults," *JETS* 60 (2017): 247-63.

[11]Peter Enns, *Exodus*, NIV Application Commentary (Grand Rapids: Zondervan, 2000), 426.

4 NOW WHAT?

[1]For example, at Sinai, the Israelites are commanded not to make altars of cut stone, but rather altars of earth or uncut stone "wherever" God authorizes them to honor him (Exodus 20:24). However, in Deuteronomy 27:5, earthen altars are not even mentioned, and in Deuteronomy 12 the centralization of worship in *one* place on *one* altar is explicitly commanded. See Michael Fishbane, *Biblical Interpretation in Ancient Israel* (Oxford: Clarendon, 1988), 252, 263. The centralization of worship motivated a new set of instructions regarding meat-eating that is unconnected with tabernacle worship. When the tribes of Israel were spread throughout the land God promised them, it was no longer feasible for meat consumption to be linked solely to religious activities. See Daniel I. Block, *Deuteronomy*, NIVAC (Grand Rapids: Zondervan, 2012), 316.

[2]See Block, "Reading the Decalogue Right to Left," 26-36. Also Kenneth A. Kitchen, *On the Reliability of the Old Testament* (Grand Rapids: Eerdmans, 2003), 243. Hittite treaties are the most similar to Israel's covenant; later neo-Assyrian treaties lack a historical prologue and blessings.

[3]The commands are addressed by default to male heads of households ("Do not covet your neighbor's *wife*"), but with implications for each member of the family.

[4]Ronald S. Hendel, "Sacrifice as a Cultural System: The Ritual Symbolism of Exodus 24,3-8," *Zeitschrift für die alttestementliche Wissenschaft* 101 (1989): 385-88.

[5]Hendel, "Sacrifice as a Cultural System," 379.

[6]Cornelis Houtman, *Exodus*, trans. Sierd Woudstra, Historical Commentary on the Old Testament (Leuven, Belgium: Peeters, 2000), 3:643.

[7]Credit for this illustration goes to Tim Mackie and Jon Collins; see "The Book of Leviticus," YouTube, 7:21, "The Bible Project," May 6, 2015, www.youtube .com/watch?v=WmvyrLXoQio&t=16s.

[8]The logic behind the clean and unclean food laws is difficult to discern, but Daniel Block makes a very plausible suggestion that the Israelites are invited to eat those things that Yahweh also accepts as sacrifices while they are prohibited from eating exotic or wild animals that have no part in tabernacle worship. Daniel I. Block, *Deuteronomy*, NIV Application Commentary (Grand Rapids: Zondervan, 2012), 345-50.

[9]For an explanation of how ritual works, see Victor Turner, "Liminality and *cummunitas*," 74-84 in Bradshaw and Melloh, *Foundations in Ritual Studies*.

[10]William H. C. Propp, *Exodus 19–40*, Anchor Bible 2A (New York: Doubleday, 2006), 528.

[11]Menahem Haran, *Temples and Temple-Service in Ancient Israel: An Inquiry into Biblical Cult Phenomena and the Historical Setting of the Priestly School* (Winona Lake, IN: Eisenbrauns, 1985), 164-65. See also Imes, *Bearing YHWH's Name at Sinai*, 157.

5 READY TO ROLL

[1]A. W. Tozer, *The Knowledge of the Holy* (New York: HarperSanFrancisco, 1961), 1.

[2]Duncan P. Westwood, "Risk and Resilience in Our God Image," paper presented at the Member Care Conference at Providence University and Seminary, May 28, 2016.

[3]Duncan P. Westwood, "God-Image as a Component of MHI/IHM's Health Screening and Diagnostic Protocols," Window on God Exercise presented at the Missionary Health Institute / International Health Management Staff Development meetings, June 21, 2013.

[4]Austin Surls argues that rather than trying to figure out the meaning of the name Yahweh at the burning bush, we should direct our attention to Exodus 34:6-7, where God's character is expressed. Austin D. Surls, *Making Sense of the Divine Name in the Book of Exodus: From Etymology to Literary*

Onomastics, Bulletin for Biblical Research, Supplements 17 (Winona Lake, IN: Eisenbrauns, 2017).

[5]See Muhammad A. Dandamaev, *Slavery in Babylonia: From Nabopolassar to Alexander the Great (626–331 B.C.)*, ed. M. A. Powell and D. B. Weisberg, trans. V. A. Powell (DeKalb, IL: Northern Illinois University Press, 1984), 229-34, 488-89; Nili S. Fox, "Marked for Servitude: Mesopotamia and the Bible," in *A Common Cultural Heritage: Studies on Mesopotamia and the Biblical World in Honor of Barry L. Eichler*, ed. Grant Frame et al. (Bethesda, MD: CDL Press, 2011), 268; Sandra Jacobs, *The Body as Property: Physical Disfigurement in Biblical Law*, Library of Hebrew Bible/Old Testament Studies 582 (London: Bloomsbury, 2014), 205-14.

[6]See John E. Hartley, *Leviticus*, Word Biblical Commentary 4 (Dallas: Word, 1992), 362. Jacob Milgrom sees vv. 31-33 as applying to the entire chapter, because of the inclusio in v. 2, or even to the entirety of God's commands. Milgrom, *Leviticus 17–22*, AB 3A (New York: Doubleday, 2000), 1887.

[7]Steven B. Sample, *The Contrarian's Guide to Leadership* (San Francisco: Jossey-Bass, 2002), 145.

INTERMISSION

[1]For more on this painting, see Flavio Febbraro and Burkhard Schwetje, *How to Read World History in Art: From the Code of Hammurabit to September 11* (New York: Abrams, 2010).

6 STRIKING OUT

[1]See Daniel I. Block, *Deuteronomy*, NIVAC (Grand Rapids: Zondervan, 2012), 624-29.

[2]For a full-scale study of the altar on Mount Ebal, see Ralph K. Hawkins, *The Iron Age I Structure on Mt. Ebal*, Bulletin for Biblical Research, Supplements 6 (Winona Lake, IN: Eisenbrauns, 2012).

[3]Sandra L. Richter, *The Deuteronomistic History and the Name Theology: Lᵉšakkēn Šᵉmô Šām in the Bible and the Ancient Near East*. Beihefte zur Zeitschrift für die alttestementliche Wissenschaft 318 (Berlin: de Gruyter, 2002).

[4]A unique form of *amar* in the hiphil stem, occurring only here, functions as a declarative speech act. In the language of speech-act theory, the statement's perlocutionary effect is the enacting of a new level of covenant commitment. For a full defense of this translation, see Stephen Guest, *Deuteronomy 26:16-19 as the Central Focus of the Covenantal Framework of Deuteronomy* (PhD diss., The Southern Baptist Theological Seminary, 2009).

208 NOTES TO PAGES 110-120

[5]David M. Howard, *Joshua*, New American Commentary 5 (Nashville: Broadman & Holman, 1998), 103. Rahab also roughly mimics Exodus 15:14-16, when she speaks of "dread," "rulers," and "melting away." In short, her confession embodies classic Deuteronomic theology, despite the lack of a comparable expression from the Israelites in Joshua. See Robert G. Boling, *Joshua: A New Translation with Notes and Commentary*, Anchor Bible 6 (New York: Doubleday, 1982), 146-47.

[6]John Goldingay, *Israel's Gospel*, vol. 1 of *Old Testament Theology* (Downers Grove, IL: IVP Academic, 2003), 464-65, 510-11. The parallels between these accounts are noted by Richard S. Hess, *Joshua: An Introduction and Commentary*, Tyndale Old Testament Commentary (Downers Grove, IL: InterVarsity Press, 1996), 177; Richard D. Nelson, *Joshua*, Old Testament Library (Louisville: Westminster John Knox, 1997), 131-32.

[7]See David G. Firth, *1 & 2 Samuel*, AOTC (Downers Grove, IL: InterVarsity Press, 2009), 115-16.

[8]A recently discovered Ugaritic text speaks of the goddess 'Athtartu as the "name of Ba'alu" who also wielded his name as a mighty weapon. See Theodore J. Lewis, "'Athtartu's Incantations and the Use of Divine Names as Weapons," *Journal of Near Eastern Studies* 70 (2011): 207-27.

[9]2 Samuel 7 has attracted much scholarly attention as to its source(s) and perspective on Davidic kingship and the temple. For a thorough discussion, see P. Kyle McCarter Jr., *II Samuel*, Anchor Bible 9 (New Haven: Yale University Press, 1984), 209-31. However the textual history is construed, the canonical text affirms that David's "name" is a gift from Yahweh and that David understands his task as that of magnifying Yahweh's name among the nations.

[10]1 Kings 3:2; 5:3, 5; 8:16-21, 29, 33, 35, 44, 48.

[11]Noted by Jeffrey Niehaus, *God at Sinai: Covenant and Theophany in the Bible and Ancient Near East*, Studies in Old Testament Biblical Theology (Grand Rapids: Zondervan, 1995), 243.

7 WHAT YAHWEH SEES

[1]One of my students, Joel Schultz, deserves special recognition for the insights in this paragraph. He gave an excellent presentation to our class on 1 Kings 18.

[2]"The 'Aqhatu Legend," trans. Dennis Pardee (*Context of Scripture* 1.103:351).

[3]Peter Leithart, *1 & 2 Kings*, Brazos Theological Commentary on the Bible (Grand Rapids: Brazos, 2006), 141.

[4]The NIV reads "den of robbers," which distances the hearers from the problem. The temple is not a den full of other robbers; it has become a den for the people themselves, who are robbing God and one another.

[5]See Daniel I. Block, *Beyond the River Chebar: Studies in Kingship and Eschatology in Ezekiel* (Eugene, OR: Cascade, 2013), 154-55. Block points to Isaiah 40:1-5 as a clear example that the covenant renewal is related to the outpouring of the spirit.

[6]For renaming as a sign of redemption, see Isaiah 58:12 ("Repairer of Broken Walls"); 60:14 ("City of Yahweh"); 61:3 ("oaks of righteousness"); 61:6 ("priests of Yahweh"); 62:4 ("Hephzibah" and "Beulah"); 62:12 ("Holy People," "Redeemed," and "Sought After"). For reversion to old names, see Isaiah 47:1, 5; 48:8.

[7]The Hebrew word *tov* describes Israel's responsibility to do that which is good in the eyes of Yahweh as well as Yahweh's blessing in response ("for your good"). For a longer catalog of covenant language from Deuteronomy, see Weinfeld, *Deuteronomy and the Deuteronomic School*, 335, 343, 345, 346.

[8]The words "not," "not," and "oh" make a *lo', lo', lu'* sequence, while the pairs "called" and "split" (*niqra'* and *qara'ta*) and "name" and "heavens" (*shimka* and *shamayim*) both share two consonants. The overall effect in Hebrew is striking: *lo' niqra' shimka 'aleyhem // lu' qara'ta shamayim*. In Hebrew the chapter break comes later.

[9]Author's translation. English translations are split over how to render 63:19. The NIV and a few others read it as a contrast between Israel and the nations: "We are yours from of old; but you have not ruled over them, they have not been called by your name." However, if Israel's elect status ("called by your name") has not been lost (63:19), then the plea for a return to Sinai in 64:1 makes little sense.

[10]The New Testament book of Hebrews confirms this assessment. It reads, "If there had been nothing wrong with that first covenant, no place would have been sought for another. But God found fault *with the people*" (Hebrews 8:7-8, emphasis added). The problem with the covenant is the people's failure to keep it.

[11]2 Corinthians 3:6-10 is also a challenge. It says that the ministry of the old covenant brought death. But in what sense? Paul elsewhere affirms that "the law is holy, and the commandment is holy, righteous and good" (Romans 7:12) so the deficiency is not with the law itself. Scott Hafemann explains, "Moses' ministry brought about death to those who received the law (v. 7) because it declared and effected God's sentence of condemnation on those who broke the covenant (v. 9a)." *2 Corinthians*, NIVAC (Grand Rapids: Zondervan, 2000), 150. The Sinai covenant is called "transitory" because of its constant need for renewal.

The problem is not with Moses and his covenant, but with those whose hearts have not yet been transformed (2 Corinthians 3:14-16).

8 JUST GIVE ME JESUS

[1]For discussion, see R. Kendall Soulen, *The Divine Name(s) and the Holy Trinity: Distinguishing the Voices* (Louisville: Westminster John Knox, 2011).

[2]I owe this insight to Daniel Block, through personal conversation.

[3]Moises Silva, ed., *New International Dictionary of New Testament Theology and Exegesis*, 2nd ed. (Grand Rapids: Zondervan, 2014), 2:527-29.

[4]R. T. France, *The Gospel of Matthew*, New International Commentary on the New Testament (Grand Rapids: Eerdmans, 2007), 53.

[5]Raymond Brown recognizes the connection with the wider biblical theme of name-bearing when he suggests that since Jesus replaced the temple, he is now the "place where God has put His name" (cf. Deut 12:5). Brown, *The Gospel According to John (XIII-XXI)*, Anchor Bible (Garden City, NY: Doubleday, 1970), 754.

[6]For a full defense of this view, see Daniel I. Block, "A Prophet Like Moses: Another Look at Deuteronomy 18:9-22," in *The Triumph of Grace: Literary and Theological Studies in Deuteronomy and Deuteronomic Themes* (Eugene, OR: Cascade, 2017), 349-73.

[7]You can read the whole story in 1 Samuel 21.

[8]The word could be translated either personally or impersonally.

[9]France, *Matthew*, 648.

[10]France, *Matthew*, 648. See Malachi 4:5 and Deuteronomy 18:15-19.

[11]France, *Matthew*, 644.

[12]France, *Matthew*, 645.

[13]Michael Harrison Kibbe, "Our Future in the Face of Jesus," *Christianity Today*, July/August 2017, 68

9 BLOB TAG

[1]See Darrell Bock, *Acts*, Baker Exegetical Commentary on the New Testament (Grand Rapids: Baker Academic, 2007), 118; Craig S. Keener, *Acts: An Exegetical Commentary* (Grand Rapids: Baker Academic, 2012), 1:920-23.

[2]For an illuminating discussion, see Richard Bauckham, *Jesus and the God of Israel: God Crucified and Other Studies on the New Testament's Christology of Divine Identity* (Grand Rapids: Eerdmans, 2008), 41-45. Paul also quotes Joel 2:32 in Romans 10:13 with similar results. See Daniel I. Block, "Who Do Commentators Say 'The Lord' Is? The Scandalous Rock of Romans 10:13," in *On the Writing of New Testament Commentaries: Festschrift for Grant R.*

Osborne on the Occasion of His 70th Birthday, ed. Stanley Porter and Eckhard J. Schnabel, Text and Editions for New Testament Study 8 (Leiden: Brill, 2013), 173-92.

[3]See Gordon D. Fee, *Paul's Letter to the Philippians*, New International Commentary on the New Testament (Grand Rapids: Eerdmans, 1995), 221-26.

[4]See Hans-Joachim Kraus, *Psalms 60–150*, trans. Hilton C. Oswald, Continental Commentary (Minneapolis: Fortress, 1993), 287.

[5]It is not certain what makes the name secret. It's possible that the idea of secrecy arose from centuries of refusal to say the name Yahweh aloud. Greg Beale insists that "secret" does not imply that the name has not yet been revealed to the elect. That is, it is not necessarily a name other than Yahweh. G. K. Beale, *The Book of Revelation: A Commentary on the Greek Text*, New International Greek Testament Commentary (Grand Rapids: Eerdmans, 1999), 257-58.

[6]"Jesus Prays for Himself (John 17)," sermon at Mt. Olive Evangelical Free Church, Three Hills, Alberta, March 11, 2018.

[7]We usually call him Paul, but that name is only used when he is in Greek-speaking contexts. Saul is his Jewish name. If you read Acts carefully, you'll see that his name is not changed in this story, as is so often taught. See Stephen B. Chapman, "Saul/Paul: Onomastics, Typology, and Christian Scripture," in *The Word Leaps the Gap: Essays on Scripture and Theology in Honor of Richard B. Hays*, ed. J. Ross Wagner, C. Kavin Rowe, and A. Katherine Greib (Grand Rapids: Eerdmans, 2008), 214-43.

[8]The NIV reads "proclaim my name," but this translation obscures the connection with the theme of bearing Yahweh's name. The word is *bastazo*, which means "to bear" or "to carry."

[9]For further discussion of this phrase, see Imes, *Bearing YHWH's Name at Sinai*, 49-61.

[10]Richard B. Hays, *Echoes of Scripture in the Gospels* (Waco, TX: Baylor University Press, 2016), 145.

[11]Hays, *Echoes of Scripture in the Gospels*, 145.

[12]See Karen Jobes, *1 Peter*, Baker Exegetical Commentary on the New Testament (Grand Rapids: Baker Academic, 2005), 287.

[13]From the hymn by Thomas Chisholm, "Great is Thy Faithfulness," penned in 1923.

[14]Daniel I. Block, "Reading Galatians with Moses: Paul as a Second and Seconding Moses," in *The Triumph of Grace: Literary and Theological Studies in Deuteronomy and Deuteronomic Themes* (Eugene, OR: Cascade, 2017), 375.

[15]See Block, "Reading Galatians with Moses," 387-90.

[16]Details regarding the seismic and eruptive activity of the volcano may be accessed in *The 1980 Eruptions of Mt. Saint Helens, Washington*, US Geological Survey, 1981 this US Geological Survey, https://pubs.usgs.gov/pp/1250 /report.pdf. On Harry R. Truman, see https://en.wikipedia.org/wiki/Harry_R. _Truman and www.usatoday.com/story/news/nation-now/2015/05/17/mount -st-helens-people-stayed/27311467.

[17]Michael Harrison Kibbe, *Godly Fear or Ungodly Failure? Hebrews 12 and the Sinai Theophanies*, Beihefte zur Zeitschrift für die neutestamentliche Wissenschaft 216 (Berlin: de Gruyter, 2016), 215.

[18]Kibbe, *Godly Fear or Ungodly Failure?*, 214.

[19]For a fuller discussion, see Ryan S. Peterson, *The Imago Dei as Human Identity: A Theological Interpretation*, Journal of Theological Interpretation Supplement 14 (Winona Lake, IN: Eisenbrauns, 2016); Catherine L. McDowell, *The Image of God in the Garden of Eden: The Creation of Humankind in Genesis 2:5–3:24 in Light of mīs pî pīt pî and wpt-r Rituals of Mesopotamia and Ancient Egypt*, Siphrut 15 (Winona Lake, IN: Eisenbrauns, 2015).

[20]John H. Walton, *The Lost World of Genesis One: Ancient Cosmology and the Origins Debate* (Downers Grove, IL: IVP Academic, 2009).

[21]Suzanne McDonald conflates creational and covenantal election, but on the whole her theology of election is refreshing and helpful. See her *Re-Imaging Election: Divine Election as Representing God to Others and Others to God* (Grand Rapids: Eerdmans, 2010).

10 WHO LET YOU IN?

[1]See Exodus 19:5 for an example of this contrast.

[2]For further discussion, see C. K. Barrett, *A Critical and Exegetical Commentary on the Acts of the Apostles*, 2 vols., International Critical Commentary (Edinburgh: T&T Clark, 1998), 2:724; F. F. Bruce, *The Book of the Acts*, rev. ed., New International Commentary on the New Testament (Grand Rapids: Eerdmans, 1988), 293; Richard Bauckham, "James and the Gentiles (Acts 15:13-21)," in *History, Literature, and Society in the Book of Acts*, ed. Ben Witherington (New York: Cambridge University Press, 1996), 154-84.

[3]The Hebrew reads, "that they may possess the remnant of Edom and all the nations upon whom my Name will be invoked" (author's translation). This could imply military domination. The Greek Septuagint reads, "that the remnant of humankind, and all the Gentiles who are called by my name, may earnestly seek me." Rather than military domination, the Greek translation suggests global conversion. Still, both versions refer to the Gentiles

as those "over whom my Name is invoked," which is the principal point on which James depends. In Hebrew, "Edom" and "humankind" are almost identical, as are "possess" and "seek," which partly explains the Greek translation.

[4]Bauckham, "James and the Gentiles," 169. Zechariah 2:11 is another potential example: "Many nations will join themselves to Yahweh on that day and they will be my people" (author's translation). However, to "join themselves to Yahweh" may imply conversion to Judaism

[5]Richard Hays contends that this chapter contains the teaching of Romans in a nutshell. Hays points out that not only is Israel's "lack of faith" in view in Deuteronomy, but also God's plan to include the Gentiles, the very message Paul is trying to proclaim. See *Echoes of Scripture in the Letters of Paul* (New Haven: Yale University Press, 1989), 164.

[6]Hays offers a chapter outline which is essentially the same as mine here, except he excludes verses 3-5, which I see as foundational to what follows. Hays, *Echoes*, 163-64.

[7]He does not use the word *faith* here, but in both contexts the primary sin is forsaking the worship of God and turning to idols.

[8]Walter Bauer, *A Greek-English Lexicon of the New Testament and other Early Christian Literature*, ed. Frederick William Danker, 3rd ed. (Chicago: University of Chicago Press, 2000), 945. Even if Paul's "marks" in Galatians 6:17 are physical scars of his persecution, he knew that his sufferings were "for the sake of the name" which he "bore" (Acts 9:15-16).

[9]Moisés Silva, ed. *New International Dictionary of New Testament Theology and Exegesis*, rev. ed. 4 vols. (Grand Rapids: Zondervan, 2014), 4:375-77.

[10]In English translations, it is unclear whether the angel is sealed or carries the seal. In Greek, the angel is "holding" it.

[11]I read this as a single name, that is, the divine "name above all names" bestowed on Jesus and celebrated in the confession, "Jesus is *kyrios*" (i.e., he is Yahweh; Philippians 2:9-11). Ephesians 1:3 provides an example of a similar grammatical structure: "the God and Father of our Lord Jesus Christ" clearly refers to one person, even though two titles are joined by "and." For other examples, see Nigel Turner, *Syntax*, vol. 3 of *Grammar of New Testament Greek* (Edinburgh: T&T Clark, 1963), 335.

[12]For more on Israelite architecture, see Philip J. King and Lawrence E. Stager, *Life in Biblical Israel*. Library of Ancient Israel (Louisville: Westminster John Knox, 2001) 28-35.

ACKNOWLEDGMENTS

[1]Andrew T. Le Peau and Linda Doll, *Heart. Soul. Mind. Strength: An Anecdotal History of InterVarsity Press, 1947–2007* (Downers Grove, IL: InterVarsity Press, 2006), 195.

SIDEBAR NOTES

5 HOW MANY HEBREWS?

[a]Colin J. Humphreys, "The Number of the People in the Exodus from Egypt: Decoding Mathematically the Very Large Numbers in Numbers I and XXVI," *Vetus Testamentum* 48 (1998): 197.

[b]Terence E. Fretheim, *Exodus*, Interpretation (Louisville: Westminster John Knox, 2010), 144.

[c]Humphreys, "The Number of the People in the Exodus," 202–4, citing J. A. Knudtzon, *Die El-Amama Tafeln* (Leipzig, 1915), 108.66f., 133.16f.

[d]See also Colin J. Humphreys, *The Miracles of Exodus: A Scientist's Discovery of the Extraordinary Natural Causes of the Biblical Stories* (New York: Harper-SanFrancisco, 2003), chapter 8. Retranslating *eleph* in Exodus doesn't answer all of our questions. Humphreys is forced to conclude that later scribes misunderstood the numbers in Numbers, so that while the (hypothetical) original read that the total number of Israelites was "598 [*eleph*= troops] and 5 [*eleph*= thousands] and 550 men, and the original readers understood that there were 598 troops containing 5550 men. At a later date, when the original meaning was lost, a scribe conflated the numbers and ran together the two [*eleph*] figures (598 + 5), to yield 603 thousand, not realising that two different [*eleph*] meanings were intended." See Humphreys, "The Number of the People in the Exodus," 207. We have no manuscript evidence for such a misreading, but it remains a possibility. The Old Testament was translated into Greek before New Testament times, and that translation reflects these conflated numbers, so the scribal misreading would have at least coincided with the Greek translation, if not predated it.

BIBLIOGRAPHY

Barrett, C. K. *A Critical and Exegetical Commentary on the Acts of the Apostles*. 2 vols. International Critical Commentary. Edinburgh: T&T Clark, 1998.

Bauckham, Richard. "James and the Gentiles (Acts 15:13-21)." In *History, Literature, and Society in the Book of Acts*, edited by Ben Witherington, 154-84. New York: Cambridge University Press, 1996.

———. *Jesus and the God of Israel: God Crucified and Other Studies on the New Testament's Christology of Divine Identity*. Grand Rapids: Eerdmans, 2008.

Bauer, Walter. *A Greek-English Lexicon of the New Testament and other Early Christian Literature*. Edited by Frederick William Danker. 3rd ed. Chicago: University of Chicago Press, 2000.

Beale, G. K. *The Book of Revelation: A Commentary on the Greek Text*. New International Commentary on the Greek Testament. Grand Rapids: Eerdmans, 1999.

Block, Daniel I. *Beyond the River Chebar: Studies in Kingship and Eschatology in Ezekiel*. Eugene, OR: Cascade, 2013.

———. *Deuteronomy*. NIV Application Commentary. Grand Rapids: Zondervan, 2012.

———. *How I Love Your Torah, O LORD!: Studies in the Book of Deuteronomy*. Eugene, OR: Cascade, 2011.

———. "A Prophet Like Moses: Another Look at Deuteronomy 18:9-22." Pages 349-73 in *The Triumph of Grace: Literary and Theological Studies in Deuteronomy and Deuteronomic Themes*. Eugene, OR: Cascade, 2017.

———. *The Triumph of Grace: Literary and Theological Studies in Deuteronomy and Deuteronomic Themes*. Eugene, OR: Cascade, 2017.

———. "Who Do Commentators Say 'The Lord' Is? The Scandalous Rock of Romans 10:13." In *On the Writing of New Testament Commentaries: Festschrift for Grant R. Osborne on the Occasion of His 70th Birthday*, edited by Stanley Porter and Eckhard J. Schnabel, 173-92. Texts and Editions for New Testament Study 8. Leiden: Brill, 2013.

Bock, Darrell. *Acts*. Baker Exegetical Commentary on the New Testament. Grand Rapids: Baker Academic, 2007.

Boling, Robert G. *Joshua: A New Translation with Notes and Commentary*. Anchor Bible 6. New York: Doubleday, 1982.

Bradshaw, Paul, and John Melloh, eds. *Foundations in Ritual Studies: A Reader for Students of Christian Worship*. Grand Rapids: Baker Academic, 2007.

Brown, Raymond E. *The Gospel According to John (XIII-XXI)*. Anchor Bible 29A. Garden City, NY: Doubleday, 1970.

Bruce, F. F. *The Book of the Acts*. Rev. ed. New International Commentary on the New Testament. Grand Rapids: Eerdmans, 1988.

Chapman, Stephen B. "Saul/Paul: Onomastics, Typology, and Christian Scripture." In *The Word Leaps the Gap: Essays on Scripture and Theology in Honor of Richard B. Hays*, edited by J. Ross Wagner, C. Kavin Rowe, and A. Katherine Greib, 214-43. Grand Rapids: Eerdmans, 2008.

Clines, David J. A., ed. *The Dictionary of Classical Hebrew*. 8 vols. Sheffield: Sheffield Academic, 1993.

Cohn, Robert L. *The Shape of Sacred Space: Four Biblical Studies*. AAR Studies in Religion 23. Chico, CA: Scholars Press, 1981.

Cross, Frank Moore. *Canaanite Myth and Hebrew Epic: Essays in the History of the Religion of Israel*. Cambridge, MA: Harvard University Press, 1973.

Dandamaev, Muhammad A. *Slavery in Babylonia: From Nabopolassar to Alexander the Great (626–331 B.C.)*. Edited by M. A. Powell and D. B. Weisberg. Translated by V. A. Powell. DeKalb, IL: Northern Illinois University Press, 1984.

Enns, Peter. *Exodus*. NIV Application Commentary. Grand Rapids: Zondervan, 2000.

Febbraro, Flavio, and Burkhard Schwetje. *How to Read World History in Art: From the Code of Hammurabi to September 11*. New York: Harry N. Abrams, 2010.

Fee, Gordon D. *Paul's Letter to the Philippians*. New International Commentary on the New Testament. Grand Rapids: Eerdmans, 1995.

Firth, David G. *1 & 2 Samuel*. Apollos Old Testament Commentary. Downers Grove, IL: IVP Academic, 2009.

Fishbane, Michael. *Biblical Interpretation in Ancient Israel*. Oxford: Clarendon, 1988.

Fokkelman, J. P. *Reading Biblical Narrative: An Introductory Guide*. Louisville: Westminster John Knox, 1999.

Foster, Benjamin R. *Before the Muses: An Anthology of Akkadian Literature*. 3rd ed. Bethesda, MD: CDL, 2005.

Fox, Nili S. "Marked for Servitude: Mesopotamia and the Bible." In *A Common Cultural Heritage: Studies on Mesopotamia and the Biblical World in Honor of Barry L. Eichler*. Edited by Grant Frame, Erle Leichty, Karen Sonik, Jeffrey Tigay, and Steve Tinney, 267-78. Bethesda, MD: CDL Press, 2011.

France, R. T. *The Gospel of Matthew*. New International Commentary on the New Testament. Grand Rapids: Eerdmans, 2007.

Fretheim, Terence E. *Exodus*. Interpretation. Louisville: Westminster John Knox, 2010.

———. *What Kind of God?: Collected Essays of Terence E. Fretheim*. Edited by Michael J. Chan and Brent A. Strawn. Siphrut 14. Winona Lake, IN: Eisenbrauns, 2015.

Gane, Roy. *Old Testament Law for Christians: Original Context and Enduring Application*. Grand Rapids: Baker, 2017.

Goldingay, John. *Israel's Gospel*, vol. 1 of *Old Testament Theology*. Downers Grove, IL: IVP Academic, 2003.

Greenberg, Moshe. "Hebrew Sᵉgullā : Akkadian Sikiltu." *Journal of the American Oriental Society* 71 (1951): 172-74.

Greenstein, Edward L. "The Rhetoric of the Ten Commandments." In *The Decalogue in Jewish and Christian Tradition*. Edited by Henning Graf Reventlow and Yair Hoffman,

1-12. Library of Hebrew Bible/Old Testament Studies 509. New York: T&T Clark, 2011.

Grossfeld, Bernard, trans. *Targum Onqelos to Exodus*. Aramaic Bible 7. Wilmington, DE: Glazier, 1988.

Guest, Stephen. *Deuteronomy 26:16-19 as the Central Focus of the Covenantal Framework of Deuteronomy*. PhD diss., The Southern Baptist Theological Seminary, 2009.

Hafemann, Scott. *2 Corinthians*. NIVAC. Grand Rapids: Zondervan, 2000.

Hall, Calvin S., Gardner Lindzey, and John B. Campbell. *Theories of Personality*. 4th ed. New York: John Wiley & Sons, 1998.

Hallo, William, and K. Lawson Younger, eds. *Context of Scripture*. Leiden: Brill, 2003.

Haran, Menahem. *Temples and Temple-Service in Ancient Israel: An Inquiry into Biblical Cult Phenomena and the Historical Setting of the Priestly School*. Winona Lake, IN: Eisenbrauns, 1985.

Hartley, John E. *Leviticus*. Word Biblical Commentary 4. Dallas: Word, 1992.

Hawkins, Ralph K. *The Iron Age I Structure on Mt. Ebal*. Bulletin for Biblical Research, Supplements 6. Winona Lake, IN: Eisenbrauns, 2012.

Hays, Richard B. *Echoes of Scripture in the Gospels*. Waco, TX: Baylor University Press, 2016.

———. *Echoes of Scripture in the Letters of Paul*. New Haven: Yale University Press, 1989.

Hendel, Ronald S. "Sacrifice as a Cultural System: The Ritual Symbolism of Exodus 24, 3-8." *Zeitschrift für die alttestementliche Wissenschaft* 101 (1989): 366-90.

Hess, Richard S. *Joshua: An Introduction and Commentary*. Tyndale Old Testament Commentaries. Downers Grove, IL: InterVarsity Press, 1996.

Houtman, Cornelis. *Exodus*. Translated by Sierd Woudstra. Historical Commentary on the Old Testament. Leuven, Belgium: Peeters, 2000.

Howard, David M. *Joshua*. New American Commentary 5. Nashville: Broadman & Holman, 1998.

Huffmon, Herbert, and Simon Parker. "A Further Note on the Treaty Background of Hebrew *Yada*." *Bulletin of the American Schools of Oriental Research* 184 (1966): 36-38.

Humphreys, Colin J. *The Miracles of Exodus: A Scientist's Discovery of the Extraordinary Natural Causes of the Biblical Stories*. New York: HarperSanFrancisco, 2003.

———. "The Number of the People in the Exodus from Egypt: Decoding Mathematically the Very Large Numbers in Numbers I and XXVI." *Vetus Testamentum* 48.2 (1998): 196-213.

Imes, Carmen Joy. *Bearing YHWH's Name at Sinai: A Reexamination of the Name Command of the Decalogue*. Bulletin for Biblical Research Supplements 19. University Park, PA: Eisenbrauns, 2018.

———. "*Treasured Possession*": Peter's Use of the Old Testament in 1 Peter 2:9-10. MA thesis, Gordon-Conwell Theological Seminary, 2011.

Jacobs, Sandra. *The Body as Property: Physical Disfigurement in Biblical Law*. Library of Hebrew Bible/Old Testament Studies 582. London: Bloomsbury, 2014.

Jobes, Karen. *1 Peter*. Baker Exegetical Commentary on the New Testament. Grand Rapids: Baker Academic, 2005.

Kalluveettil, Paul. *Declaration and Covenant: A Comprehensive Review of Covenant Formulae from the Old Testament and the Ancient Near East*. Analecta Biblica 88. Rome: Biblical Institute Press, 1982.

Keener, Craig S. *Acts: An Exegetical Commentary*. 4 vols. Grand Rapids: Baker Academic, 2012.

Kibbe, Michael Harrison. *Godly Fear or Ungodly Failure?: Hebrews 12 and the Sinai Theophanies*. Beihefte zur Zeitschrift für die neutestamentliche Wissenschaft 216. Berlin: de Gruyter, 2016.

———. "Our Future in the Face of Jesus." *Christianity Today*. July/August 2017, 66-69.

King, Philip J., and Lawrence E. Stager. *Life in Biblical Israel*. Library of Ancient Israel. Louisville: Westminster John Knox, 2001.

Kitchen, Kenneth A. *On the Reliability of the Old Testament*. Grand Rapids: Eerdmans, 2003.

Kitchen, Kenneth A., and Paul J. N. Lawrence. *Treaty, Law and Covenant in the Ancient Near East*. 3 vols. Wiesbaden: Harrassowitz, 2012.

Kraus, Hans-Joachim. *Psalms 60–150*. Translated by Hilton C. Oswald. Continental Commentary. Minneapolis: Fortress, 1993.

Lauinger, Jacob. "Esarhaddon's Succession Treaty at Tayinat: A Biographical Sketch." Paper presented at the annual meeting of the Society of Biblical Literature, Chicago, 2012.

LeFebvre, Michael. *Collections, Codes, and Torah: The Re-Characterization of Israel's Written Law*. Library of Hebrew Bible/Old Testament Studies 451. New York: T&T Clark, 2006.

Leithart, Peter. *1 & 2 Kings*. Brazos Theological Commentary on the Bible. Grand Rapids: Brazos, 2006.

Le Peau, Andrew T. and Linda Doll. *Heart. Soul. Mind. Strength: An Anecdotal History of InterVarsity Press, 1947–2007*. Downers Grove, IL: InterVarsity Press, 2006.

Lewis, Theodore J. "'Athtartu's Incantations and the Use of Divine Names as Weapons." *Journal of Near Eastern Studies* 70 (2011): 207-27.

McCarter, Jr., P. Kyle. *II Samuel*. Anchor Bible 9. New Haven: Yale University Press, 1984.

McDonald, Suzanne. *Re-Imaging Election: Divine Election as Representing God to Others and Others to God*. Grand Rapids: Eerdmans, 2010.

McDowell, Catherine L. *The Image of God in the Garden of Eden: The Creation of Humankind in Genesis 2:5—3:24 in Light of mīs pî pīt pî and wpt-r Rituals of Mesopotamia and Ancient Egypt*. Siphrut 15. Winona Lake, IN: Eisenbrauns, 2015.

Milgrom, Jacob. *Leviticus 17–22*. Anchor Bible 3A. New York: Doubleday, 2000.

Nelson, Richard D. *Joshua*. Old Testament Library. Louisville: Westminster John Knox, 1997.

Niehaus, Jeffrey. *God at Sinai: Covenant and Theophany in the Bible and Ancient Near East*. Studies in Old Testament Biblical Theology. Grand Rapids: Zondervan, 1995.

Parpola, Simo, and Kazuko Watanabe. *Neo-Assyrian Treaties and Loyalty Oaths*. State Archives of Assyria 2. Helsinki: Helsinki University Press, 1988.

Peterson, Ryan S. *The Imago Dei as Human Identity: A Theological Interpretation*. Journal of Theological Interpretation Supplement 14. Winona Lake, IN: Eisenbrauns, 2016.

Propp, William H. C. *Exodus 19–40*. Anchor Bible 2A. New York: Doubleday, 2006.

Richter, Sandra L. *The Deuteronomistic History and the Name Theology: Lᵉšakkēn Šᵉmô Šām in the Bible and the Ancient Near East.* Beihefte zur Zeitschrift für die alttestementliche Wissenschaft 318. Berlin: de Gruyter, 2002.

Sample, Steven B. *The Contrarian's Guide to Leadership.* San Francisco: Jossey-Bass, 2002.

Silva, Moises, ed. *New International Dictionary of New Testament Theology and Exegesis.* 2nd ed. Grand Rapids: Zondervan, 2014.

Smith, Mark S. *The Pilgrimage Pattern in Exodus.* Journal for the Study of the Old Testament Supplement Series 239. Sheffield: Sheffield Academic, 1997.

Soulen, R. Kendall. *The Divine Name(s) and the Holy Trinity: Distinguishing the Voices.* Louisville: Westminster John Knox, 2011.

Surls, Austin D. *Making Sense of the Divine Name in the Book of Exodus: From Etymology to Literary Onomastics.* Bulletin for Biblical Research, Supplements 17. Winona Lake, IN: Eisenbrauns, 2017.

Tozer, A. W. *The Knowledge of the Holy.* New York: HarperSanFrancisco, 1961.

Trimm, Charlie. "Honor Your Parents: A Command for Adults." *Journal of the Evangelical Theological Society* 60 (2017): 247-63.

Turner, Nigel. *Syntax.* Vol. 3 of *Grammar of New Testament Greek.* Edinburgh: T&T Clark, 1963.

Walton, John H. *Ancient Near Eastern Thought and the Old Testament: Introducing the Conceptual World of the Hebrew Bible.* Grand Rapids: Baker Academic, 2006.

———. *The Lost World of Genesis One: Ancient Cosmology and the Origins Debate.* Downers Grove, IL: IVP Academic, 2009.

Weinfeld, Moshe. *Deuteronomy and the Deuteronomic School.* Oxford: Oxford University Press, 1972.

Wenham, Gordon J. *Genesis 1-15.* Word Biblical Commentary. Dallas: Word, 1987.

Westbrook, Raymond, ed. *A History of Ancient Near Eastern Law.* 2 vols. Leiden: Brill, 2003.

Westwood, Duncan P. "God-Image as a Component of MHI/IHM's Health Screening and Diagnostic Protocols." Window on God Exercise presented at the Missionary Health Institute / International Health Management Staff Development meetings. June 21, 2013.

———. "Risk and Resilience in Our God Image." Paper presented at the Member Care Conference at Providence University and Seminary. May 28, 2016.

Wright, Christopher J. H. *The Mission of God: Unlocking the Bible's Grand Narrative.* Downers Grove, IL: IVP Academic, 2006.

IMAGE CREDITS

Figure 1.1. Leonardo da Vinci, *The Last Supper* (restored), Santa Maria delle Grazie, Milan, Italy / Wikimedia Commons.

Figure 1.2. Sinai narratives drawing by Carmen Joy Imes and Abigail Guthrie.

Figure 4.1. Comparison drawing by Carmen Joy Imes.

Figure 4.2. Diagram of the tabernacle drawing by Danny Imes. First published in Carmen Joy Imes, *Bearing YHWH's Name at Sinai: A Reexamination of the Name Command of the Decalogue*, Bulletin for Biblical Research Supplements 19 (University Park, PA: Eisenbrauns, 2018), 125. Used courtesy of the Pennsylvania State University Press.

Figure 4.3. High priestly garments drawing by Carmen Joy Imes. First published in Carmen Joy Imes, *Bearing YHWH's Name at Sinai: A Reexamination of the Name Command of the Decalogue*, Bulletin for Biblical Research Supplements 19 (University Park, PA: Eisenbrauns, 2018), 154. Used courtesy of the Pennsylvania State University Press.

Figure I.1. Jacques-Louis David, *The Death of Socrates*, Catharine Lorillard Wolfe Collection, Wolfe Fund, 1931, Metropolitan Museum of Art, New York / Wikimedia Commons.

SCRIPTURE INDEX

Finding the Textbook You Need

The IVP Academic Textbook Selector
is an online tool for instantly finding the IVP books
suitable for over 250 courses across 24 disciplines.

ivpacademic.com